THE GRAMMAR OF CONDUCTING

THE GRAMMAR OF CONDUCTING

A Practical Guide to Baton Technique and
Orchestral Interpretation

by

MAX RUDOLF

Second Edition

SCHIRMER BOOKS
A Division of Macmillan Publishing Co., Inc.
NEW YORK

Collier Macmillan Publishers
LONDON

Copyright © 1950, 1980 by Schirmer Books
A Division of Macmillan Publishing Co., Inc.

Schirmer Books
A Division of Macmillan Publishing Co., Inc.
866 Third Avenue, New York, N. Y. 10022

Collier Macmillan Canada, Ltd.

Library of Congress Catalog Card Number: 79-7634

Printed in the United States of America

printing number
2 3 4 5 6 7 8 9 10

Library of Congress Cataloging in Publication Data

Rudolf, Max.
    The grammar of conducting.

    1. Conducting.   I. Title.
MT85.R8   1980   781.6'35   79-7634
ISBN 0-02-872220-5

Chapter 36, Rehearsal Techniques, was first published by McGraw-Hill Book Co. in the volume
The Conductor's Art and is reproduced by permission.

CONTENTS

v

PAGE

PREFACE TO THE SECOND EDITION

Thanks to the detachment from his work that an author owes to the passing of time, I hope that this new edition of *The Grammar of Conducting* has benefited by the reexamination of judgments which I now, thirty years later, see in a different light. I have attempted to increase the text's usefulness by rewording comments that need better clarification and by adding musical examples in the interest of greater variety. In order to illustrate a point in question more effectively, twenty of the former excerpts have been replaced. Most important, the scope of the book has been widened by the addition of eight chapters. Transcending the area of baton technique, they touch upon questions of musical interpretation and render advice related to the preparation of performances.

The text's layout as a grammar has been preserved, which implies that rules and usage are compiled within a system that lends itself to class work or self-study within a gradual progression from simple to more exacting assignments. My book is not a treatise, but a methodic introduction into the techniques used in conducting an orchestra. Theoretical discussions are immediately applied to musical examples to let the student accumulate techniques as the examples increase in difficulty and variety. This explains some repetitions and the seemingly improvised nature of some chapters, much in the way of instruction in a seminar. It further explains why some of the most pertinent advice can be found in my comments on the musical examples.

The musical excerpts, brought up to date according to authentic sources, are condensed so as to offer the greatest aid to students, not for their pianistic effect. In class work, they should be played by the teacher or by a student who is able to react to the beat as an orchestra would. Although the orchestration is indicated, full scores should be consulted frequently to put the excerpts into wider perspective.

Most examples are quotations from the symphonic and operatic standard repertory. Others consist of technical exercises which enable the student to concentrate entirely on mechanical problems. Since users of the first edition did not see a need for rewriting those unpretentious bits of music, I have refrained from "modernizing" them. The exercises should be practiced at many different speeds so as to train the student to indicate contrasting tempi unmistakably. Also, I recommend arranging some exercises for a small ensemble to let students prove their ability in front of an orchestra.

Nearly all the diagrams of the first edition have been retained. When I began designing them, I observed that the very small diagrams often found in textbooks were impractical and frequently inaccurate. Consequently, I decided, as a safeguard, to draw conducting patterns on large sheets (60 x 43 cm) and to adjust the lines to fit exactly my life-size gestures. Since it was my intention to suggest techniques that followed the common practice of prominent conductors, I asked George Szell to test my patterns by conducting along their lines, while I was playing on the piano excerpts of his choice. During the stimulating discussions that ensued, he shared my thought that students would profit by transferring the printed diagrams back to large size as a device to insure self-control. Musicians studying under strict supervision are less in need of such precaution than those who proceed on their own. To the latter, I recommend the procedure explained on pages 4 to 10. It will help them achieve a clear and incisive beat.

No author could hope to pinpoint the unending diversity of motions used in conducting. My task, therefore, was to organize the principles of what we might call good usage in conducting within a workable plan and to show students how to develop a great variety of gestures, free of pedantic time beating, yet marked by the kind of self-discipline that characterizes any worthwhile artistic endeavor.

My terminology and method of teaching, with its six basic beat patterns (*non-espressivo, light-staccato, full-staccato, espressivo-legato, marcato, tenuto*), have been largely accepted by those who have studied the book's first edition. (To my pleasure,

I have seen my term "accented upbeat" appear even in music reviews.) Methods and terminologies, however, are merely tools in the hands of an educator to be used in conjunction with his estimate of each student's potential as a performer. This takes on a special meaning in the education of conductors which, unlike any other musical training, is aimed at a fusion of comprehensive musicianship with the mastery of a highly individual sign language.

Part musician, part actor, the conductor pursues a craft that cannot be easily described. Even its definition is controversial and may depend on a person's more or less biased outlook. Haven't conductors been exposed to surprisingly divergent evaluations, from a denial of their right to exist to blind adulation of the "miracle worker" on the podium? Another radical view is the not infrequently heard assertion that conducting is nothing but an innate gift and cannot be learned. True, in every profession the measure of success is inseparable from an inborn talent. Yet, when speaking of a "born surgeon," no one would suggest that a medical person, no matter how brilliant, should take charge of an operation unless he was thoroughly trained in the theory and practice of his craft.

The first edition included only occasional references to musical interpretation. The impulse to discuss it on a broader basis came from my students, especially during the three years when I taught conducting at the Curtis Institute of Music in Philadelphia. My students' interest in performance practice (an interest generally more in evidence now than a generation ago) seemed to justify the addition of chapters with the purpose of establishing a basic understanding of interpretational problems, of putting them in historical perspective, and of providing guidelines for further investigation.

The field of study related to musical interpretation is much too extended to allow, within the framework of this volume, more than an outline of the most common questions. As every performing musician knows, relatively few of them yield clearcut answers. Hence, my discussion of a number of typical cases should be regarded as a means of helping students preserve an open mind when making their own choices. I hope to meet with understanding when I consider an "open mind" not as something which is given us by nature, but as an attribute which must be acquired. In this context, I could not avoid pointing to the diversity of attitudes among performers as to how best do justice to the composer. Without claiming to have solved the problem of objectivism versus subjectivism in performing music, I believe that young conductors can be shown a path that leads in between a literal and an individualistic approach to a sort of "realism" in music making, a blend of well-founded knowledge and personal initiative.

As in the first edition, an Appendix serves to discuss the performance of complete works; some of the former selections have been replaced to cover a wider range of styles. Appendixes B and C have been added to illustrate points in connection with new chapters.

My gratitude to those who helped me with the first edition has not diminished through the years. First, I recall my unforgettable friend, George Szell. Without his encouragement, generous interest, and expert advice, it is doubtful whether my project would have become reality. Dr. Irving Kaplan contributed invaluable critical and literary assistance in the preparation of the text; Prof. Leo Kraft gave highly competent aid while I was working on the first draft. Three men, then associated with G. Schirmer, are gratefully remembered: William Schuman, who was the first to read my manuscript and believed in its worth; Nathan Broder and Felix Greissle, who gave their time unstintingly and contributed many helpful ideas.

Thanks to *The Grammar of Conducting*, I have made a large number of new friends both at home and abroad. Traveling in our country or touring around the globe, I have had numerous occasions to discuss my book with colleagues who had studied it and used it as a text for teaching. I am happy to use this opportunity to express to all of them my thanks, not only for their interest and appreciation, but for their excellent comments that have been put into use for this revision.

M.R.

INTRODUCTION

Directing an Orchestra Is a Complex Job

THE CONDUCTOR must be a trained musician, must know how to work with people in a group, and must be able to convey his intentions to his players by means of gestures.

It is very important that the conductor have a thorough knowledge of composition, and he should be familiar with various musical styles. He should also be aware of the problems of musical interpretation. A good working knowledge of instruments, both individually and in combination, is indispensable. The ability to read an orchestral score, and, if necessary, play it on the piano is a vital part of the conductor's equipment. While absolute pitch is not a prerequisite, the conductor's ear should be keen enough to recognize inaccuracy in pitch and to maintain the proper balance. The mastery of all these elements will give him the authority to be a genuine leader.

But all his musicianship and thorough study of scores will help him little unless he knows how to talk to people, work with them, and get results in a quick and direct manner. Knowledge of a few simple principles of group psychology is of great assistance in rehearsing efficiently and in stimulating the players to a good performance.

Musicianship and knowledge of psychology, however, still do not make a conductor. There is a technique of conducting just as there is a technique of playing an instrument.

The Technique of Conducting

The technique of conducting involves the use of the right arm in wielding the baton, the left arm in lending support, and the functions of the eyes. The most elementary gestures are used to set the tempo of the music and to indicate when to start and stop, including holds and interruptions. These gestures are indispensable but are in themselves hardly more than traffic signals to keep the orchestra together. To obtain an artistic result the conductor must be able to communicate nuances in dynamics, details of phrasing, articulation (legato and staccato), and general expression. For this, mere *time-beating* is not enough; the appropriate gesture for each musical expression must be mastered, before we can speak of *conducting*.

If you watch an accomplished conductor, you will be impressed by the natural unity and coherence of his gestures. His motions seem to be such a simple and direct means of evoking musical expression that you may not realize their thoroughly planned and purposeful nature. These motions constitute a technique for conveying to the orchestra a large number of musical details. In order to teach this technique, the various gestures that the conductor uses will be analyzed and discussed in this book. You may wonder why an activity that appears so easy and natural must be dissected. You may also doubt whether all conductors have worked out their techniques as methodically as this book proposes to do. Actually, if they have not done so, they have attained the same end only by a long process of trial and error.

Whether a conductor studies in the manner proposed by this book, or whether his technique evolves in the course of his experience alone, he will have to pass through a stage of development in which he becomes acutely conscious of technical problems. Most musicians rely at first on their natural feelings and may work for some time with little to guide them but their instinct. But presently they realize that technical control is indispensable to artistic mastery. Once attained, such control gives the artist that expressive simplicity which is the goal of all artistic performance. For the conductor this means that his gestures become second nature and he can give himself entirely to the music.

The Use of the Baton

A conductor who fractured his left arm would still be able to exercise complete control of his group, provided that he had a good baton technique. Therefore, a large part of this book will be devoted to advising the student how to handle the baton, the conductor's most efficient tool.

The handiest kind of baton is about twenty inches long and fairly light in weight. It should not be so thin that the point is shaky, making it hard to beat distinctly. The choice of a baton with or without a handle depends upon the individual. You must also decide for yourself what grip is the most convenient. The conductor must be able to control the baton completely and feel perfectly at ease; this is the test of a good grip. The most advisable way to hold the baton is with the thumb, first, and second fingers, and with the butt against the palm of the hand. You will feel more secure in the energetic beats if you use an even fuller grip.

Conducting Without Baton

Conducting without baton has one obvious advantage in that there are two expressive hands instead of one. But even though the baton takes some of the expressiveness from the right hand, there are advantages in using it. Remember that the player's attention is always divided between his music stand and the conductor. It is much easier for the player to follow the baton, especially if the music is unfamiliar or the part is technically difficult, or in accompaniments. The baton is even more important when there is a large ensemble, for then many of the players are quite a distance from the conductor's stand. In the interest of clarity, therefore, the student should learn to conduct with a baton. Nevertheless, the diagrams of this course can be studied without one.

General Explanation of the Diagrams

It is suggested that the student enlarge the diagrams of at least the first ten chapters. Each square of the diagram represents one square inch. The enlarged diagrams, drawn either on a sheet of paper or on a blackboard, will make it possible for the student to practice with a life-size beat.

Because of the two-dimensional nature of the diagrams, different beats along the same line can be indicated only by slight separation of the beat-lines. Straight lines which run close together on the diagram coincide in actual practice.

All counts are marked so that the played beat coincides with the written count: the baton is at ① when the 1st beat sounds, and moves so as to arrive at ② at the start of the 2nd beat.

○ The baton passes through without stopping.

□ The baton stops at this point.

[ATT] Position of attention.

There are four kinds of lines in the diagrams:

indicates the field of beating.

indicates deliberate, controlled movement.

indicates very quick movement.

indicates bouncing.

THE GRAMMAR OF CONDUCTING

Chapter 1

THE NON-ESPRESSIVO PATTERN (4-Beat)

General Training of the Right Arm

IN DIRECTING MUSIC the right arm describes certain patterns which represent the rhythm. There is a different pattern for each rhythm, and the patterns are modified according to the musical expression. The movements of the baton are: up, down, left, right, and their various combinations.

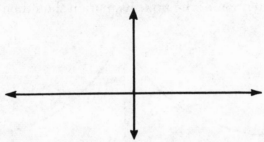

This diagram shows the up-down line and the left-right line used in beating. The general area covered by these lines is called the field of beating, and the lines are the axes of the field. The size of the field of beating may vary widely from one situation to another.

1.   Practice the up-down and left-right motions with the wrist alone, first slowly, then rapidly. To be sure that the forearm does not move, hold it firmly with the left hand. Avoid tension in the wrist and make as large a gesture as possible.

2.   There are two positions of the wrist: palm downward and palm sideways. Practice with both positions. In practicing the left-right movement you may find the palm-downward position stiff. If so, do not try to force it on the wrist; just practice the palm-sideways position. In actual conducting it is most convenient to use a position halfway between the two, or to change smoothly from one to the other.

3.   In adding the forearm motion to the wrist motion, you must be aware of a general rule: the motion increases with the distance of the moving part from the body. Thus, the point of the baton travels farther than the hand, which in turn moves more

1

4.   than the forearm. Use the left hand to hold the arm above the elbow while practicing with the forearm. In slow tempo precaution should be taken in order to achieve smooth coordination of all parts: the hand motion should always be a little behind that of the forearm. This necessitates a turn of the wrist each time the forearm changes direction. For example, suppose the forearm is moving upward and the wrist reaches its highest position; the hand will be pointing halfway down and will complete its upward motion while the arm is already moving downward. Similar relationships apply to both up-down and left-right movements.

5.   The third preliminary exercise uses the whole arm. Work for a smooth motion in which all parts of the arm blend their movements, so that no one part sticks out awkwardly. Think of the baton as an extension of the arm; its motion should be smooth and steady.

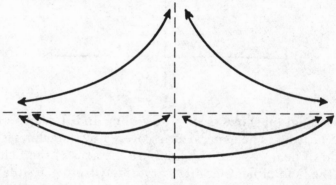

This diagram shows five swinging movements. Practice each with wrist alone, then with wrist and forearm. Vary the size and the speed of your beat, from a snap of the wrist to a slow turn.

These four preliminary exercises should be practiced before the work of each of the first ten chapters. In addition, the student should use a few warming-up exercises familiar to violinists and pianists: shaking the hands freely, lifting the arms and letting them drop suddenly, and so on.

The Non-Espressivo Pattern (4-Beat)

The first four chapters deal only with music that requires 4 beats in a measure. Several patterns of beating this rhythm will be shown, beginning with the non-espressivo pattern.

The non-espressivo beat is a plain, continuous motion. It is neutral in character and therefore uses mostly straight

*lines. It is not large in size and is done with no intensity in
the forearm motion.*

Put the enlarged Diagram I on the music stand or tack it on-   MIRROR
to the wall. Each student can find the height best suited to him
by standing before the diagram with elbow relaxed, forearm
slightly elevated, and baton extended forward. The point of the
baton should then be at the level of the left-right line. (Use the
same level for all diagrams!) Stand directly in front of the diagram and let the baton point to the intersection of the up-down
and left-right lines, approximately three inches from the surface
of the diagram.

First count aloud without beating: *One-Two-Three-Four* in
moderate tempo ($\textsf{J} = 66$). When you feel that the tempo is established, continue to count aloud and start moving the baton, following the lines exactly so that the point of the baton passes
through the number corresponding to each count. Always keep
the baton a few inches from the diagram, but close enough to
follow the lines exactly. Try to achieve a smooth motion and
avoid stopping on the counts.

A wrist motion is sufficient for this pattern. However, many
students will find that they cannot use the wrist alone without
feeling some strain. Since it is of utmost importance to feel at

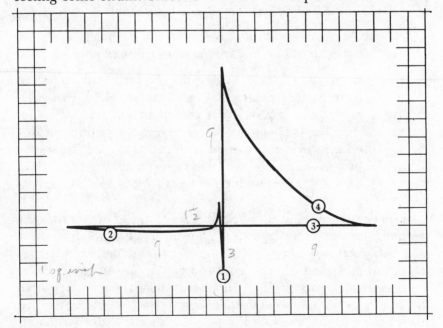

Diagram 1. 4-beat; non-espressivo

ease while beating time, a slight forearm motion may be used in addition to the wrist motion. In this case it should always be remembered that the point of the baton moves more than the hand, the hand more than the forearm. The elbow should be held still but relaxed. With practice you will gradually develop the ability to use the wrist alone.

You will observe that on the 1st count the baton is carried upward before it is turned to the left. This upward movement on the 1st count is called the rebound. You will also notice that the distance between the counts is not uniform. The distance between ③ and ④ especially is smaller than the others, while the distance between ④ and ① is much larger. Nevertheless, you will soon learn to adjust your beat automatically so as to keep it even and smooth.

When you are sure that your can follow this pattern without the help of the diagram, check yourself by using a large mirror. Now start beating, watching yourself to see that no part of your body is moving except wrist and forearm. Your whole body should be relaxed and calm. Be sure to keep the elbow quiet, but do not press it against your side. Watch your beat, keeping it clear and steady!

The Preparatory Beat at the Start

It is a general rule that the conductor gives one extra beat, strictly in tempo, before the music actually begins.

In other words, to start playing on the 1st count you must start beating one count earlier, that is to say, on *Four*. However, this beat of preparation which is shown in Diagram 2 is not merely the regular 4th beat, for it starts from the position of "attention" and has the quality of an invitation. It is equivalent to lifting the bow in the string instruments and to taking a breath in the winds. It enables the conductor to get a clean and unified attack.

Practice the preparatory beat in the following manner. Point the baton to the attention space ATT on Diagram 2 and count aloud the previous *One-Two-Three-Four*. Just before *Four*, let the baton move so that it passes through ④ as you count *Four*. Keeping strict tempo, follow the line until you reach ①, where the music presumably begins. Having mastered this, return to the mirror with both arms down and relaxed. Lift the baton and

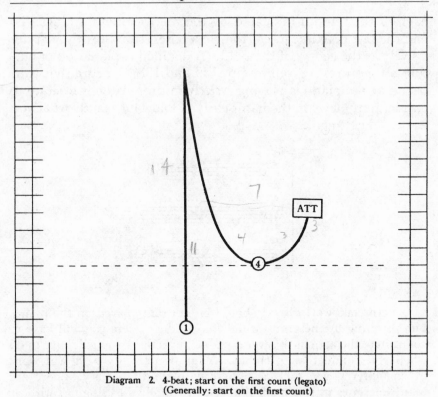

Diagram 2. 4-beat; start on the first count (legato)
(Generally: start on the first count)

assume the position of attention. Try to feel that by doing this you would really gain the attention of your group. This will be still more effective if you lift elbow and forearm slightly. Count—this time to yourself—and give the preparatory beat. When you reach ①, continue beating as you did with Diagram 1 and beat for several bars. Do this over again several times, starting each time from a completely relaxed position with the arm at the side.

Applying the Gestures to Musical Exercises

Since it is a good habit for the conductor to watch his players, you should always memorize the first few bars before starting.

Face your friend at the piano and take the position of attention. Concentrate on the tempo and be sure that you know exactly how fast your are going to beat. Then, using what you have learned so far, conduct Exx. 1 a–c. Repeat them several times in each of the tempos indicated by the metronome markings. To end the last note in each of these exercises, stop the 4th beat decisively at the center of the field. (A detailed explanation of cutting-off gestures is given on pp. 129 and 133.) Be sure that your friend at the piano is playing strictly in time. Do not hesitate to correct him; develop the habit early of knowing exactly what you want and getting it.

In class work, Ex. 1 should be not only played on the piano, but also sung by the group while you conduct. Here you will have to coordinate the actions of several people, exactly as you will have to do when you conduct an orchestra. Your preparatory beat will work much better if you take a slight breath simultaneously. There are many exercises in this book that lend themselves to singing, with or without piano accompaniment. Whenever possible the class should sing the melody in those exercises.

Exx. 2 and 3 are to be played on the piano or can be arranged for a small instrumental ensemble. Ex. 3 is marked 2/4, but use 4 beats in a measure because of the slow tempo.

So far you have conducted these exercises *p*. Now repeat them *mf*. To do this, you will have to enlarge the size of your beat. Make your gestures about a third larger than those used for *p*, but do not change their proportions. Keep checking the smoothness and clarity of your beat with the mirror. For the larger beat, use the forearm in addition to the wrist motion.

Emphasizing the Beats by "Clicking"

In Exx. 4 a–c you will find that you want to make your beat very precise because of the dotted rhythms and syncopations. Especially in slow tempo, the beats will have to be emphasized; this is done by "clicking." This is a sharp, quick wrist motion which speeds up the movement of the baton just before reaching a count. Immediately after the count, the motion continues at normal speed. This technique can be applied only when the forearm participates in moving the baton. Remember that clicking serves the purpose of emphasizing the beat and must not be used where a smooth beat is sufficiently clear.

Use Diagram 3 for practice (♩ = 66). The 1st count is now located on the left-right line, to give space to continue the motion in the same direction after the click. While practicing clicking on all 4 counts, you will feel that each beat is emphasized. Learn to do it with ease and certainty, but do not get into the habit of clicking continually!

Applying the Non-Espressivo Pattern to Musical Examples

By learning the non-espressivo beat first, you start your conducting without any emotional bias and you concentrate upon a clear presentation of the rhythm. But aside from its educational value, you will need it in actual conducting.

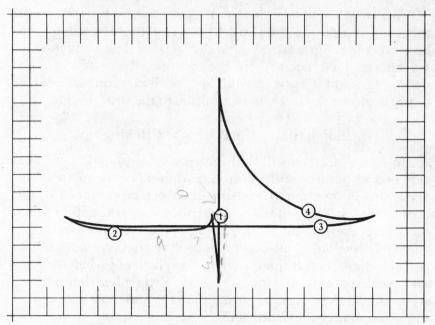

Diagram 3. 4-beat; non-espressivo with clicking on the counts

In practicing Exx. 5–9, it is a good habit to hum a few bars of the melody before starting to beat. This will fix the tempo firmly in your mind and enable you to give the preparatory beat strictly in time. Otherwise the preparation might not be in the same tempo as the succeeding beats; the players will be confused and the rhythm will be rather shaky.

Do not use the left hand in directing these examples; its use will be discussed in later chapters.

The metronome markings are those of the original scores—except for those in parentheses, which are suggested as a guide without claim to authenticity.

Ex. 5: The harp needs only a clear indication of the rhythm; the quiet flute solo certainly requires no dramatic gestures (see p. 75).

Ex. 6: Indicate the accent in the 3rd measure with a slightly larger *Three,* putting emphasis on *Four* but without slowing down. You will feel that the enlarged 3rd beat is a preparation for the accented 4th.

Ex. 7: Since the orchestra has nothing but *pp* accompaniment, the non-espressivo beat is quite adequate (see pp. 75 and 305).

Ex. 8: A minimum of gesture will be sufficient to indicate the tempo for the English horn accompanied by the string section. Here is a good chance to practice keeping the baton in continuous motion in very slow tempo.

Ex. 9: These first bars of *Fingal's Cave* set an atmosphere for the entire piece—more color than expression. For this you need the unemotional non-espressivo beat.

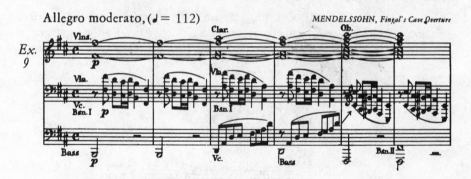

Additional examples for the study of the non-espressivo pattern (4-beat):

Beethoven: Piano Concerto No. 5, 2nd movement—bars 16–24.

Haydn: *The Creation*, No. 12 (Recitative)—bars 1–3.

Mahler: Symphony No. 1, 1st movement, beginning.

Nicolai: Overture to *The Merry Wives of Windsor*, bars 1–3, 6, 7.

Shostakovitch: Symphony No. 1, 3rd movement, beginning (the solo oboe needs no special direction).

Tchaikovsky: *Romeo and Juliet* (Overture-Fantasia), beginning.

Verdi: Prelude to *Aïda*, bars 18–23.

Wagner: *Liebestod* from *Tristan und Isolde*, bars 1–5.

Chapter 2

STACCATO PATTERNS (4-Beat)

Light-Staccato

The light-staccato beat is a quick, straight motion with a stop on each count. The gestures are small.

Diagram 4. The light-staccato beat is done by the wrist alone. In this pattern there is no rebound on the 1st count. Point the baton to 4 and set the tempo at ♩ = 126 in your mind. Then start beating: stop at each count and move very quickly between the counts. Avoid any tension, especially in the forearm. A review of the wrist exercises on pages 5 and 6 will limber you up so that your wrist will be flexible and your forearm loose. Check your appearance in the mirror to be sure that shoulder and elbow are not moving. Practice light-staccato also at ♩ = 108 and ♩ = 160.

Use Diagram 5 for the start. The motion with which you reach 4 must be very quick and decisive: a snap of the wrist. The preliminary beat is little larger than the other beats. Since this preparation indicates not only the tempo but the staccato

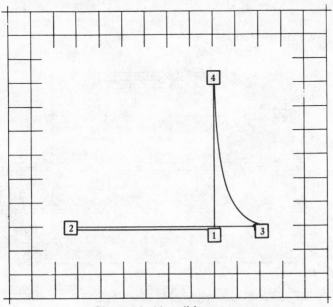

Diagram 4. 4-beat; light-staccato

11

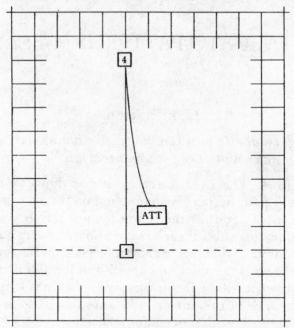

Diagram 5. 4-beat; start on the first count (light-staccato)

quality, you must be sure to make a definite stop at [4] and not to leave it until just before the downbeat.

Exx. 10–16: will give you practice in using this beat. Light-staccato is generally used with tempos of ♩ = 100 or faster. However, it can be very effective at slower tempos in *pp* passages (Ex. 13). In the latter case you must be very careful to give a precise preparation and to maintain a steady rhythm (for Exx. 14 and 16, see p. 75).

Ex. 13
♩=60
♩=80
♩=100

Ex. 14

Allegro, (♩= 152)

Vln. I

sotto voce

ROSSINI, Semiramide—Overture

Str.

Ex. 15

Im mässigen Hauptzeitmass (♩= 108)

WAGNER, Die Meistersinger-Overture

Ob.
Cl. *molto stacc.*

Tutti
ff *p*

Bsn.

molto stacc.

Ex. 16

Andante, (♪= 80-88)

MOZART, Symphony No. 35

Vln. I

p

Vln. II

Vla.
p Vc.
Bass

Additional examples for the study of the light-staccato pattern (4-beat):

Beethoven: Symphony No. 8, 2nd movement (Ex. 369).

Grieg: *Peer Gynt Suite No. 1*, 4th movement — beginning.

Haydn: Symphony No. 99, 1st movement, *Vivace assai* — beginning.

Mussorgsky-Ravel: *Pictures at an Exhibition*, No. 3 (Tuileries).

Mozart: *Le Nozze di Figaro*, No. 1, Duettino.

Shostakovitch: Symphony No. 1, 1st movement, No. 8.

Tchaikovsky: Symphony No. 6, 1st movement, *Allegro non troppo* (after the Introduction).

Tchaikovsky: *Nutcracker Suite, Danse Chinoise* (the solo flute needs no special direction).

Full-Staccato

The full-staccato beat is a quick, slightly curved motion with a stop on each count. It is snappy and energetic, with a characteristic "bouncing" on the downbeat. The size may vary from small to large.

Bouncing, a special form of the rebound, is done by a wrist motion. First, practice bouncing without the baton. Lift your forearm and jerk it downward, stopping abruptly at about the left-right line. The wrist must be completely relaxed so that, when the forearm stops, the hand continues downward and snaps up again immediately. This bouncing of the hand is a natural muscular reaction and must not be hindered by any tension in the wrist.

Diagram 6. Practice at $\quad = 80$ and $\quad = 100$.

EXECUTION IN *p:* The size of the beat corresponds to the usual enlargement of the diagram. The 1st count is at the bottom of the bounce, and the stop immediately after is on the left-right line. Use very little forearm for the 2nd and 3rd beats; a slight twist will make them snappier. On the 4th beat whip up the arm immediately after the count.

EXECUTION IN *f:* Since the pattern is now about one and one-half times as large as in *p*, use an energetic motion of the forearm for the 2nd and 3rd beats.

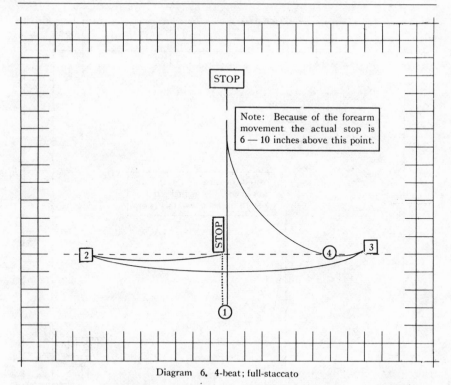

STOP

Note: Because of the forearm movement the actual stop is 6 — 10 inches above this point.

STOP

2   4   3

1

Diagram 6. 4-beat; full-staccato

As indicated on Diag. 6, the 4th count does not coincide with STOP at the top, though ④ is only a split second from STOP . By making the experiment of beating *Four* at the very top, you will see that it involves a special effort and thus indicates an accent on the 4th count (*accented upbeat*). However, this is an exceptional case (see Diag. 21) and must be avoided in the regular pattern. But remember that, in the light-staccato, the 4th count actually comes on the highest stop because of the limited size of that beat.

Diagram 7 shows the preliminary beat in full-staccato. In applying it to the exercises, always prepare the tempo in your own mind by counting before you start beating.

Exx. 17 and 18: (each of them to be repeated at least once), practiced in the different speeds and dynamics, will train you in the full-staccato. You will help the players by beating very sharply on the rests, so that they can enter precisely on the small-value notes.

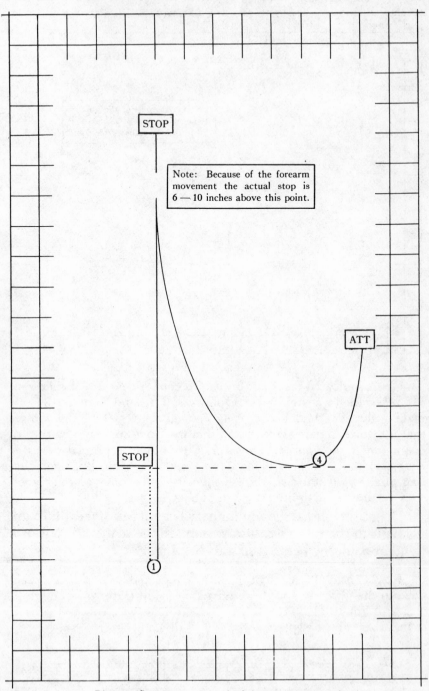

Note: Because of the forearm movement the actual stop is 6 — 10 inches above this point.

Diagram 7. 4-beat; start on the first count (full-staccato)

Full-staccato is applied in Exx. 19–21.

Additional examples for the study of the full-staccato pattern (4-beat):

Bach: *Brandenburg Concerto No. 3*, 2nd movement.

Bizet: *L'Arlésienne Suite No. 1*, 1st movement — beginning.

Brahms: *Academic Festival Overture, L'istesso tempo, un poco maestoso*.

Haydn: *The Creation*, No. 3 (Recitative) — *Allegro assai*.

Mahler: Symphony No. 6, 1st movement.

Mendelssohn: *Fingal's Cave Overture*, passage starting with bar 76 (one measure before B).

Roussel: *Bacchus et Ariane*, Suite No. 1, beginning.

Tchaikovsky: Violin Concerto, 1st movement, *Moderato assai* (after E).

Vivaldi: Concerto Grosso in A minor, RV 522 (Op. 3 No. 8).

Chapter 3

THE ESPRESSIVO-LEGATO PATTERN
(4-Beat)

The espressivo-legato beat is a curved, continuous motion. It is done with a certain tension in the forearm. The intensity and degree of curve vary with the emotional quality of the music. The size may be anywhere from fairly small to very large.

Diagram 8. Start with the preparatory beat of Diagram 2, but a little larger and with more sweep. Practice with metronome $\jmath = 72$, using wrist and forearm. Since the purpose of this pattern is to express a more or less emotional melodic line, you should feel the intensity in the forearm — without too much muscular tension! — and the baton should move as if it were encountering some resistance, a motion similar to the intense drawing of the violin bow in a lyric passage.

The usual enlargement of Diagram 8 gives the size of the *p* beat; practice *mf* with a beat half again as large, and *f* with a beat twice as large. For *f* and *ff* use your whole arm.

While you will have to move the elbow, avoid the mistake of letting it become the center of your conducting motion. Only the tip of the baton offers a clear point of orientation to the players, and movements of the wrist, forearm, and elbow are subordinate to those of the baton. The shoulder must remain still but never tense.

There are many degrees of expression between non-espressivo and molto espressivo, and you should have a wide enough variety of beats to indicate all the shades of intensity. It is therefore important to realize that the espressivo beat is a development of the non-espressivo beat. For poco espressivo, for instance, the pattern of the lines will be bent only slightly, as suggested in Diagram 8a; 8 indicates more intensity, and 8b is still more expressive. A highly passionate passage needs an even larger and more curved gesture. Practice before the mirror; start with *p* non-espressivo and, referring to Diagrams 8a and b, work up gradually to *f* molto espressivo.

19

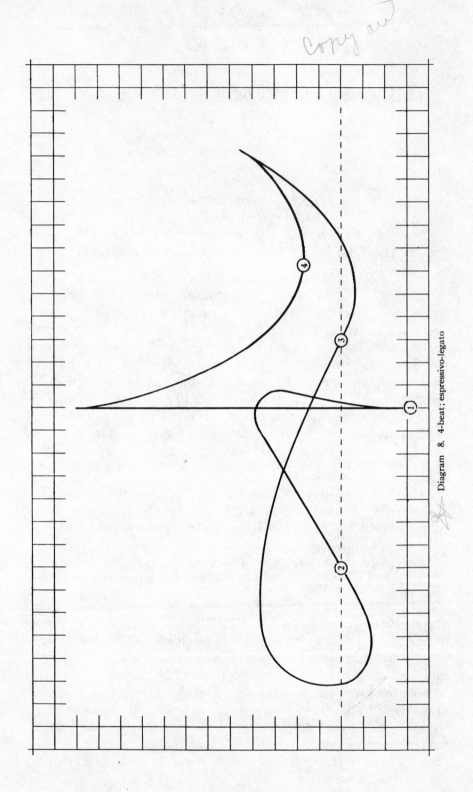

Diagram 8. 4-beat; espressivo-legato

20

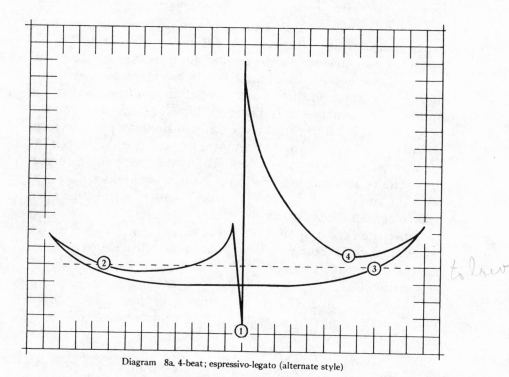

Diagram 8a. 4-beat; espressivo-legato (alternate style)

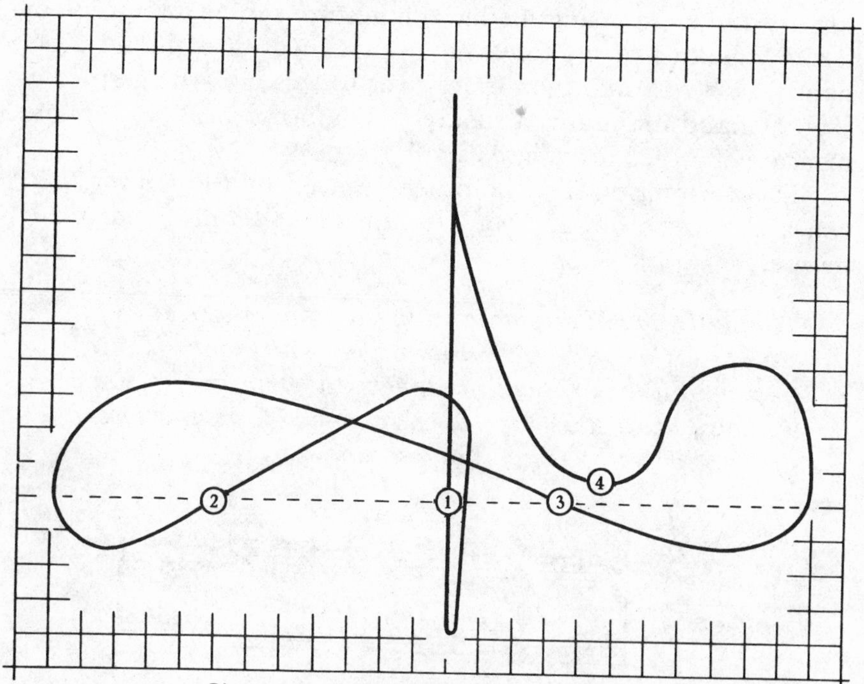

Diagram 8b. 4-beat; espressivo-legato (alternate style)

The relatively neutral patterns of the first two chapters have a quite similar appearance with different conductors. The espressivo beat, however, is more individual; its execution will differ from one conductor to another, but the freedom you gain must not be misused. The orchestra will be confused unless you indicate the counts clearly. There will be occasions when you will need clicking with this beat, especially in slow tempo. The *location* of ①, ②, ③, and ④ remains the same, even though the manner of *connecting* them depends on the musical interpretation. The connecting gestures must be flexible and varied to express the nuances of the melody, which sometimes change from beat to beat in the same bar.

Since the execution of this pattern must be well balanced and graceful, a conductor with very long arms will have to be more careful to control the size of his beat than one with relatively short arms.

The last bar in Ex. 22 needs special attention. The sustained note does not require an espressivo beat; non-espressivo is sufficient. When playing f, however, a gesture of the left hand is needed to prevent the orchestra from playing $f >$. The palm faces upward or inward, and the fingers are somewhat bent. The quality of demand contained in this gesture can be intensified by a slight shaking of the forearm. In other words, while the right hand just beats time (non-espressivo) in this bar, the gesture of the left hand maintains a steady f. The last 2 beats in the 2nd measure of Ex. 23 are treated similarly.

These exercises, like the others written by the author, give you a chance to develop your feeling for a definite and steady tempo.

The skill you gain by practicing the same music at different speeds will prove invaluable in your conducting experience. It is worthwhile to take great pains with the preliminary beat; students have a tendency to rush it in very slow tempo and to drag it in fast tempo.

Ex. 24: By starting with a somewhat larger beat than the usual *p*, you will be able to build the musical phrases. Then you will express the decreasing intensity of the 2nd bar by the decreasing intensity of your gesture. *Four* in the 2nd and 4th bars is like a preliminary beat, preparing the following phrase. The emphasized 3rd beat in the last measure should also be prepared (without delaying the tempo!); carry the 2nd beat farther to the left, and you will naturally give more expression to the 3rd beat.

Ex. 25: In the 2nd measure, use a very small gesture for *Three*—then on *Four* prepare for the next bar. The intensity in the forearm, usually characteristic of the espressivo beat, would be too heavy for this graceful music. Therefore lead the melody with a light forearm, poco espressivo.

Ex. 26: The conductor must devote as much attention to the counterpoint in the cellos as to the melody. All the beats must be espressivo and the intensity of the gesture should express the rise and fall of the melody.

Ex. 27: While guiding the strings with an espressivo beat, the conductor must not lose sight of the triplets in the brass. For an accurate indication of the rhythm, emphasize the counts whenever needed. The crescendo in the 4th measure requires an increasing gesture.

Ex. 28: The character of this music indicates a light and graceful gesture. Here, again, you should not "feel" your forearm.

Additional examples for the study of the espressivo-legato pattern (4-beat):

Berg: *Lulu Suite,* Rondo.

Brahms: Symphony No. 3, 2nd movement—passage starting at F.

Delius: *A Song of Summer*—passage starting at bar 48.

Elgar: *Enigma Variations, Op. 36,* Variation No. 5—beginning.

Franck: Symphony in D minor, 1st movement—*Lento.*

Ives: Symphony No. 4, 3rd movement.

Mahler: Symphony No. 4, 3rd movement.

Rachmaninoff: Symphony No. 2, 3rd movement.

Tchaikovsky: Symphony No. 6, 1st movement—*Andante* in D major.

Verdi: Overture to *La Forza del Destino, Andante mosso* at C.

Chapter 4

STARTING ON OTHER COUNTS

ACCORDING TO THE RULE on page 4, you are supposed to give one extra beat, strictly in tempo, before the first "played" beat. Thus, if the music starts on the 4th count, start beating *Three*; if it starts on the 3rd count, start beating *Two*; if it starts on the 2nd count, start beating *One*. Your preparation must also include the dynamics: a larger gesture prepares *f*, a smaller gesture *p*.

Start on the 4th Count

Diagram 9. It has been pointed out that the preliminary beat, because of its quality of invitation, is not identical with the regular pattern. Even in non-espressivo it is slightly curved, unlike the usual straight line. The more expressive the music, the more expressive the preparation should be. But do not give too

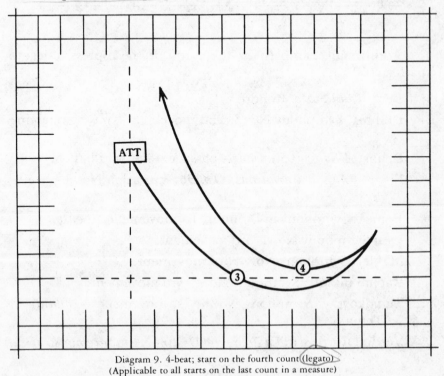

Diagram 9. 4-beat; start on the fourth count (legato)
(Applicable to all starts on the last count in a measure)

much weight to the preliminary beat, which is always gentler than the first played beat. Apply these ideas to your practice of Ex. 29.

Diagram 10. As in all staccato beats, use a snappy and decisive motion in the preparation. You can indicate the tempo clearly only by making a definite stop at ③ ; otherwise the staccato quality is lost and the players do not get a precise feeling of the tempo. Keep this in mind while practicing Ex. 30.

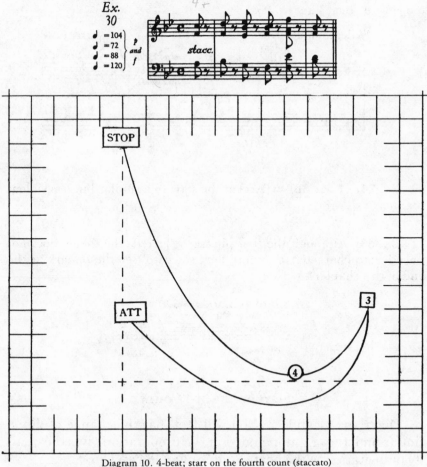

Diagram 10. 4-beat; start on the fourth count (staccato)
(Applicable to all starts on the last count in a measure)

Ex. 31: Use poco espressivo and a small beat. The metronome indication follows Carl Czerny's suggestion (see Ch. 34). Usually, this movement is performed at a slightly slower pace, ♩ = 54–56.

Ex. 32: For this very energetic start, raise the whole arm on the preparatory beat (the baton pointing downward!), while the elbow may go slightly backwards to increase the impetus of the start. Check in the mirror to be sure that the gesture appears convincing but not too violent. Beat staccato *ff*.

Ex. 247 (1 bar only): Accent the start in a similar but less violent manner.

Ex. 33: Although the first phrase is slurred, the theme does not have legato character, therefore beat staccato (see the remark at the end of this chapter).

Start on the 3rd Count

Diagrams 11 and 12. You will feel that the change of direction from left to right included in the preparation gives the quality of invitation to the beat. Practice Exx. 34 and 35.

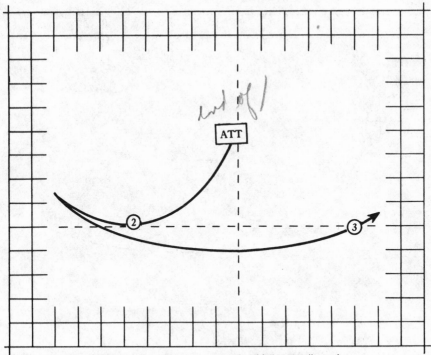

Diagram 11. 4-beat; start on the third count (legato)

Ex.
34

♩ =88
♩ =60 } *p*
♩ =100 } *and*
♩ =112 } *f*

Ex.
35

Andante, ♪ =112
Andante moderato, ♪ =96 } *p*
Adagio, ♪ =80 } *and f*

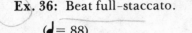

Ex. 36: Beat full–staccato.

(♩ = 88)

BACH, *Easter Oratorio*

Ex.
36

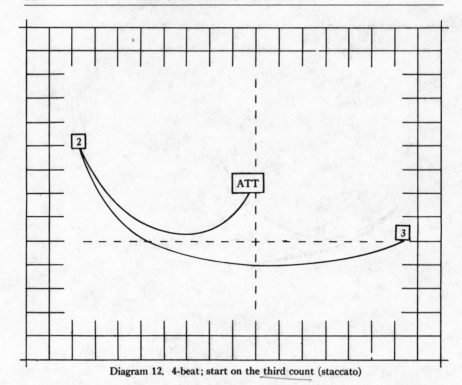

Diagram 12. 4-beat; start on the third count (staccato)

Ex. 37: Beat in 4 in spite of the time-signature ℂ. The first two notes are detached, the rest legato; beat accordingly. Your preparatory gesture should be very gentle, to match the graceful music (see p. 339).

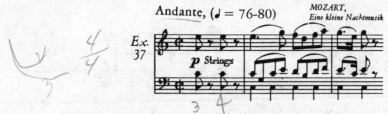

Ex. 38: Vigorous staccato.

Ex. 39: *f* legato.

MENDELSSOHN, *Elijah*

Start on the 2nd Count

Diagrams 13 and 14. Again the change of direction leads the players into their attack. The staccato preparation in this case requires a large bounce, but should be very elastic and by no means heavy. Lifting the forearm slightly on the rebound will emphasize the introductory character. In light-staccato, however, use the wrist only. The gesture then is considerably smaller. For training, use Exx. 40 and 41.

Ex. 42: Start *p* legato, crescendo to *f*. After a large downbeat (*fp*) make the 2nd beat much smaller and crescendo again (see p. 249).

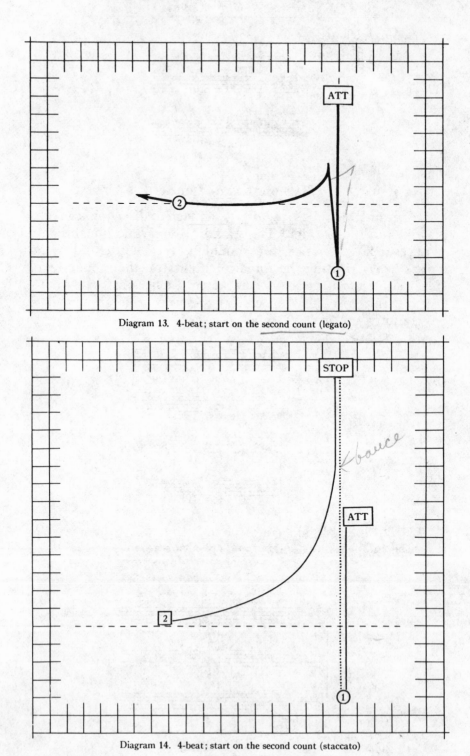

Diagram 13. 4-beat; start on the second count (legato)

Diagram 14. 4-beat; start on the second count (staccato)

Exx. 43 and 44: *p* legato, poco espressivo. The quarter-rest on *One* does not affect the manner of preparation (do not prepare *One*!).

Ex. 45: *f* staccato, but not too sharp, since the music is solemn and the bowing should not be too detached.

Keep in mind the various positions of attention! Once you lift the baton, do not leave the position of attention until you give the preparatory beat. Before lifting the baton, be sure where to point it. Remember this simple rule: *when the attack is on the 1st count, point the baton to the right. To start on the other counts point it to the center.* There is one exception. For a spectacular attack on the 4th count, point the baton to the left. This position allows a very large preliminary beat (whole-arm gesture). Try it, but do not use it too often.

Additional examples:

Start on the 4th count:

Beethoven: Symphony No. 3, 2nd movement.

Brahms: Symphony No. 2, 2nd movement.

Haydn: *The Creation*, No. 24—Aria.

Mahler: Symphony No. 4, 4th movement.

Mozart: *Die Zauberflöte*, No. 21—Finale.

Puccini: *Madama Butterfly*, 2nd act—beginning.

Verdi: *Il Trovatore*, 2nd act (No. 4—Chorus).

Start on the 3rd count:

Haydn: *The Seasons*, No. 34—Cavatina.

Mozart: *Così fan tutte*, No. 25—*Rondo* (often conducted with subdivision, see Ch. 14).

Prokofiev: *Classical Symphony*, 3rd movement.

Start on the 2nd count:

Bach: Cantata No. 21 (*Ich hatte viel Bekümmernis*), No. 3—Aria for Soprano.

Bach: Cantata No. 106 (*Gottes Zeit ist die allerbeste Zeit*), No. 4—Coro.

Bartók: Piano Concerto No. 3, 2nd movement.

Rachmaninoff: Symphony No. 2, 1st movement.

Verdi: *Falstaff*, 1st act—beginning.

Chapter 5

THE 3-BEAT

Non-Espressivo and Espressivo-Legato

Diagram 15. Apply the same procedure as for Diagram 1. To start on the 1st count, use Diagram 2 (changing the figure ④ to ③) and practice before the mirror at different tempos.

Ex. 46: Non-espressivo.

Diagram 16. The explanations of Chapter 3 apply to this pattern. Diagrams 16a and b show poco espressivo and molto espressivo. Enlarge according to dynamics.

Ex. 47: Practice with poco espressivo to molto espressivo.

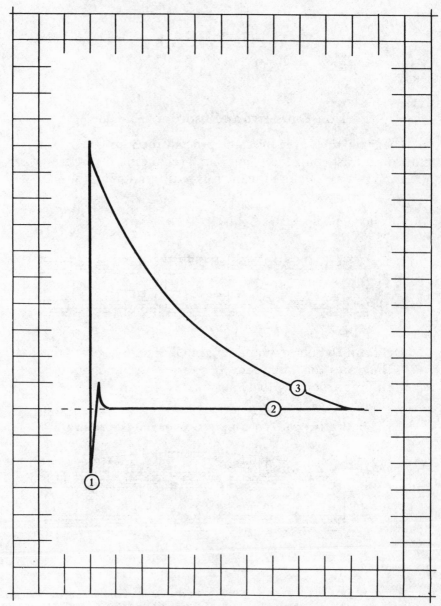

Diagram 15.   3-beat; non-espressivo

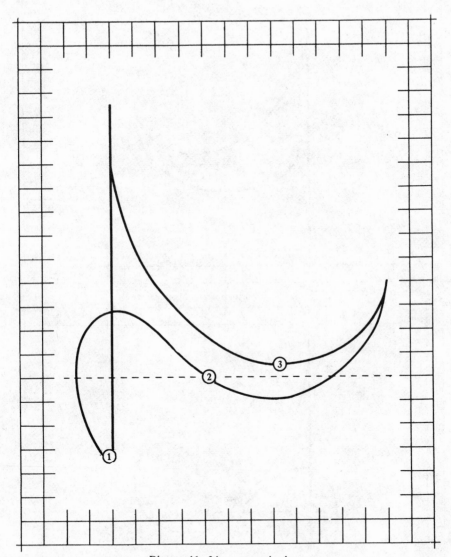

Diagram 16. 3-beat; espressivo-legato

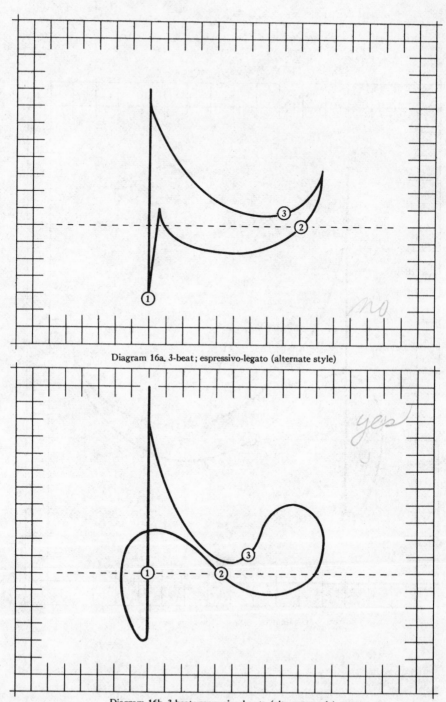

Diagram 16a. 3-beat; espressivo-legato (alternate style)

Diagram 16b. 3-beat; espressivo-legato (alternate style)

Ex. 48: Beat in 3, indicating each ♩ with one beat. Use non-espressivo.

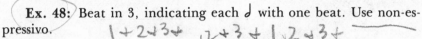

Lento, (♩ = 46)   VAUGHAN WILLIAMS, *A London Symphony*

Ex. 48 — Str. Harp. Org.

Reprinted by permission of the copyright owners, Stainer & Bell, Ltd., London

Ex. 49: Very small non-espressivo.

Allegro moderato, (♩ = 116-120)

SCHUBERT, *Symphony No. 8*

Ex. 49

Ex. 50: Molto espressivo.

Andante sostenuto, ♩ = 54   MASCAGNI, *Cavalleria Rusticana*

Ex. 50

Light-Staccato and Full-Staccato

Diagrams 17 and 18. Compare the explanations of Chapter 2. For the start, apply Diagram 5 (light-staccato) and Diagram 7 (full-staccato), changing the figure ④ to ③ . Practice at different speeds.

For training in 3-beat staccato use Exx. 51 and 52.

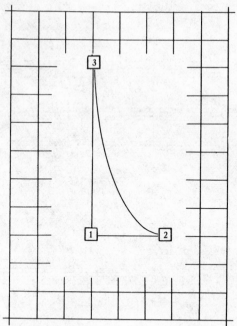

Diagram 17. 3-beat; light-staccato

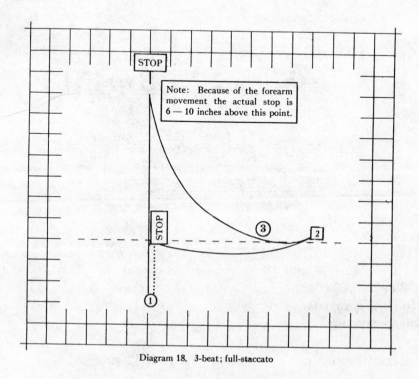

STOP

Note: Because of the forearm movement the actual stop is 6 — 10 inches above this point.

STOP

Diagram 18. 3-beat; full-staccato

Ex. 53a Light-staccato. The legato in the flutes (bar 4) does not affect the beat, which remains staccato. Staccato patterns are often applied to fast passages when slurring is primarily a matter of articulation and a strong feeling for the rhythm prevails (cf. p. 76).

Andantino quasi Allegretto, ♩ = 100   BIZET, *Carmen.*

Ex. 53b: 2 bars full-staccato (not too large), followed by 2 bars light-staccato.

BIZET, *Carmen*

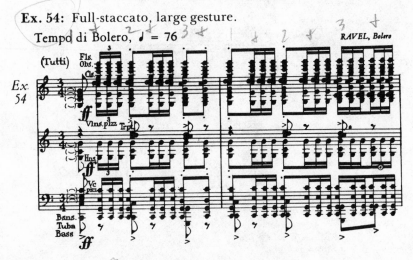

Ex. 54: Full-staccato, large gesture.

Tempo di Bolero, ♩ = 76   RAVEL, *Bolero*

Ex. 55: Light-staccato. Make your preparation sufficiently fast. Here, as in the first 2 bars of Ex. 53a, the strings are playing pizzicato, which often requires staccato beating.

Start on the 2nd and 3rd Counts

Use Diagrams 19 and 20 for the start on the 2nd count, Diagrams 9 and 10 for the start on the 3rd count (changing figures as usual). Practice Exx. 56–59.

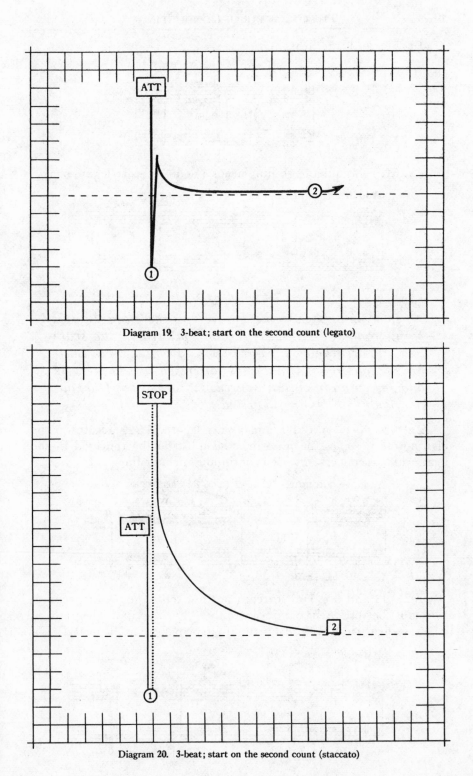

Diagram 19. 3-beat; start on the second count (legato)

Diagram 20. 3-beat; start on the second count (staccato)

Ex. 60: Full-staccato.

(♩ = 138) GLUCK, *Orphée et Euridice—Chaconne*

breath ↓ with stick at same time

Ex. 61: This quiet beginning needs a non-espressivo legato beat.

Andante tranquillo, (♩= 63-69)

MENDELSSOHN, *Midsummer Night's Dream—Nocturne*

60= 1001 + a little speed

In some of the Beethoven excerpts there are two sets of metronome markings: the one printed in the score and, in parentheses, the one that is now often used. Beethoven's metronome markings, discussed in Chapters 32 and 34, are an important source of information. Only minor modifications are suggested.

Ex. 62: Poco espressivo and always legato. The staccato on the eighth-note C serves the phrasing and must not be reflected in the beat, which is concerned with a continuous melodic line.

Andante con moto, ♪ = 92 (♪ = 84) BEETHOVEN, *Symphony No. 5*

Exx. 63 and 64: Full-staccato but not too large. Your preparation must be very precise to indicate the correct tempo: Allegretto in Ex. 63, Allegro in Ex. 64. All turns are to be played on the beat.

Allegretto, (♩ = 138)

HAYDN, *Symphony No. 88*

Additional examples for the study of 3-beat:

Non-espressivo:

Beethoven: Symphony No. 5, 2nd movement — bars 39–46.

Elgar: *Enigma Variations, Op. 36*, Variation No. 9 — beginning.

Rimsky-Korsakov: *Capriccio Espagnol*, 2nd movement — beginning.

Stravinsky: *L'Oiseau de Feu* (Suite), Finale — beginning.

Espressivo-legato:

Bizet: Symphony, 2nd movement.

Fauré: *Pelléas et Mélisande Suite*, 1st movement.

Grieg: Piano Concerto, 2nd movement.

Nielsen: Symphony No. 4, 1st movement.

Prokofiev: Symphony No. 5, 1st movement until No. 6; 3rd movement at No. 60.

Tchaikovsky: Serenade for Strings, 3rd movement.

Tchaikovsky: *Manfred*, 1st movement — *Andante*.

Wagner: Overture to *Tannhäuser*, bars 17–31.

Light-staccato:

Dukas: *L'Apprenti Sorcier*, 3 bars before No. 2 — (*Vif*).

Haydn: Symphony No. 97, 3rd movement — Trio.

Rossini: Overture to *La Gazza Ladra, Allegro*.

Stravinsky: *Feu d'Artifice*, beginning.

Tchaikovsky: *Nutcracker Suite, Danse Arabe* — beginning.

Full-staccato:

Brahms: Symphony No. 4, 4th movement — passage starting at C.

Mussorgsky: Polonaise from *Boris Godunov*

Offenbach: *Les Contes d'Hoffmannn*, 2nd act—Minuet in A major.

Shostakovitch: *The Golden Age*, 1st movement—passage starting at No. 2.

Strauss, Richard: *Salome, Dance of the Seven Veils*—beginning.

Tchaikovsky, Symphony No. 3, 5th movement.

Start on the 2nd count:

Ravel: *Rapsodie Espagnole*—beginning.

Start on the 3rd count:

Beethoven: Symphony No. 8, 3rd movement.

Brahms: *Ein deutsches Requiem*, 2nd movement.

Franck: Symphony in D minor, 2nd movement.

Handel: *Messiah*, Aria—*The trumpet shall sound.*

Mahler: Symphony No. 7, 3rd movement.

Schumann: Symphony No. 1, 2nd movement.

Chapter 6

SUDDEN CHANGES OF DYNAMICS
AND ARTICULATION

Sudden Change from *p* to *f* and Vice Versa

IT HAS ALREADY been pointed out that the dynamics of the music can be expressed by the size of the gesture. There are two other ways of indicating volume of sound, and all three will be discussed in this chapter.

(1) Changing the Size of the Beat

Exx. 65 and 66: The danger here is that you may over-emphasize the last *p* beat, preparing for the *f*. This can be avoided by using a field of beating in the *p* bars that is about 6 inches higher than the normal. You will then have ample room for a large *f* downbeat. The transition from *f* to *p* (in the repeats!) is done simply by a sudden diminution of the downbeat. Use non-espressivo for *p* and espressivo for *f*. The preliminary gesture is small in Ex. 65; large in Ex. 66.

Ex. 67: The last *p* beat must be somewhat larger to prepare for the *f*, but must not appear to indicate a crescendo. On the rest in bar 4, beat *p* to prepare the repeat. For *p* staccato, use the light-staccato or full-staccato. Maintain your tempo, do not speed up in *f*, and do not slow down when changing back to *p* !

47

Ex. 68: Beat *f* on the rest in the 4th measure to prepare the repeat.

These exercises offer practice in the sudden change of dynamics on the 1st count in a measure. Changes on the other counts, which are less difficult to execute, are directed in a similar manner.

(2) Using the Left Hand

It has already been demonstrated how to indicate *f* with the left hand (p. 22). In the gesture which expresses *p,* the palm of the hand, fingers together, faces the orchestra. These two gestures do not take the place of indicating dynamics with the beat, but are rather supporting gestures. (The one exception is in an *f* passage with sustained notes, as in Ex. 22, in which a large and cumbersome baton motion is usually avoided by means of an *f* gesture in the left hand.)

Repeat Exx. 65-68, using the left hand. The *f* gesture of the left hand must come exactly on the first *f* beat; the *p* gesture, however, should come a little ahead of the *p* beat. In other words, the left-hand gesture, following the last *f* beat immediately, indicates a sudden warning before the *p* passage begins. Practice turning your left hand quickly on the last eighth-note of the measure.

In staccato, use the left hand to indicate the change to *p* only, and not for the change to *f*. Avoid time-beating movements in the left hand!

(3) Moving the Right Hand Nearer To or Farther Away From the Body

The right hand may beat close to the body, or it may move away a considerable distance. To emphasize an *f* beat, the right hand may move away from the body suddenly. Likewise, a sudden retreat of the hand close to the body makes the change to *p* more effective.

Apply this to the examples without using the left hand. Support by the left hand and motion by the right hand as described are rarely used together. Their combination is a very powerful dramatic gesture and should be reserved for great climaxes.

The following examples may be used for applying the various techniques.

Ex. 69 Allegro, (♩ = 126) BEETHOVEN, *Piano Concerto No. 5*

Ex. 70 Allegretto (♩ = 80) *CÉSAR FRANCK, Symphony in D minor*

Ex. 71 Andante maestoso, ♩ = 120 KODÁLY, *Háry János Suite*

Andante cantabile con moto, ♪ = 120 (♪ = 104)   BEETHOVEN, *Symphony No. 1*

Ex. 72

Additional examples for the study of sudden dynamic changes:

4-beat:

Haydn: Symphony No. 101, 2nd movement—bars 11–12.

Mozart: Symphony No. 39, K. 543—2nd movement.

Mozart: Violin Concerto No. 5, K. 219—2nd movement.

Tchaikovsky: Symphony No. 5, 4th movement—at C and 9 bars after C.

Tchaikovsky: Symphony No. 6, 1st movement—at 0.

Wagner: *Tristan und Isolde, Liebestod*—bars 44–46, 54.

3-beat:

Bartók: Divertimento for String Orchestra, 1st movement—bars 59–62.

Beethoven: Symphony No. 5, 2nd movement.

Brahms: Symphony No. 2, 1st movement (see Ex. 319a).

Haydn: Symphony No. 92, 1st movement—*Allegro*.

Rimsky-Korsakoff: *Capriccio Espagnol, Variazioni*—16 bars before the end.

Tchaikovsky: Symphony No. 4, 1st movement—5 bars after B and at E.

Change from Legato to Staccato and Vice Versa

Experiment by having your friend at the piano play Ex. 73 (♩ = 66) while you are beating the 1st bar staccato and the 2nd legato, contrary to the music. The player will neither feel comfortable in his legato line nor be sure of the rhythm of the staccato chords. This experiment, better than a long explanation, proves the necessity of articulating the beat in agreement with the music—in spite of certain exceptions already mentioned and others to be discussed later on.

As to the execution of the transitions, you will not find it difficult to go from legato to staccato. Just begin to beat staccato on the count at which the detached playing begins; if this is the 1st count, use "bouncing." To change from staccato to legato, beat staccato as usual on the last staccato count, but instead of waiting on the ⟨STOP⟩ during the count, let the hand *immediately* continue in a legato motion to the next count. Practice this technique in slow tempo until you feel able to apply it to the faster metronome markings.

—— **Exx. 73–79:** Practice all the transitions from legato to staccato and vice versa by doing all the repeats.

There are different ways of performing staccato: from very short and sharply attacked notes to moderately detached playing; from a vigorous *f* staccato to a very gentle touch. A conductor can make his players understand what kind of staccato he wants by his beat alone. Furthermore, learn to articulate so distinctly that, when your friend at the piano is playing some simple passage, such as a scale, he will know when to play legato or staccato just by following your baton. To do this, you will have to think ahead; if you are not sure of what you want, your gesture will not convince the player.

Chapter 7

CRESCENDO AND DECRESCENDO

IN CHAPTER 6 you practiced the *sudden* change from *p* to *f* and vice versa. This discussion deals with the *gradual* change.

Changing the Size of the Beat

As the dynamics gradually increase or decrease, your gesture changes its size. If there is a crescendo from *p* to *f* in one measure, the 2nd beat will be markedly larger than the 1st, the 3rd still larger, and the 4th will indicate *f*. But if you have two or more bars at your disposal, the increase of size is sometimes so slow (crescendo poco a poco) that the change from beat to beat is hardly noticeable. The same applies to decrescendo.

Practice first before the mirror, beating in 4 and 3 (♩ = 80) and indicating *p* ⟞ *f* in one measure, then in two measures, finally in three or more measures. In legato, start non-espressivo or poco espressivo. As a rule, the non-espressivo pattern is not suited for very large gestures because it then looks awkward. Therefore, do not carry this beat too far in crescendo, but change to espressivo. This also applies to light-staccato, which should change gradually to full-staccato. Practice similarly *f* ⟞ *p*.

Now use Exx. 80-83. Each of these has 4 different dynamic markings. Thorough practice will make your beat flexible and improve your control considerably. Be economical in the use of your arm and avoid exaggerated gestures. To direct *p* ⟨⟩ *p*, it is often sufficient to add some forearm motion to the wrist movement used to lead the *p*.

53

Using the Left Hand

Crescendo is indicated by lifting the left hand, palm facing upward, from the level of the hip to eye level. The hand is held up as long as you want to maintain *f*. For decrescendo, turn the hand *slowly* so that the palm faces the players; then start dropping the hand gradually, the palm still towards the orchestra, until it reaches the starting position. (The reason for turning the left hand slowly is that a sudden turn would indicate sudden *p* instead of decrescendo!)

Practice these movements by allowing yourself first one measure, then two, then three or more measures for crescendo.

Count aloud in 4 and in 3. Practice decrescendo the same way. Take great care not to make any time-beating movements with the left hand. The up-and-down motions must be absolutely smooth and continuous. Students sometimes have trouble in achieving this smoothness in the left hand while the right hand is beating time. Practice the coordination of both hands and check in the mirror.

In applying the left-hand gestures to Exx. 80 through 83, you should realize that they constitute a very strong support. Therefore you will not need beats as large as those you used with the right hand alone. Try to balance the movements of both hands and avoid exaggerations. Crescendo in staccato does not need the expressive left-hand gesture. However, the left hand is considerably more effective than the right in securing a diminuendo or *p* subito in both legato and staccato.

Another point that must be considered is connected with the psychology of the orchestra. Many players have a tendency to play loudly at once when they see "cresc." and softly when their parts indicate "decresc." or "dimin." On the other hand, the orchestra does not easily give all its strength to the climax of a crescendo unless stimulated by the leader. So you will have to be fairly restrained at the beginning of a crescendo but very energetic at the climax.

The conductor must not yield to the temptation to increase the tempo when directing a crescendo or to slow down during a diminuendo passage.

Ex. 84: In most editions the time signature for this movement is C. However, both Beethoven's manuscript and the first print have ₵. Moreover, Carl Czerny, who performed the work's premiere under the composer's supervision, pointed out that this *alla breve* movement must not drag.

Still, the *Adagio un poco moto* is directed with a 4-beat (Czerny suggested ♩ = 60). Diag. 8a is recommended for the beginning. During the 4th bar, lift the left hand halfway to indicate *f* espressivo in bar 5 (see p. 22), while the beat increases in expressiveness (Diag. 8). Turn the palm during the 1st beat of bar 6 and drop the hand slightly. With the 1st beat in bar 7, the left hand moves back to indicate *f*; it is turned again during the 3rd beat and dropped slowly. The *right hand* uses the 4th beat in bar 4 (quarter-rest) for a fairly large and very expressive preparation for the following *f*. In the 6th measure use small gestures for the 2nd and 3rd beats, but a larger preparatory beat to attack the second *f* entry. The 8th bar requires restrained gestures (cf. pp. 130 and 159).

Ex. 85: Beat espressivo. In the 3rd measure, gradually put the left hand into action. After the climax in the 5th bar a strong diminuendo follows, which requires convincing gestures of both hands.

Ex. 86: Increasing intensity of the gestures indicates the increase in the volume and sonority of the string orchestra. A strongly contrasted motion is needed for the *p* subito.

Ex. 87: In a case like this, do not enlarge your beat for the crescendo in the drum; it is much more effective to save the first large gesture for the preparatory beat (full-staccato) needed on *Three* for the *ff* attack on *Four*. Small beats will do to start the drum player and to beat the first 2 counts.

Ex. 88: Full-staccato. It is not advisable to use beats that are too large in staccato when the tempo is lively, because the gestures would become too hectic. Instead, indicate the crescendo by increasing the intensity and sharpness of your staccato beat. Support the climax with the left hand.

Ex. 89: Poco espressivo. Increase the size of the beat in the 5th bar only slightly and gradually; then use the left hand to indicate the sudden *p* in bar 7. Keep your gestures small and graceful (see p. 349).

Ex. 90: Start beating non-espressivo with restrained gestures, and indicate the 3 small crescendos (bars 2–6) with slightly enlarged beats. For the crescendo starting in the 7th measure, use either of the methods you have learned, but be economical with your gestures! If you have exhausted your resources by bar 13 (*f*), nothing is left to build up the climax in bar 25. This *ff* requires a special preparation, made by beating the last beat in bar 24 full-staccato with *Three* on STOP . This is the *accented upbeat* mentioned in Ch. 2 (p. 15); see Diag. 21 and comments on p. 76.

A general remark may be added here. The detailed suggestions made in this and the following chapters are to some extent a matter of individual interpretation. It is not assumed that they constitute the only right way of execution, for there are often several "right" ways to conduct a particular piece of music. Nevertheless, it is important that the student be shown at least one of the right ways, and thus get a start on the road which leads away from mere time-beating and toward a development of his ability to convey artistic intentions to his players.

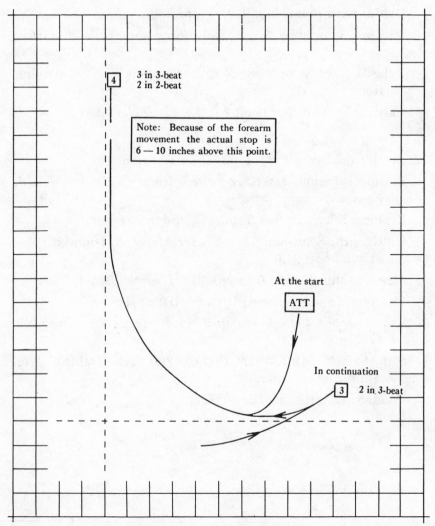

Diagram 21. Accented up-beat

Additional examples for the study of crescendo and decrescendo:

4-beat:

Beethoven: Symphony No. 6, 2nd movement.
Bizet: *L'Arlésienne Suite No. 1,* 1st movement — last 10 bars.
Bruckner: Symphony No. 7, 2nd movement — at H and S.
Debussy: *Sirènes* (also *p* subito).

Dvořák: Symphony No. 9, 2nd movement — after No. 4.

Sibelius: Symphony No. 2, 2nd movement — passage starting at D.

Tchaikovsky: Symphony No. 5, 1st movement — Introduction.

Verdi: *Messa da Requiem*, No. 1 — *Kyrie eleison*.

3-beat:

Beethoven: Symphony No. 2, 2nd movement.

Berlioz: *Menuet des Feux-Follets* from *La Damnation de Faust*.

Brahms: *Ein deutsches Requiem*, 2nd movement.

Hindemith: Symphony *Mathis der Maler*, 3rd movement — *Sehr lebhaft* 9/8.

Mendelssohn: *Elijah*, Aria No. 21 — *Hear ye, Israel*.

Puccini: *Manon Lescaut*, 4th act — bars 1–4.

Ravel: *Daphnis et Chloé*, Suite No. 2 — from No. 156 to No. 170.

Saint-Saëns: *Samson et Dalila*, 2nd act — Dalila's aria, *Amour, viens aider*.

Wagner: Overture to *Tannhäuser*.

Chapter 8

THE 2-BEAT

Non-Espressivo and Espressivo-Legato

DIAGRAM 22. In 2-beat it is absolutely essential to follow the diagram exactly. Otherwise it is easy to slip into a habit that is confusing to the players—namely, to use almost identical gestures for the 1st and 2nd beats. Avoid carrying the rebound of the 1st beat too far up (see Diag. 22a). ② must be *on* the left-right line, not below! It will help you in practicing to imagine that you are lifting something off the left-right line with the point of the baton at ② .

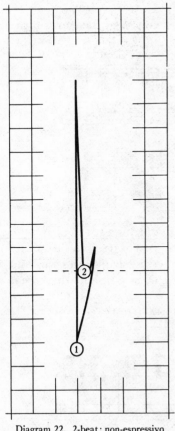

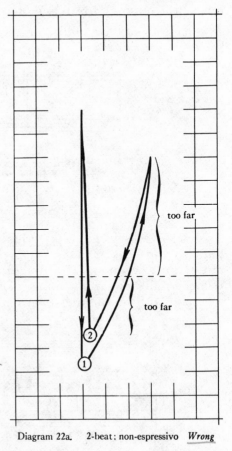

Diagram 22. 2-beat; non-espressivo

Diagram 22a. 2-beat: non-espressivo *Wrong*

61

For the start on the 1st count, use the preliminary beat of Diagram 2. Practice Ex. 91.

Diagram 23. Use this pattern in slow and very expressive music. The double curve looks almost like a subdivided 2nd beat (*Two-and*), but there is no rhythmic subdivision here; the double curve gives more space to execute the 2nd beat smoothly and fluently. Diagram 23a is used often, especially in a tempo faster than ♩ = 60. Diagram 23b is recommended for molto espressivo.

All of these diagrams, both non-espressivo and espressivo-legato, can be applied only in slow and moderate tempos. The legato gestures for 2-beat in rapid tempo are discussed in the chapters on the tenuto pattern and on free style.

Practice Exx. 92 and 93. For the latter you need the start on the 2nd count shown in Diag. 24.

Ex. 94: Most violinists perform this *Andante* at a speed of ♪ = 96. Still, beating 6 counts to the measure would be contrary to the nature of this quiet beginning. Use a 2-beat, non-espressivo, with calm and well-controlled gestures. (In the course of this movement, the 2-beat alternates with 6-beat subdivision.)

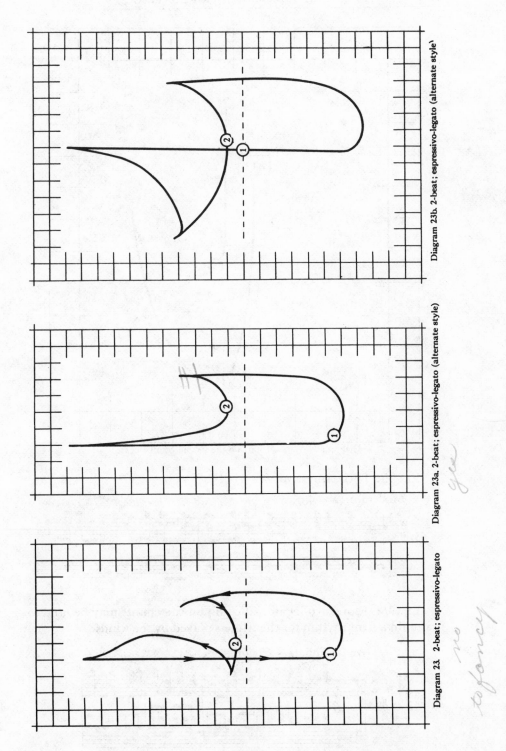

Diagram 23b. 2-beat; espressivo-legato (alternate style)

Diagram 23a. 2-beat; espressivo-legato (alternate style)

Diagram 23 2-beat; espressivo-legato

63

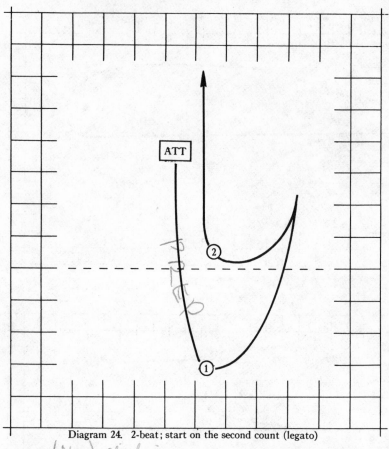

Diagram 24. 2-beat; start on the second count (legato)

Ex. 95: Poco espressivo.

Moderato, ($\downarrow$. = 48)   OFFENBACH, Les Contes d'Hoffmann

Ex. 96: Espressivo-legato. Clicking on the counts may be used to maintain a firm rhythm for the triplets played by the winds.

Andantino, ($\downarrow$ = 69-76)   TCHAIKOVSKY, Symphony No. 4

Ex. 97: Start on the 2nd count; use a very intense espressivo gesture (cf. p. 213).

Light-Staccato and Full-Staccato

Diagrams 25 and 26 show the patterns for staccato. Use Ex. 98 for practicing light-staccato and full-staccato. Ex. 99 starts on the 2nd count. On the preliminary beat (Diag. 27), lift the fore-

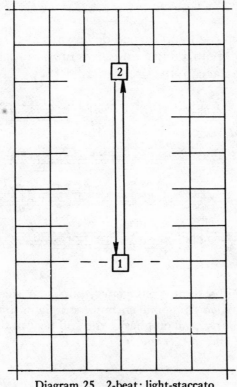

Diagram 25. 2-beat; light-staccato

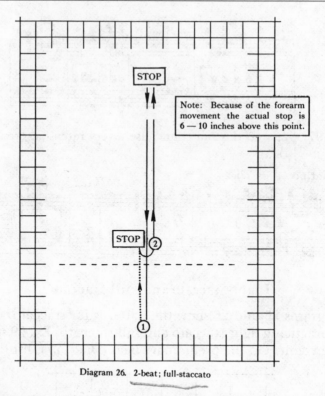

Diagram 26. 2-beat; full-staccato

arm swiftly with the hand turned downward at the lower $\boxed{\text{STOP}}$. Thus the baton points down and gives more impetus to the *f* attack. For light-staccato the size is smaller.

Ex. 100: Full-staccato, energetic gestures. A sharp 2nd beat in bar 2 will get a good trombone entrance strictly in time. Beat *One* in the 4th bar similarly, and emphasize the 2nd beat in the 5th bar after which the horns and violas come in.

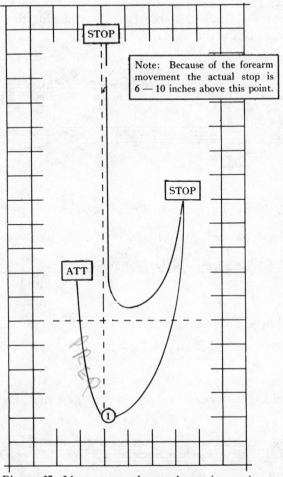

Note: Because of the forearm movement the actual stop is 6 — 10 inches above this point.

Diagram 27. 2-beat; start on the second count (staccato)

Allegretto, ♩. = 69   *RIMSKY-KORSAKOV, Capriccio Espagnol*

Ex. 100

Ex. 101: <u>Light-staccato.</u> Your small but distinct movements should be seen equally well by the 1st violins playing the theme, and the 2nd violins playing the staccato counterpoint.

Ex. 102: Beginning in bar 6, use full-staccato (see p. 90).

Copyright 1945 by Boosey & Hawkes, Ltd. Renewed 1973.
Reprinted by permission of Boosey & Hawkes, Inc.

Ex. 103: Light-staccato, in spite of the legato marking.

Ex. 104a: Full-staccato.

Ex. 104b Light-staccato.

Exx. 105 and 106: Both start on the 2nd count—Ex. 105 in full-staccato, Ex. 106 in light-staccato. Beat the preparation in the correct tempo!

Dynamic Changes

For dynamic changes, review the explanations of Chapters 6 and 7. Practice Ex. 107; in order to indicate the dynamics exactly as they occur in the music, your mind must always be ahead of your hand.

Ex. 108: An excellent opportunity to practice the coordination of both hands. In bars 5 and 6, use the right hand alone. In bar 7, use the left hand again. Apply the pattern of Diag. 23a, with clicking on the accented beats.

Allegretto pastorale, ♩. = 60

GRIEG, *Peer Gynt Suite No. 1*

Ex. 109: In the 3rd and 7th measures, the 1st beat is large, the 2nd small.

Allegro con anima, ♩. = 104

TCHAIKOVSKY, *Symphony No. 5*

Ex. 110: For the sudden *p* in the 3rd bar, put up the left hand just in time to announce the change without affecting the last *f* eighth-note. After the legato beat in the first 3 measures, change to a gentle staccato, becoming somewhat sharper with the gradual crescendo. Reverse this procedure for the diminuendo.

Allegro ma non troppo, ♩ = 66 (♩ = 116–120) BEETHOVEN, *Symphony No. 6*

Ex. 111: For the articulation, see Ex. 110. In cases like this, it helps to think of the structure of the music (periods of 4 bars each) in building up a gradual crescendo. Do not forget the cues!

Change From Legato to Staccato

The explanations of Chapter 6 apply to the following exercises:

Additional examples for the study of 2-beat:

Non-espressivo:

Bruckner: Symphony No. 4, 1st movement—beginning.

Dvořák: Symphony No. 7, 1st movement—beginning.

Strauss: *Tod und Verklärung*—passage beginning 18 bars after L.

Stravinsky: *L'Oiseau de Feu* (Suite), *Ronde des princesses*—beginning and last 19 bars.

Tchaikovsky: Serenade for Strings, 4th movement—beginning.

Espressivo-legato:

Borodin: Symphony No. 2, 2nd movement—passage starting at F.

Brahms: Symphony No. 4, 1st movement (see Appendix A, No. 5).

Janáček: *Sinfonietta*, 3rd movement.

Mascagni: *Cavalleria Rusticana*, Santuzza's aria, *Voi lo sapete*—Introduction.

Rachmaninoff: Piano Concerto No. 2, 3rd movement—*Maestoso* (second theme).

Smetana: *The Moldau*, passage starting at bar 40.

Verdi: Overture to *I Vespri Siciliani*, passage starting at I (bars 185–199).

Light-staccato:

Beethoven: Symphony No. 6, 4th movement—beginning.

Mendelssohn: Overture to *A Midsummer Night's Dream*.

Mozart: Overture to *Le Nozze di Figaro*, beginning.

Prokofiev: Symphony No. 5, 4th movement—at No. 80.

Rimsky-Korsakov: *The Flight of the Bumble-Bee*.

Rossini: *Il Barbiere di Siviglia*, 2nd act—Tempest Music.

Tchaikovsky: *Nutcracker Suite: Ouverture miniature*, and *Danse des Mirlitons*.

Full-staccato

Bach: *Brandenburg Concerto No. 1*, 3rd movement.

Berlioz: *Marche Hongroise (Rakóczy March)* from *La Damnation de Faust*.

Berlioz: *Symphonie fantastique*, 4th movement.

Brahms: Symphony No. 2, 4th movement—passage starting at A.

Dvořák: *Carneval Overture.*

Franck: Symphony in D minor, 1st movement, *Allegro non troppo.*

Rimsky-Korsakov: *Capriccio Espagnol*, passage starting at M.

Roussel: Suite in F major, 1st movement (see Ex. 214).

Start on the 2nd count:

Bach: Suite No. 2 in B minor, Badinerie.

Beethoven: Symphony No. 8, 4th movement.

Gluck: *Orphée et Euridice*, 2nd act, 2nd scene — *Cet asile* (*Grazioso* 6/8).

Gounod: *Faust*, 1st act, 2nd scene — No. 3 (Chorus).

Haydn: Symphony No. 103, 1st movement — *Allegro con spirito.*

Mozart: *Don Giovanni*, 1st act — No. 2, Duet (*Fuggi, crudele*).

Rachmaninoff: *Rhapsody on a theme of Paganini* — beginning.

Dynamic changes:

Beethoven: Symphony No. 4, 1st and 4th movements.

Berlioz: Overture *Le Carnaval Romain, Allegro vivace.*

Berlioz: *Symphonie fantastique*, 1st movement — *Allegro* section.

Bizet: *Carmen*, Prelude to the 1st act.

Falla: *Three-Cornered Hat*, Suite No. 2 — *Danse du Meunier* and *Danse final.*

Haydn: Symphony No. 88, 4th movement.

Mozart: Overture to *Le Nozze di Figaro.*

Rossini: Overture to *Guillaume Tell, Allegro vivace* 2/4.

Chapter 9

FACING THE ORCHESTRA

Orchestral Seating Arrangement

THIS CHAPTER REQUIRES a bit of imagination on the part of the student. A young actor not only memorizes his part and acquaints himself with the poetic and spiritual values of the play; he prepares himself by imagining that he is acting his part on the stage. Self-training of this kind is very useful for the young conductor. When you apply your baton technique to the study of scores, you should act as though facing an orchestra. It is of minor importance which of the several different seating arrangements you have in mind while practicing. It will increase your flexibility if you think of one seating plan now, and of another the next time you practice.

Cuing

The question of when to cue in the players will be discussed in greater detail in Chapter 24, but whether you give a cue or not, you should be aware of the entries. This means that you must know the score so well that you know what each instrument is doing all the time.

There are three ways of giving a cue: with the eyes, with the baton, and with the left hand.

Some conductors like to show their superior knowledge of the score by throwing the left hand in the direction of the entering instruments as the first note of the entry is played. The players dislike it, and quite justifiably. Cuing is helpful only if done a little in advance of the entry and, while a spectacular gesture may impress the public, it is apt to make the players nervous. Do not get into the habit of giving all cues by pointing. The left hand should be used primarily to indicate a special kind of attack or the expression with which the particular entry is to be played.

In directing your baton toward a group of entering instruments, you can address the players effectively by turning and facing them. This technique should be used, however, only when *[handwritten margin notes: "prep type gesture"; "opposed = { tutti to melody / wait / long rests"]*

a very dramatic entrance is required. If used too often the repeated change of the field of beating upsets the clarity of the beat, as any strong gesture used too frequently loses its effectiveness. Moreover, indication of entries by stretching the whole arm, as though you wanted to stab the players, is not a good habit.

Most of the time, the best way of cuing in your players is to look at them. Turn your eyes toward the players 1 count in advance in moderate tempo, and about 2 counts in fast tempo. Using your eyes is best for two reasons: first, you should not use more motion than you need in conducting; second, the expression of your eyes and your general facial expression can tell the players more about your intentions than fancy hand-waving.

A review of some of the exercises will give you an opportunity to combine the picture of the orchestral set-up with your conducting technique and to use your eyes for cuing in the players.

Ex. 5: Shortly after assuming the position of attention, look at the harp, then start. Not too soon, but not later than the 4th beat in bar 2, turn your eyes toward the flute.

Ex. 7: Since the orchestra pauses in the 1st bar, your beats are small but distinct in order to keep the rhythm clear. In the 4th beat, include an unobtrusive preparation for the horns by turning your eyes toward them. The G-minor chord in the next bar is played by the strings without 1st violins; turn the head toward the other sections. At the same time think about the grace notes (G, B♭, A) in the solo violin while beating the last count in bar 2, so as to start bar 3 exactly with the soloist (see p. 305).

Ex. 9: To start, address the string section in a general way without pointing out any special group. You may have to prevent the double-basses from starting too loudly, as they sometimes do: put your left hand unobtrusively in p position. Watch the entries of clarinets, oboes, and 2nd bassoon.

Ex. 14: After attention, turn the body and baton halfway to the left. This establishes closer contact with the 1st violins, which is desirable when they have a passage of solo-like quality. Be sure that the rest of the orchestra can see the beat.

Ex. 16: Do not turn your baton to the left, since it would be awkward to move the field of beating a few seconds later to address the other string groups.

Exx. 53a and 55: In this fast tempo, turn your eye toward the flutes in Ex. 53a and to the 1st violins in Ex. 55 at least 2 beats before the entries.

Ex. 90: Address the violins and then the violas (+ bassoons) for the small crescendos. In the 13th bar there are simultaneous entries of the oboes, horns, and trombones. During the preceding bar, look at the oboes and horns, then concentrate on the accented trombone entry. Your beats on the accented counts, played alternately by trombones and clarinets, should be especially sharp. Cue in the flutes; 4 bars later the kettle-drum; and, on the *ff*, the trumpets.

Conducting a Complete Work

At this point the student will have sufficient command of the elements of conducting to apply his training to an entire composition. To conduct a piece of music, one must know it intimately. This knowledge must include not only the notes but also the dynamics, the orchestration, and the harmonic and formal structure; nor can the importance of rhythm be emphasized too much.

Only if the conductor approaches his task with a definite idea of the rhythmic requirements for each instrument can he control a rehearsal efficiently and direct a good performance.

The use of a good phonograph recording is quite stimulating, because it supplements the musical imagination. It is helpful in memorizing the score and in giving a vivid picture of the orchestration. But using a record for practice gives you only a passive experience, for you tend to follow rather than to lead. The best active practice is to hum or sing while you conduct or to be assisted by a skillful pianist who can follow your beat intelligently. This develops the feeling for leading, while following the record does not.

When playing recordings, students must insure accurate pitch. Tonal deviations affect the speed of the music and can, therefore, distort the pacing intended by the performer. Misrepresentations of this sort are not uncommon when recorded music is heard in radio broadcasts.

At the beginning of your practice, put yourself into the mood of the music. Fix the rhythm firmly in your mind by humming the first few bars or thinking them to yourself. Then call your imaginary orchestra to attention. The authority of this gesture must be in keeping with the particular character of the opening, which may vary from quiet and contemplative to vivacious and energetic.

Study and practice scores Nos. 1 and 2 discussed in the Appendix. In class work, a small string orchestra should be made available. It is also recommended that class sessions be videotaped. Students will benefit greatly by the replay of their performances and by watching their gestures and appearance.

Chapter 10

THE 1-BEAT

WHEN THE TEMPO of a piece of music is very fast, the conductor will be unable to give all the beats without confusing the players. In many classic scherzos, the written tempo of 3/4 is so fast that it is much more convenient to give only 1 beat in a measure. The same is true for most waltzes. Many classic pieces with the time-signature 2/4 are also done in this way, as are a number of modern pieces written in 4-time and even 6-time (Sibelius, Symphony No. 2, 3rd movement in 6/8, see Ex. 332; Stravinsky, *L'Oiseau de Feu, Danse infernale* in 6/4).

Non-Espressivo

Diagram 28. The diagram shows that the downward movement is quicker than the upward movement. Avoid any stop at the top of the beat. For the start use Diagram 29 or Diagram 2; the choice between the two is a matter of personal preference.

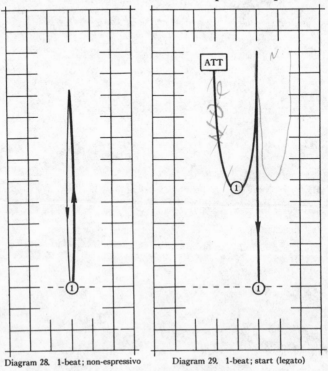

Diagram 28. 1-beat; non-espressivo   Diagram 29. 1-beat; start (legato)

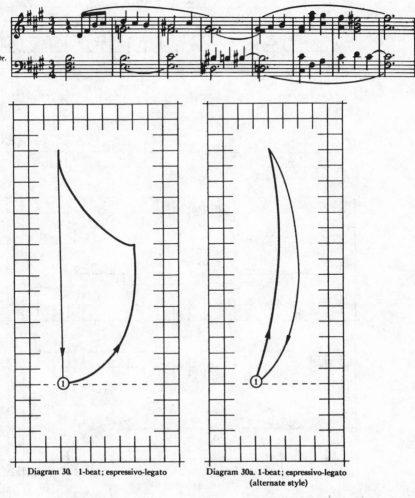

Espressivo-Legato

Diagram 30. This pattern implies a subdivision into 3-time; when that is not desired, use Diagram 30a. In any case, do not stress any part of the beat except ① . Since the execution of the beat depends upon the individual gesture and the character of the music, feel free to vary the pattern, which is only one of several possibilities.

Diagram 30. 1-beat; espressivo-legato

Diagram 30a. 1-beat; espressivo-legato (alternate style)

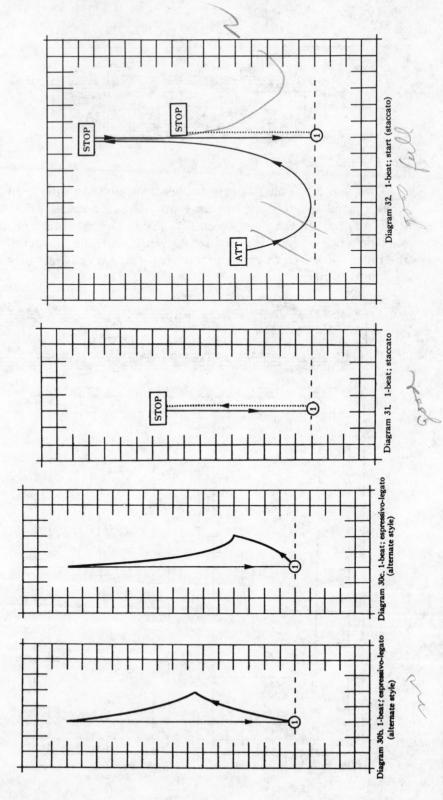

Diagram 32. 1-beat; start (staccato)

Diagram 31. 1-beat; staccato

Diagram 30c. 1-beat; espressivo-legato (alternate style)

Diagram 30b. 1-beat; espressivo-legato (alternate style)

80

Staccato

Diagram 31. This pattern covers both light-staccato and full-staccato. For full-staccato the size is larger and the bounce sharper, with more arm movement. The intensity of the beat depends upon the speed with which you snap the baton up. If this movement is moderately slow, the staccato is rather gentle; if you make a special effort to whip the baton up, the orchestra will play very sharply. In practicing the start (Diag. 32, also 5 or 7), remember that the preliminary beat must express the type of staccato you want from the players. Exx. 116 and 117 give you varied practice.

Dynamic Changes and Change From Legato to Staccato

Ex. 118: Practice first with the right hand alone, then support with the left hand.

Ex. 119: The technique explained in Ch. 6 is used here.

Musical Examples

Ex. 120: Beating this in 3 would disturb the smooth flow of the melody, therefore 1-beat is always used here. Beat the first 8 bars legato non-espressivo, the following accompaniment figure staccato, very gently.

Ex. 121: A graceful espressivo beat is recommended. The non-espressivo 1-beat pattern would be too dull, while beating 3 beats in a measure would be too agitated. For the start, see Ch. 12.

Ex. 122: A flexible espressivo beat is needed to build up the melodic line.

Exx. 123 and 124: Very small but precise light-staccato.

Copyright©1941 G. Schirmer, Inc.
Used by permission.

Ex. 125: Full-staccato. Do not be too quick with the diminuendo, since the orchestra is apt to quiet down too suddenly.

Ex. 126: Because of the strong rhythmic element, beat staccato, first gently, but with full-staccato at *ff* (see p. 380).

Ex. 127: 4 bars legato, 2 bars full-staccato, then sudden change to light-staccato.

Ex. 128: 1st bar full-staccato, 2nd bar light-staccato with the character of a preparation for the 3rd; light-staccato in bars 4–7, and full-staccato in the 8th measure.

Additional examples for the study of 1-beat:

Non-espressivo:

Beethoven: Symphony No. 5, 3rd movement—passage starting at bar 324.

Bizet: Symphony, 3rd movement—passage at No. 38.

Brahms: *Variations on a Theme by Haydn*, Variation No. 8.

Chausson: Symphony Op. 20, 1st movement (also espressivo-legato and staccato).

Delius: *Brigg Fair* — passage at No. 2.

Dvořák: *Scherzo Capriccioso*, bars 7-16.

Espressivo-legato:

Bruckner: Symphony No. 7, 3rd movement — Trio.

Gounod: *Faust*, Ballet No. 1 (A major) — starting at the double bar.

Ravel: *La Valse*-passage at No. 30 (also dynamic changes).

Strauss, Johann: *Emperor Waltz* — No. 1.

Verdi: Overture to *La Forza del Destino*, *Allegro agitato* 3/8.

Weber-Berlioz: *Invitation to the Dance*, passage starting at No. 7.

Staccato:

Beethoven: Symphony No. 9, 2nd movement.

Bruckner: Symphony No. 9, 2nd movement.

Dukas: *L'Apprenti Sorcier*, starting at No. 6.

Dvořák: Symphony No. 9, 3rd movement.

Elgar: *Enigma Variations, Op. 36*, Variation No. 4.

Handel: Concerto Grosso No. 5, 3rd movement (*Presto* 3/8).

Rossini: *Il Barbiere di Siviglia*, 1st act — Finale I, *Allegro* 3/4 in E-flat major.

Schubert: Symphony No. 2, 4th movement.

Schubert: Symphony No. 6, 3rd movement.

Dynamic changes:

Beethoven: Symphony No. 5, 3rd movement.

Berlioz: *Symphonie Fantastique*, 2nd movement (*Un Bal*).

Dvořák: *Slavonic Dance in C major, Op. 46, No. 1*.

Mahler: *Das Lied von der Erde,* 1st movement.

Schubert: Symphony No. 9, 4th movement.

Schumann: Symphony No. 1, 3rd movement — Trios I and II.

Strauss: *Burleske* (also non-espressivo, espressivo-legato, and staccato).

Tchaikovsky: *Nutcracker Suite*, No. 3 — *Valse des Fleurs*.

Chapter 11

THE MARCATO PATTERN

The marcato beat is a heavy motion with a stop on each count. It is forceful, sometimes aggressive in character, and medium to large in size. The gestures connecting the counts are slower than in staccato; they are either straight or curved (espressivo) depending on the music.

There are two types of marcato, both done with a strong and vigorous gesture. For the first type, which uses straight lines to connect the counts, apply Diagram 4. Since marcato is used only in loud dynamics (*mf* to *ff*), the size will have to be at least three times that of the light-staccato pattern. Also remember that you must not move too quickly. $\boxed{4}$ at the top of the field of beating is characteristic of this type of marcato. To gain the impetus needed for a start on the 1st count, use the accented upbeat of Diagram 21. Start on the other counts with a full-staccato preliminary beat.

Diagrams 17 and 25 are applied in a similar manner for marcato in 3-beat and in 2-beat. Diagram 33 shows the execution of 1-beat marcato. It is characterized by an intense holding on to $\boxed{1}$ and a quick but energetic up-down motion which gives the impetus for the next marcato attack.

Ex. 129: An excellent example for practicing marcato with straight lines. Conduct the entire *Hallelujah*. Try to find a few instrumentalists to assist the class, which sings the chorus. Conduct legato, beginning with the words "The kingdom of this world," 7½ bars in all.

Allegro, (♩ = 104-112)

HANDEL, *The Messiah*

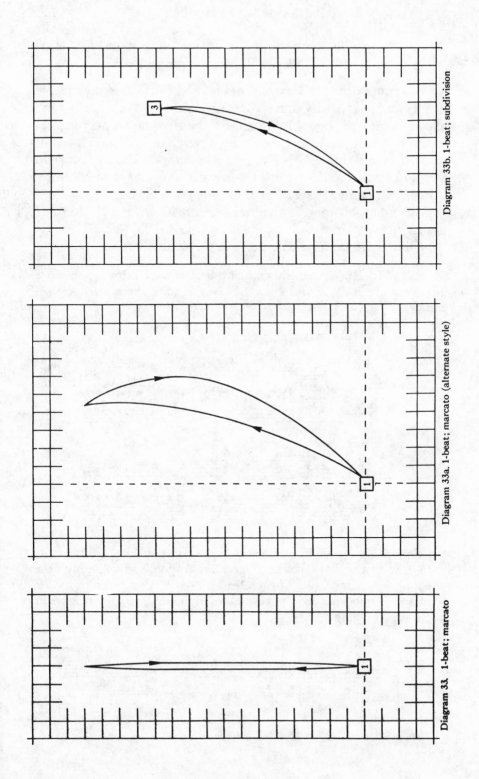

Diagram 33b. 1-beat; subdivision

Diagram 33a. 1-beat; marcato (alternate style)

Diagram 33. 1-beat; marcato

87

Since *The Star-Spangled Banner* is in every conductor's repertoire, practice it now, beating marcato in the first and last parts.

The marcato with curved lines is used for rather slow music of passionate intensity and strong rhythm. It combines the lyric expressiveness of the legato beat with the rhythmical decisiveness of the staccato. In 4-beat, apply Diagram 8 or 8b, making a full stop on each count. The slowness of the tempo permits you to do this and still have time for an espressivo movement to the next count. Remember that, while the connection between counts depends somewhat upon individual interpretation, the location of the counts remains fixed. Apply Diagrams 16, 23, and 30 for this type of marcato in 3-beat, 2-beat, and 1-beat, respectively.

Ex. 130: The curved-line marcato beat at once expresses the lyric quality of the melody and gives a heavy, definite rhythm for the accompaniment (see p. 142).

Ex. 131: Gradual intensification from non-espressivo (*pp*) to marcato (*ff*). Start with a fairly small gesture; gradually increase both the size and the accentuation of each beat till bar 5. Use the straight-line marcato. Do not wait for the 16th-notes in the brass; only a strict beat precludes dragging.

Ex. 132: Similar to Ex. 130 but in 3-beat. The advantage of marcato in such cases over espressivo (even with clicking) is that it keeps the heavy brasses from dragging, as they are otherwise likely to do.

Ex. 133: The heavy brass chords and syncopated strings demand the marcato (see p. 118).

Ex. 102: The downbeats in each of the first 5 measures require marcato gestures. *Two* in these bars always serves as preparation; use the same preparatory beat as you would in staccato. With the entrance of the woodwinds, the beat changes to full-staccato.

Ex. 134: Though the time-signature is 4/4, this music is beaten alla breve (2-beat). Experiment by beating legato; try it again staccato. You will not be very comfortable either way, and only the marcato beat will give you the feeling that you are in control of this music. Think of the different orchestral groups as you conduct and cue them in.

Ex. 135: 1-beat. The heavy chords starting with the 2nd bar require a strong marcato beat. Decrease not only the size but the heaviness of the beat until you reach *p* non-espressivo.

Ex. 136: 1-beat marcato with a very lively connecting motion.

Additional examples for the study of the marcato pattern:

4-beat:

Bach: *Brandenburg Concerto No. 1*, 1st movement.

Liszt: *Les Préludes, Andante maestoso* 12/8.

Shostakovitch: Symphony No. 5, 3rd movement—passage starting at No. 89.

Wagner: Funeral March from *Götterdämmerung, ff* passages.

3-beat:

Brahms: *Ein deutsches Requiem,* 2nd movement—13 bars after B.

Britten: *The Young Person's Guide to the Orchestra*—Theme.

Handel: Concerto grosso, Op. 6, No. 6, 3rd movement (*Musette*)—passage starting at bar 81 (see Appendix A, No. 1).

Prokofiev: Symphony No. 5, 1st movement, at No. 23; 3rd movement, at No. 71.

Puccini: *Tosca,* 1st act—beginning.

Sibelius: Symphony No. 2, 4th movement—3 bars before B (*Pesante*).

2-beat:

Beethoven: Symphony No. 5, 4th movement—beginning.

Liszt: *Hungarian Rhapsody No. 2*, 4th bar from the end (*Andante*).

Mendelssohn: Symphony No. 5, 4th movement—last 19 bars.

Rachmaninoff: Piano Concerto No. 2, 1st movement—beginning.

Rimsky-Korsakoff: *Scheherazade,* 1st movement—beginning.

Saint-Saëns: Symphony No. 3, 2nd movement—at T.

Stravinsky: *L'Oiseau de Feu* (Suite), Finale—5 bars beginning at No. 20.

Verdi: *Messa da Requiem,* No. 2 (*Dies Irae*)—beginning.

1-beat:

Brahms: Piano Concerto No. 2, 2nd movement—passage starting 38 bars after C.

Mahler: Symphony No. 1, 2nd movement—beginning (if played not faster than indicated by the composer, ♩. = 66, the marcato beat emphasizes the half-notes; in the revised edition, the 2nd note in violins and violas was changed from an eighth to a sixteenth).

Mussorgsky-Ravel: *Pictures at an Exhibition*, No. 10 (*La Grande Porte de Kiev*)—at No. 115.

Chapter 12

START AFTER THE COUNT

IF THE MUSIC DOES NOT START on the count but on a fractional value, ignore the fraction in your beating and give the same rhythmic preparation that you would if the music began on the next full count. Do not try to beat the fractions, but rather feel them within the regular preparatory beat.

In class work Ex. 137 should be sung. There is a risk that the singers may not enter correctly, although the beat is right. However, the valuable experience gained by the student as a result of direct contact with the group is easily worth the time spent in interrupting and repeating.

In Exx. 137 a–g, give the preparation as though the music began on the 1st count; in h–j as though it began on the 2nd count; in k and l prepare the 3rd count; and in m the 4th. If you have a firm feeling for the rhythm, you can give a convincing preparation, and then the fractional values will come out correctly and automatically. Each of these short exercises should be repeated immediately in different tempos.

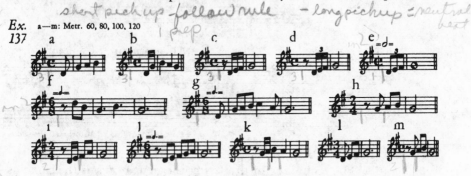

Ex. a—m: Metr. 60, 80, 100, 120
137

Exx. 138 and 139: Eighth-note before the 1st count. The preliminary beat is *pp* legato in Ex. 138 and *f* staccato in Ex. 139.

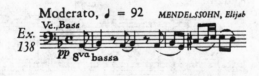

Moderato, ♩ = 92   MENDELSSOHN, *Elijah*
Vc., Bass
Ex.
138
pp 8ᵛᵃ bassa

Exx. 140 and 141 (1 bar only): The two openings are similar. But while the attack works easily in fast tempo, it is more difficult in slow tempo. The attack of Ex. 141 can be handled in several different ways: (1) Strictly according to rule: the staccato preparation has the value of a quarter-note (do not wait for the ♪, but keep going without hesitation!). (2) The preliminary beat has the value of an eighth-note. (3) Free style: make the preparation as though the ♪ were on *One*; this technique is successful if all the players have a definite feeling for the short-long rhythm. (Another way of conducting openings of this type is explained at the end of Ch. 24.)

Some musicians believe that the baroque practice of shortening upbeat notes, regardless of the music's tempo, applies to these kinds of double chords in post-baroque music, including the early nineteenth century.

no neutral beat

Ex. 142: The allegro section follows a pause and starts after the 3rd count. The technique of preparing the new attack is the same as that used at an opening start. During the pause, point the baton to the left to get a clear preliminary beat on *Three*.

Exx. 143–145: The downbeat should express the solemn dignity of the music in Ex. 143, while the preparation for Exx. 144 and 145 is a very snappy full-staccato. (To conform to baroque practice, the eighth-note in Ex. 143 must be shortened. The same applies to the 16th-notes.)

Ex. 146: Poco espressivo, legato.

Ex. 147: Light-staccato.

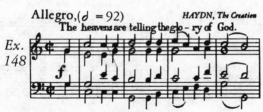

Ex. 148: *f* marcato.

Ex. 363 (bar 1): A sharp upbeat secures a precise ♪ at the attack.

Exx. 149, 150, and 151: Similar techniques, contrasting tempi.

RIMSKY-KORSAKOV, *Scheherazade*

DVOŘÁK, *Symphony No. 7*

MOZART, *Don Giovanni*

Ex. 152: Very energetic staccato.

SMETANA, *The Bartered Bride—Overture*

Exx. 153 and 154: Same rhythm, different tempos and dynamics. The preparation has the character of an upbeat.

SCHUBERT, *Symphony No. 2*

Exx. 155 and 156: 1-beat in 2/4 time. Ex. 155 requires light-staccato, Ex. 156 full-staccato. The preparatory gesture again has the character of an upbeat. (In Ex. 155 the second violin may not be authentic.)

Exx. 157, 158, and 257a: In these examples the entrance occurs immediately after the downbeat. Proceed in strict tempo and without hesitation from the first downbeat to the next. Do not wait unnecessarily for the notes in the 1st bar to be played, or the tempo will drag. The preparation here does not feel like an upbeat but has the solidity of an actual strong beat.

Use of an Extra Beat

Because of the difficulty of executing certain starts after the count, especially in fast tempo, conductors sometimes give an extra beat to secure precision.

Thus in Ex. 159 you may beat *One-Two* to establish the tempo with certainty.

MOZART, *Eine kleine Nachtmusik*

Ex. 160: You may beat *Two-One*, but a very small *Two*, no more than a flick of the wrist at the top of the field of beating, followed by a large staccato downbeat (*One*).

In a similar way, extra beats are sometimes used for Exx. 147, 150, 151, 154, 157, and 257a. Remember: use the extra beat only if you cannot get a satisfactory result without it. If you want to use the extra beat, you have to inform the players.

Occasionally the left hand can be used for extra beats to set up the tempo for tricky attacks. For the start in Ex. 154, for instance, small left-hand motions may indicate *One-Two-Three-Four*, each motion at the pulse of one measure. Exactly on *Four*, the baton gives the upbeat.

Additional examples for the study of the start after the count:

4-beat

After the 1st count:

Bach: Cantata No. 31 (*Der Himmel lacht, die Erde jubilieret*), No. 2 — Coro; No. 6 — Aria.

Beethoven: *Fidelio*, No. 5 — Terzett.

Schumann: Overture to *Manfred*.

Verdi: *Aïda*, 4th act — 2nd scene.

Weber: *Der Freischütz*, No. 9 — Terzett.

After the 2nd count:

Bach: Cantata No. 80 (*Ein feste Burg ist unser Gott*), No. 4 — Aria

Haydn: Symphony No. 86, 4th movement.

After the 3rd count:

Brahms: *Ein deutsches Requiem*, 5th movement.

Stravinsky: *Ragtime*.

After the 4th count:

Enesco: *Roumanian Rhapsody No. 1.*

Handel: Concerto Grosso, Op. 6, No. 8 (*Allemande*).

Haydn: Symphony No. 59, 1st movement.

Haydn: Symphony No. 83, 4th movement.

Rossini: *Il Barbiere di Siviglia*, 1st act — Finale I.

3-beat

After the 1st count:

Bach: *St. Matthew Passion*, No. 49 — Chorus.

Berwald: Symphony No. 4, 1st movement.

Vivaldi: Concerto Grosso in D minor, RV 565 (Op. 3, No. 11).

After the 2nd count:

Bach: Suite No. 4 in D major, Réjouissance.

Haydn: *The Seasons*, No. 21 — Introduction (*Autumn*).

Rossini: *Il Barbiere di Siviglia*, 1st act—Rosina's Cavatina.

Weber: *Der Freischütz*, No. 2—Terzett mit Chor.

After the 3rd count:

Barber: Overture to *The School for Scandal*.

Handel: *Messiah*, Part II, Aria—*Thou art gone up on high*.

Respighi: *Feste Romane*, beginning.

Wagner: *Die Walküre*, 3rd act—*Ride of the Valkyries*.

2-beat

After the 1st count:

Bach: Cantata No. 31 (*Der Himmel lacht, die Erde jubilieret*), No. 1—Sonata.

Mendelssohn: Overture to *Ruy Blas, Allegro molto*.

Mozart: *Così fan tutte*, No. 22—Quartetto.

Rachmaninoff: Symphony No. 2, 2nd movement.

Tchaikovsky: Symphony No. 4, 2nd movement.

Tchaikovsky: Suite No. 3, *Scherzo*.

Verdi: *Messa da Requiem*, No. 3—*Offertorio*.

Wagner: Overture to *Der Fliegende Holländer*, 6 bars before L (after the General Pause).

After the 2nd count:

Beethoven: Symphony No. 2, 4th movement.

Brahms: Symphony No. 4, 1st movement.

Dvořák: String Serenade, Op. 22, Finale.

Haydn: Symphony No. 80, 4th movement (with syncopation).

Haydn: Symphony No. 85 (*La Reine*), 4th movement.

Mozart: Piano Concerto K. 449, 3rd movement.

Mozart: *Così fan tutte*, No. 8—Coro; No. 12-Aria; No. 15—Aria; No. 28—Aria.

Puccini: *La Bohème*, 3rd act, beginning.

1-beat

Beethoven: Symphony No. 5, 3rd movement.

Brahms: Serenade No. 1 in D major, *Scherzo* I.

Dvořák: Symphony No. 8, 3rd movement.

Elgar: *Enigma Variations*, Variation No. 2.

Mahler: Symphony No. 6, 2nd movement.

Mozart: *Così fan tutte*, No. 13—Sestetto, at *Allegro* 3/4.

Schubert: Symphonies Nos. 3 and 6, 3rd movements.

Stravinsky: *Pulcinella Suite*, at No. 53 (to set the tempo for the *Tarantella*, ♩. = 88, a 2-beat, ♩. = 176, can be used for the first bar).

Tchaikovsky: Serenade for Strings, 2nd movement.

Chapter 13

THE 6-BEAT

Two STYLES are used in beating 6-time: the so-called German style, taught in most textbooks and used by the majority of conductors until recently; and the Italian style, now becoming more popular. The choice between them is a matter of personal preference; in general, you will find the German style useful for slow and expressive music, while the Italian is handier in quick tempo. Especially in operatic conducting, the economy of gesture gives the Italian style the advantage. The student should study both styles to find out from personal experience which is better suited to him or whether he will desire to make use of both.

German Style

Diagram 34. Think of ② and ⑤ as being interpolated into the 4-beat pattern. Use the wrist alone for these two "added" beats except in very expressive passages. For the espressivo patterns, see Diagram 35. Practice before the mirror in a fairly slow tempo; then use Ex. 161.

Ex. 161
♪ =92) pp
♪ =112 } mf
♪ =72) f espr.

Diagrams 36 and 37 show the staccato beat (whether to use 36 or 36a is a matter of choice). Practice with Ex. 162.

Ex. 162
♪ =104) p
♪ =126 } and
♪ =88) ff

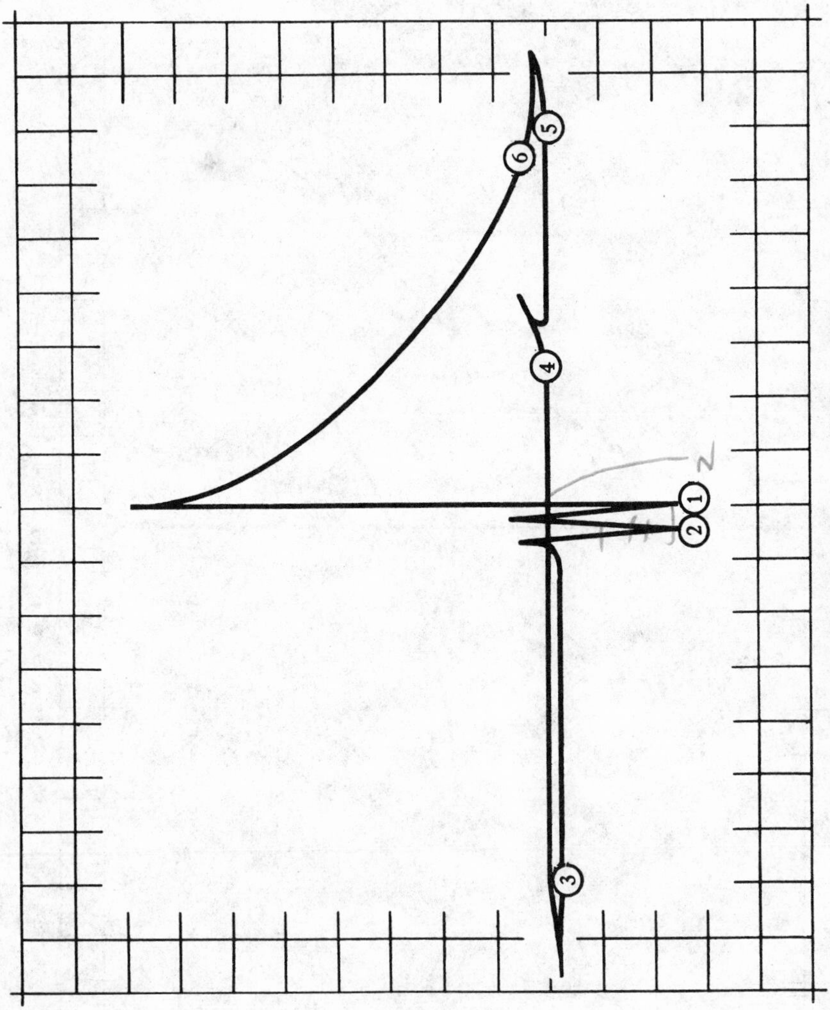

Diagram 34. 6-beat (German style); non-espressivo

103

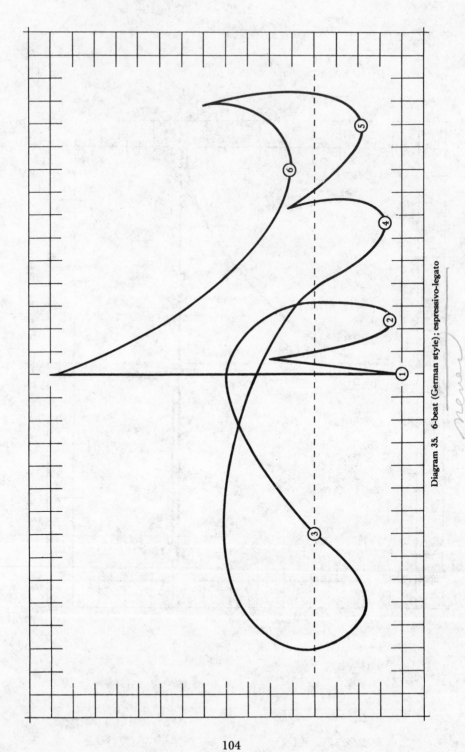

Diagram 35. 6-beat (German style); espressivo-legato

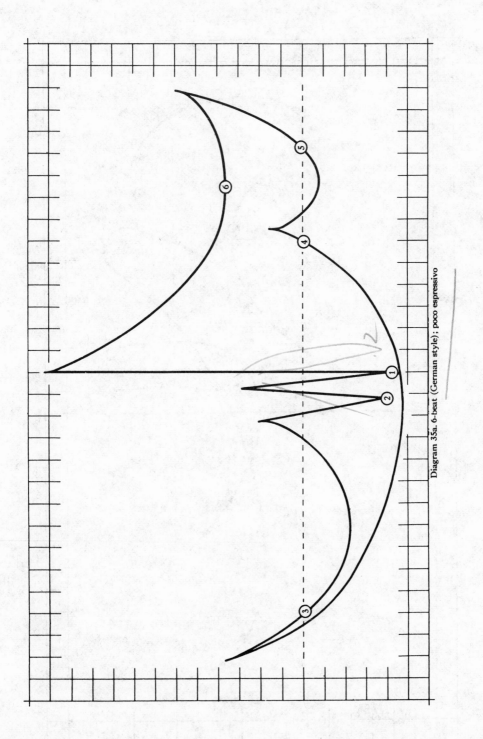

Diagram 35a. 6-beat (German style); poco espressivo

105

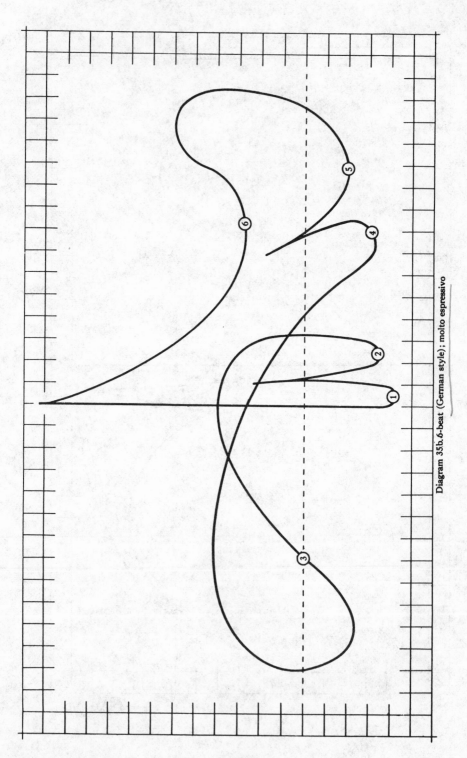

Diagram 35.b. 6-beat (German style) ; molto espressivo

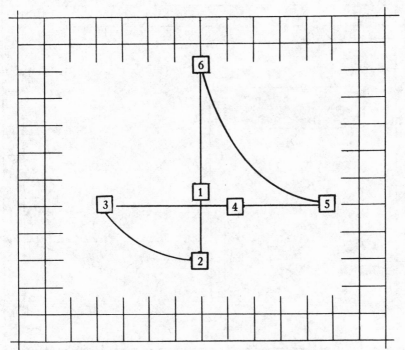

Diagram 36. 6-beat (German style); light-staccato

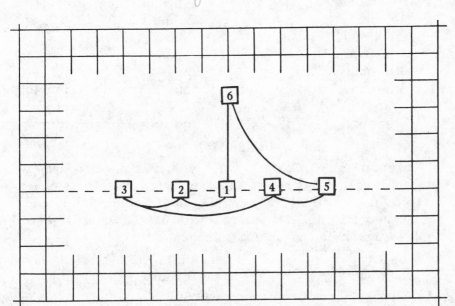

Diagram 36a. 6-beat (German style); light-staccato (alternate style)

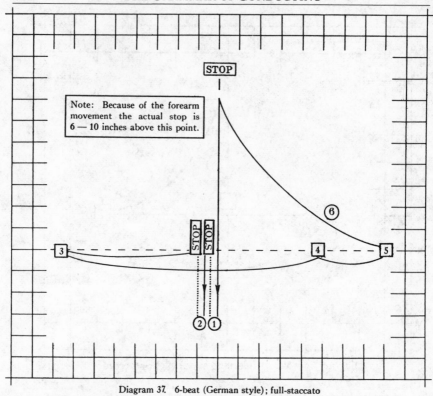

Diagram 37. 6-beat (German style); full-staccato

To start on the	apply diagrams
1st count	2, 5, and 7
2nd count	28 and 32
3rd count	13 and 14
4th count	11 and 12
5th count	11 and 12 (slightly farther to the right)
6th count	9 and 10

Italian Style

Diagram 38. This pattern is fairly close to a subdivided 2, which means that the 1st and 4th counts are considerably more marked than the others. By enlarging the pattern and adding to the curves of the lines, you can easily work out the espressivo.

Diagrams 39 and 40 demonstrate the staccato.

To start on the	apply diagrams
1st count	2, 5, and 7
2nd count	28 and 32
3rd count	28 and 32
4th count	9 and 10
5th count	11 and 12
6th count	9 and 10

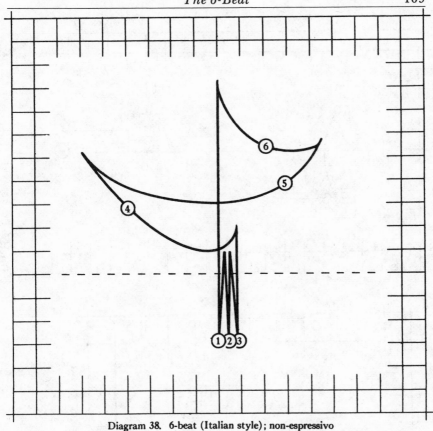

Diagram 38. 6-beat (Italian style); non-espressivo

Ex. 163a: Marcato, not too heavy and fairly small; with the diminuendo, change to non-espressivo. **Ex. 163b:** Full-staccato, accented upbeat on ⑥ in bar 1. **Ex. 163c:** Molto espressivo, legato.

dimenuedo

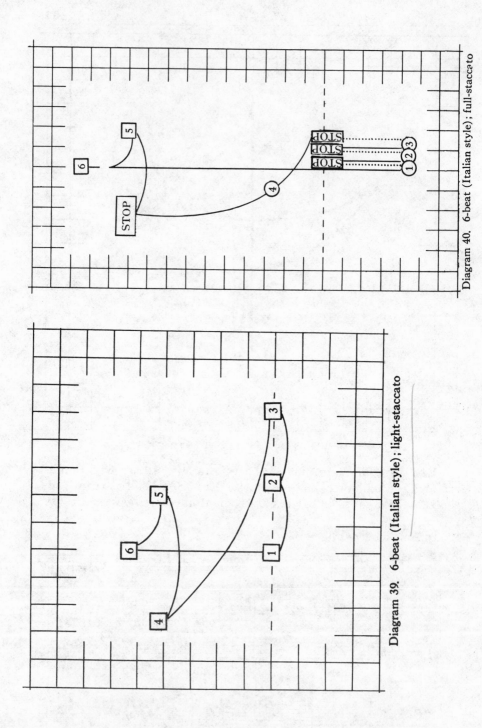

Diagram 39. 6-beat (Italian style); light-staccato

Diagram 40. 6-beat (Italian style); full-staccato

110

malto espresso legato (handwritten, left margin)

Ex. 163 c　Strings　poco f

Ex. 164: The woodwind entry requires a certain emphasis on *One* in bar 2; then beat very quietly non-espressivo. The 5th beat in bar 3 is used for a cut-off (discussed in Ch. 15).

Langsam und schmachtend, (♪ = 76)

Ex. 164

WAGNER, *Tristan und Isolde*

Ex. 165: Legato poco espressivo; the gesture must be very graceful.

German 1 3 4 6 emphasized (handwritten)

Andante,(♪ = 100)

HAYDN, *Symphony No. 95*

Ex. 165　Strings p

Ex. 166: Gentle staccato for the strings; use the 3rd beat to prepare the entrance of the winds (non-espressivo).

Andantino,(♪ = 112)

Ex. 166　p Strings　Hn.

MOZART, *Die Zauberflöte*

Ex. 475: To accompany the singer, a non-espressivo beat leads the sustained wind chords beginning in the 2nd bar. When the same theme is played in the Overture of the opera, a more expressive gesture is needed for the crescendo and decrescendo.

Ex. 167: Start after the count. Give the preparation as though the music would start on the 6th count.

Additional examples for the study of 6-beat:

Non-espressivo:

Berlioz: *Symphonie Fantastique*, 3rd movement (also espressivo-legato, staccato, and dynamic changes).

Brahms: Symphony No. 1, 1st movement, 1st and 2nd bars after A.

Debussy: *La Mer*, beginning.

Mozart: Piano Concerto in A major, K.488, 2nd movement (also poco espressivo).

Verdi: *Aïda*, 3rd act, Aïda's aria starting at D.

Espressivo-legato:

Debussy: *Nuages.*

Hindemith: *Sinfonische Metamorphosen—Andantino.*

Massenet: *Manon*, 1st act, Prelude, *Andante sostenuto.*

Mendelssohn: *Elijah*, No. 37—Arioso.

Puccini: *Madama Butterfly*, 1st act, No. 116–118 (alternating with subdivided 3/4); *Largamente* before No. 135 to No. 136.

Schubert: Symphony No. 5, 2nd movement (also non-espressivo).

Verdi: *Messa da Requiem*, No. 2, *Quid sum miser* at No. 24 (poco espressivo).

Wagner: *Die Meistersinger von Nürnberg*, 3rd act, 4th scene—Quintet.

Staccato:

Bach: Cantata No. 62 (*Nun komm, der Heiden Heiland*), No. 1 — Chorale.

Britten: *Spring Symphony — The Driving Boy.*

Kodály: *Psalmus Hungaricus*, passage starting at No. 25.

Liszt: *Mazeppa*, beginning.

Mozart: *Die Zauberflöte*, No. 16 — Terzett (for this lively tempo, use Diag. 39).

Mozart: *Don Giovanni*, No. 15 — Terzetto.

Rossini: Overture to *Semiramide*, passage starting at the 20th bar of *Andantino*, 6/8.

Tchaikovsky: *Capriccio Italien*, at B.

Marcato:

Bach: Cantata No. 11 (*Lobet Gott in seinen Reichen*), No. 11 — Chorale.

Saint-Saëns: Symphony No. 3, 2nd movement, *Maestoso* after R.

Wagner: Prelude to *Parsifal*, passage for brass instruments, 6/4.

Dynamic changes:

Brahms: Symphony No. 1, 1st movement — passage starting at bar 9.

Delius: *On Hearing the First Cuckoo in Spring.*

Dukas: *La Péri.*

Haydn: Symphony No. 96, 2nd movement.

Mozart: Symphony No. 38, K.504 ("*Prague*"), 2nd movement.

Reger: Variations on a Theme by Mozart — Variation No. 8.

Verdi: *Aïda*, 1st act, 1st scene — Radames's aria, starting at B.

Chapter 14

SUBDIVISION

WHEN THE MUSIC is so slow that the regular beat would not give the conductor enough control or intensity, the beat is divided into fractional parts. This chapter deals mainly with the execution of the subdivided patterns; their application will be discussed in greater detail in Chapters 25 and 26.

The general principle is that, unless the musical expression demands otherwise, the main beats are larger and more emphatic than the subdivisions. To start in subdivided time, always give the preliminary beat in terms of the smallest unit that you are actually beating.

8 Beats in a Measure

Diagram 41. The weaker beats ②, ④, and ⑥ are usually done with wrist motion only. Conductors differ in their manner of beating ⑦ and ⑧. Some always beat ⑦ at the top of the field. The main reason for not doing so is that it emphasizes the 7th beat and destroys the smooth flow. Use this technique only when you want to accent the 7th beat.

The various patterns (staccato, espressivo, etc.) can be deduced easily from the diagram. In some cases it will add to the distinctness to click on the main counts: ①③⑤⑦ .

Ex. 168: Non-espressivo; the preliminary beat has the value of an eighth-note. Conduct the strings as accompaniment, but know exactly what is going on in the oboe solo. The conductor must be able to deal with fractional values very easily in order to correct his players. The study of Bach will train the conductor's mind to recognize these small values quickly even in the most complicated passages. (Bach's violin sonatas afford especially good practice.)

Adagio assai, (♪ = 76)　　　　BACH, Cantata No. 21

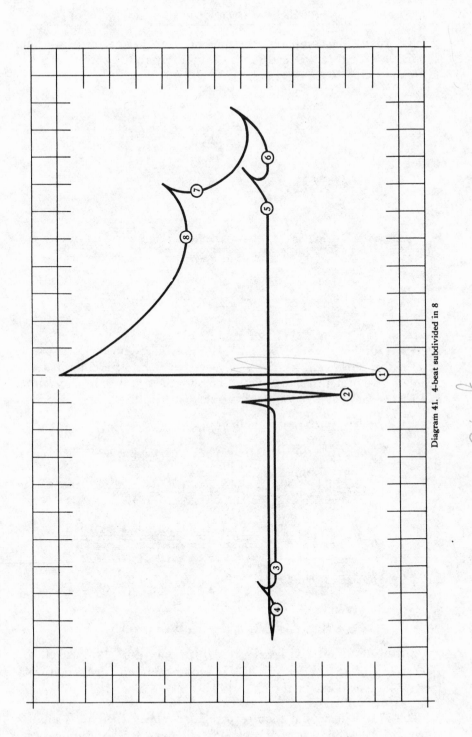

Diagram 41. 4-beat subdivided in 8

115

Ex. 169: The composer's metronome refers to quarter-beats, but subdivision is needed to lead the violas securely and to coordinate the xylophone entry in bar 4.

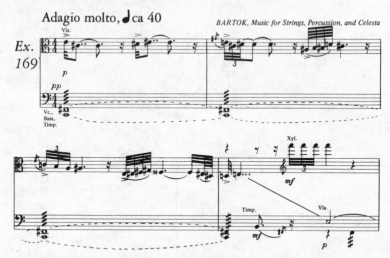

Ex. 170: For the start, see Ex. 141. (Rossini did not write an overture to the *Barber of Seville*. The piece exists in different versions. Scholars give preference to the original one, the overture to *Aureliano in Palmira*, but not all conductors agree. See p. 130.)

4 Beats as a Result of Subdivision

2-time with subdivision is shown in Diagrams 42a and 42b. The style shown in Diagram 42b is recommended for transitions from a 4-beat to a 2-beat (see p. 147).

Ex. 171: The 1st bar requires a regular 4-beat; then use a subdivided 2/4 (=4/8) to lead the melody. In bars 3–5 the subdivision should be hardly noticeable; use it in bars 6 and 7.

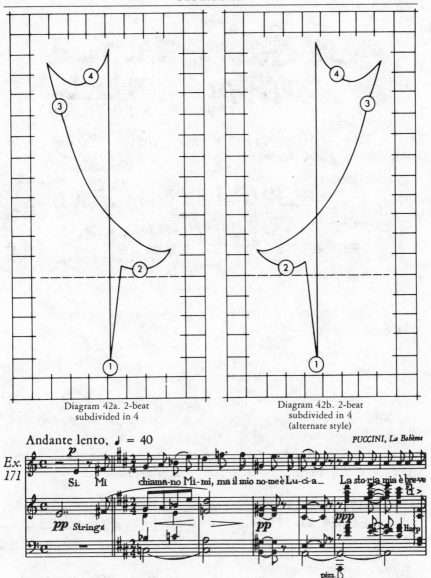

Diagram 42a. 2-beat
subdivided in 4

Diagram 42b. 2-beat
subdivided in 4
(alternate style)

Ex. 172: Subdivision applies only to bars 9 and 10. Here it helps to bring out the *sf* and to lead the 32nd-groups with a decisive beat.

Ex. 173: Here the subdivision, starting with *ff*, is the best way to control the accented ritenuto (see p. 194).

Ex. 133: The most effective way of directing the allargando is to subdivide the beat.

12 Beats in a Measure

4-time with each beat subdivided triply is shown in Diagram 43. Now it is even more important to keep the main beats— ① ④ ⑦ ⑩ —clear and distinct, to avoid any misunderstanding on the part of the players. For this reason, a number of conductors prefer the slightly different pattern of Diagram 43a.

Exx. 174 and 175: Use slightly curved motions for the graceful music of Ex. 174. The restrained mood of Ex. 175 requires small neutral beats.

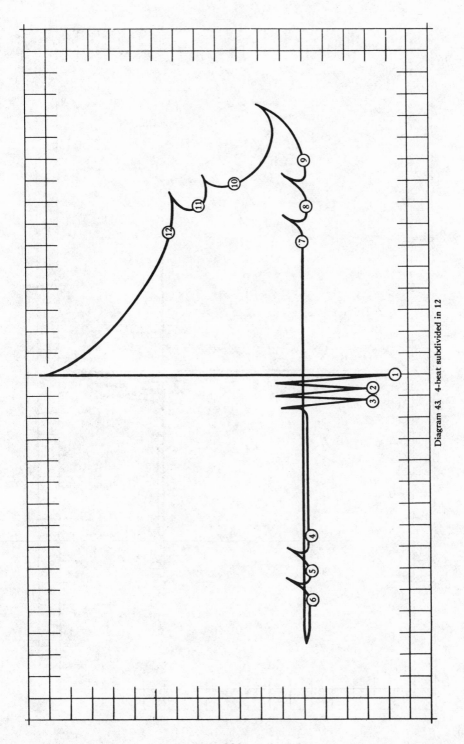

Diagram 4.3   4-beat subdivided in 12

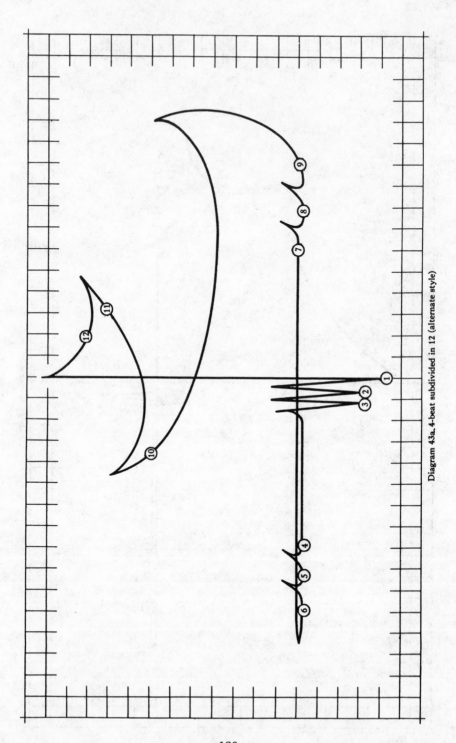

Diagram 43a. 4-beat subdivided in 12 (alternate style)

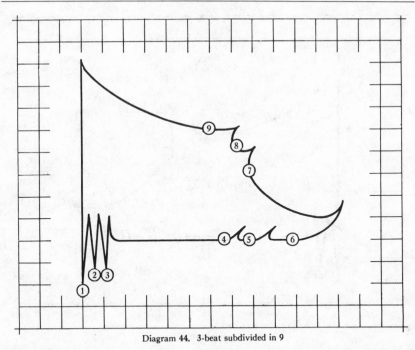

Diagram 44. 3-beat subdivided in 9

Ex. 176: This should be sung and the various entries indicated precisely by the conductor.

9 Beats in a Measure

Diagram 44. This pattern is 3-time with each beat subdivided triply.

Ex. 177 (bar 1): Non-espressivo (see p. 255).

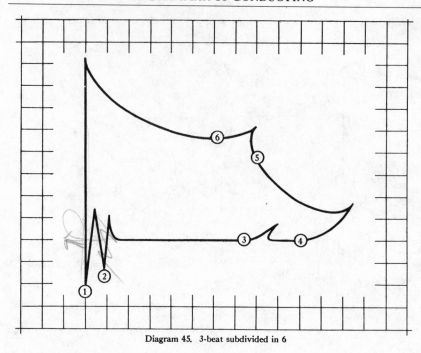

Diagram 45. 3-beat subdivided in 6

Ex. 178: The 2nd measure requires 9 beats, legato.

6 Beats as a Result of Subdivision

6-beats resulting from subdivision is different from regular 6-beat; it is 3-time or 2-time subdivided.

(1) The pattern for 3-time subdivided is shown in Diagram 45.

Ex. 179: The subdividing gestures must not disturb the feeling of 3 pulses per measure (see the comments on Mozart's tempi in Ch. 33). Subdivision serves to lead the 32nd-notes in the melody and to prepare the *f* chords.

Andante cantabile, (♪ = 96) MOZART, *Symphony No. 41*
Ex. 179

Ex. 180: Start with non-espressivo; on the 2nd eighth-beat in bar 2, suddenly enlarge the gesture, which then becomes smaller while you direct the diminuendo.

Adagio, ♪ = 76 BERLIOZ, *Harold en Italie*
Ex. 180

Ex 181a: In bar 1, use strong marcato gestures for the main counts while the subdivided beats serve as preparation.

Ex. 181b: The character of the music requires emphatic motions on each of the 6 beats, but keep the pattern unmistakably clear.

Larghissimo, ♩ = 40 WILLIAM SCHUMAN, *Symphony for Strings*
Ex. 181 a

(2) 2-time with each beat subdivided triply is shown in Diagram 46 (compare the different Italian pattern for 6-beat).

Ex. 182: Regular 6-beat, especially in the German style, would be too academic and would not conform to the pulsation of the music. Start with relatively small gestures and bring out the crescendo.

Andante sostenuto, ♩. = 42 PUCCINI, *Tosca*
Ex. 182

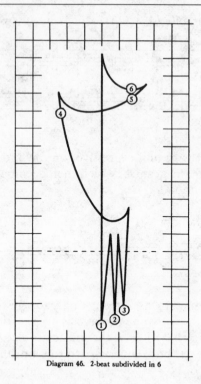

Diagram 46. 2-beat subdivided in 6

Ex. 183: Start beating in 2; with the first (optional) rallentando, subdivide, and at "rall. molto" use the regular 6-beat pattern (Italian style). Return to beating 2 beats in a measure for the last bar.

1-Beat with Subdivision

1-beat with subdivision occurs only in fairly fast 3-time; it is used when the regular 3-beat would be awkward and the regular 1-beat would lack distinctness or intensity. It can be done in 3 different ways.

Although the student will be referred to the espressivo patterns of Diag. 30, there is a marked distinction between 1-beat espressivo and 1-beat with subdivision. The object of the former is to add expression to the simple 1-beat, but without rhythmic accentuation. Consequently, a very smooth and relatively large gesture is used. In the subdivided 1-beat, the fractions of the rhythm are clearly indicated with a more or less staccato quality of the gesture. Thus, even though the motions may be small, there is no doubt as to the fractional parts of each measure.

(1) As a special case of 3-beat, the gesture is very small, and the 2nd beat, instead of going to the right, goes upward at a very small angle (Diag. 30b). This pattern is useful when an occasional indication of the 3 beats is needed, although the rhythm is felt primarily as one pulse to the measure.

Ex. 184: The syncopations in bars 5-7 require small, but clear, subdivision. Return to 1-beat in bar 9.

(2) When the pulsation felt is *One-Two(-three)*, apply Diagram 30. The gesture indicating the 3rd count is not only very small but weak. The outline of each bar is practically a 2-beat in 3-time, in which each bar can be considered as ♩ ♩ |.

(3) When the pulsation felt is *One-(two)-Three*, use Diagram 30c, or apply a regular 2-beat. The outline of each bar can be considered as |♩   ♩|.

Ex. 185: Neither a regular 3-beat nor a regular 1-beat would do justice to this music, both being too academic. *One- (two)-Three* is felt in bars 1–8, *One-Two(-three)* in bars 9–12; beat accordingly.

Additional examples for the study of the subdivided patterns:

12 beats in a measure:

Bach: *St Matthew Passion*, No. 47 — Aria.

Debussy: *Prélude à l'Après-midi d'un faune*, at No. 3.

Messiaen: *L'Ascension,* 1st movement.

Prokofiev: Violin Concerto No. 2, 2nd movement.

Verdi: *Rigoletto*, No. 14, *Duetto finale* — passage starting with the 25th bar of *Andante* in D-flat major (subdivision helps to coordinate the off-beat notes of the first violins with the pizzicato of the second violins).

9 beats in a measure:

Brahms: Symphony No. 1, 1st movement — bar 8.

Dukas: *La Péri*, at No. 1 and after No. 6.

Saint-Saëns: Symphony No. 2, 2nd movement, at S.

Strauss: *Also sprach Zarathustra*, at No. 18 (9/4, ♩ = 160, change to 3-beat, ♩. = 54, once the rhythm has been established).

Wagner: Prelude to *Parsifal*, passage starting at *sehr gehalten.*

8 beats in a measure:

Bach: Cantata No. 12 (*Weinen, Klagen, Sorgen, Zagen*) — Sinfonia.

Bartók: Divertimento for String Orchestra, 2nd movement.

Handel: Concerto Grosso, Op. 6, No. 12, 1st movement.

Haydn: Symphony No. 104, 1st movement — Introduction.

Hindemith: *Nobilissima Visione*, beginning.

Rossini: *Il Barbiere di Siviglia*, 2nd act — Quintet.

Schoenberg: Piano Concerto Op. 42, bars 297–325.

Schubert: Symphony No. 2, 1st movement — Largo.

6 beats in a measure (3-time):

Beethoven: Symphony No. 4, 2nd movement

Brahms: *Academic Festival Overture — Maestoso* 3/4.

Copland: *A Lincoln Portrait*, beginning.

Haydn: *The Creation*, No. 29 (Recitative) — Prelude to Part III.

Prokofiev: *Romeo and Juliet* Suite II, No. 5 — at No. 42.

Rachmaninoff: Piano Concerto No. 2, 2nd movement — bars 13, 16, etc.

Sibelius: Symphony No. 3, 1st movement — 7th bar after No. 4, 2nd bar after No. 12, etc.

6 beats in a measure (2-time):

Brahms: Piano Concerto No. 1, 1st movement, bars 175–225.

Enesco: *Roumanian Rhapsody No. 1*, passage starting at No. 7, *Posato.*

Mascagni: *Cavalleria Rusticana*, Prelude — bars 20–27.

Wagner: Overture to *Der Fliegende Holländer*, passage of 3 bars at *Un poco ritenuto* (four times).

4 beats in a measure (2-time):

Britten: *Sea Interludes*, No. 1, *Dawn* (the intended tempo is indicated by $\flat = 44$ and confirmed by the composer's recording; use subdivision whenever needed for coordination, but do not alter the pace of the music).

Haydn: Symphony No. 104, 2nd movement.

Schoenberg: Kammersymphonie, bars 75–79.

Schubert: Symphony No. 2, 2nd movement.

Tchaikovsky: Serenade for Strings, 1st movement — bar 8.

Verdi: Overture to *I Vespri Siciliani*, *Allegro agitato*. (Start beating 2 but subdivide whenever necessary to lead the sixteenth-passages and the syncopations; the subdivision ends 7 bars before D but is resumed at E.)

1-beat with subdivision:

Bizet: *L'Arlésienne Suite No. 1*, 2nd movement, middle section.

Debussy: *Ibéria*, beginning.

Debussy: *La Mer*, 2nd movement — passage beginning at No. 16.

Dvořák: Symphony No. 9, 3rd movement — after the double bar.

Falla: *The Three-Cornered Hat*, Suite No. 2, *Danse Finale* — at No. 11, *Giocoso*.

Prokofiev: Piano Concerto No. 3, 3rd movement.

Strauss, Johann: *Tales from the Vienna Woods*, Waltz No. 1, at *poco ritenuto*.

Study and practice scores Nos. 3 and 4 discussed in the Appendix.

Chapter 15

RESTS

PROPER HANDLING of rests is part of conductorial skill. There are three different uses for beats where no music is sounding: (1) to cut off the tones preceding the rest when necessary, (2) to indicate counts during the pause, (3) to prepare the next attack.

(1) The cut-off is used only after a sustained tone, not after a detached one. However, not every sustained tone followed by a rest needs a cut-off; use it only when a unified release is difficult to achieve automatically. This occurs more often in slow tempo than in fast, and more often in loud passages than in soft.

You may cut off with the right hand alone, either by clicking or by making a definite stop on the rest. The left hand may also be used, and in several different ways. The effect of the gesture is that of a command: be quiet! Some conductors move the arm in toward the body, palm inward, closing the hand simultaneously. Another effective motion is a quick downward turn of the left hand.

(2) A small non-espressivo beat is usually sufficient to indicate the rests when neither cut-off nor preparation is needed.

(3) When a rest is followed by an attack, use the rest for preparation, especially if it is the last of several in succession. In most cases the preparatory gesture will not have to be as emphatic as at the start, since the rhythm is already established.

Ex. 186: The first rest is for cut-off (in slow tempo), the second for a slight preparation. In the 3rd measure, cut off on *Two*, mark the time on *Three*, and prepare on *Four*. Follow this procedure throughout the example and do not forget that the half-note in bar 5 ends exactly on *Four*.

Ex. 187a: No cut-off because of staccato. Do not yield to the temptation of beating staccato during the rests, except of course for preparation.

Ex. 84: The 4th beats in bars 3 and 4 must indicate a clear release and, at the same time, maintain a continuous crescendo.

Ex. 170: Use the left hand, which supported the *ff* for an incisive cut-off, allowing the right hand to find the most convenient position for the light-staccato that follows. Use the rests in the 2nd bar for preparation. In bar 3, beat the first 2 eighth-rests small, non-espressivo; beat the following (preparatory) eighth sharply and further to the left, to make room for a large gesture to attack the *ff* chord.

Ex. 179: Review this, applying what you have just learned.

Ex. 188: Three conducting patterns alternate in this movement: 3-beat, 1-beat, and subdivided 1-beat. Most conductors begin with a 3-beat. The gesture on the first rest may be quite small, even skipped if you are very sure of the rhythm. Here are two different types of preparation on rests; *Three* in bar 1 is an accented upbeat for *f* staccato, *Three* in bar 2 prepares *p* legato.

Ex. 189: Subdivided 3-beat. The preparation at the end of bar 3 should also include the *sf* at the beginning of bar 4.

Ex. 190: 2 beats to a measure. Use the 2nd beat in bar 2 to prepare the staccato. *Two* in bar 14 is non-staccato.

Allegro con brio, (♩ = 84)

BEETHOVEN, *Coriolanus Overture*

Ex. 191: The drum-roll requires no big gesture while the other instruments rest. Beat full-staccato to prepare the chords (see p. 185).

Molto vivace, (♩ = 132)

Moderato assai, (♩ = 84)

TCHAIKOVSKY, *Symphony No. 5*

Ex. 192: Be sure that the time-marking beats in bar 3 are neutral and do not lead the 1st violins into a false entry—as has happened in prominent orchestras! Beat light-staccato in the 4th measure.

Allegro,(♩ = 138)

MOZART, *Symphony No. 39*

Ex. 193: 1-beat. The first and second G.P.'s (General Pauses) are used for preparation. Mark time in the 7th bar and prepare in the 8th. A time-beater, not a conductor, would use the same large downbeats throughout this example.

Molto vivace, ♩· = 116

BEETHOVEN, *Symphony No. 9*

Ex. 194: The 2nd and 3rd beats must be hardly noticeable. This increases the tension of the music and the attention of the orchestra.

Ex. 195: A new section with change of tempo begins here. To establish the rhythm and character of the *Allegretto vivace*, beat the rests light-staccato. In such cases the neutral beat would not give the conductor the needed control.

Rests at the Beginning of a Piece

There is no rule explaining how to beat when a piece starts with several rests. Since the rests appear in the parts and are counted by all the players, including those who do not come in at the very start, skipping could cause confusion. Whether to beat the rests in a neutral manner or with some kind of expression depends upon the character of the opening. In any event, do not beat the rests in a way that could lead the players into a premature attack. If you decide to skip beats, the change must be entered in the orchestra parts.

Exx. 196 and 197: While no special treatment is needed in 196, a non-espressivo start in 197 would lack tension; start light-staccato, and beat full-staccato on the 4th count (preparation).

TCHAIKOVSKY, Overture "1812"

Ex. 198: To get a good pizzicato entry, beat both quarter-rests staccato.

Ex. 199: A completely neutral 1st beat would lose the drama of the opening; directly from ATT at the top of the field of beating, give a fairly large but not too emphatic downbeat, and continue with a preparatory staccato on *Two*. (If *One* is too emphatic, the horn players may mistake it for the preparation!)

TCHAIKOVSKY, *Piano Concerto No. 1*

Rests at the End of a Piece

Rests often occur after the last played note of a piece, either to fill up the last bar or, where the last bar is part of a group, to fill out the metrical balance. Naturally, rests of this kind do not require any beat at all. The last beat is for the last played note, with cut-off if needed.

The concluding cut-off is done by moving the baton downward or sidewise with a very quick gesture. In *f* it is sharper and more forceful than in *p*. The *p* ending may be done with a quick turn of the wrist or by drawing the baton swiftly toward the body. In both *p* and *f* the cut-off gesture must not suggest any accent. The left hand may support the right-hand movements in *f* with an energetic gesture, in *p* in the way described on p. 129.

Ex. 200: The concluding chord is usually played tenuto and therefore requires a cut-off gesture (see p. 159).

Rests in Accompaniment

The following two examples show the special care with which rests must be treated in accompaniments.

Ex. 201: Neutral beats in the 1st bar. Be sure you are in time, or even a little ahead, on the 2nd beat in bar 2, and synchronize your preparatory 3rd beat with the triplet in the solo violin, to be in position for the 4th beat. Give a sharp beat before each of the syncopated chords with neutral beats between. Prepare the last measure (*fp*) by picking up the beat from the violin.

Ex. 202: Here it is very important to know the words as well as the music, and to be sure which syllable falls on which beat. The preparatory beats must be flexible, because the singer is allowed a certain liberty in recitative. Your downbeat in the 3rd bar coincides with "cin-," followed by 2 secco chords in strict tempo. If necessary, wait on *Four* so as to be sure that the next downbeat comes exactly on "dir-." Do not drag the neutral beats, and be ready for the next downbeat! The singer traditionally holds the high A♭; wait for him on *Two* and time your preparatory beat to be with "-to" precisely on *Three*. Use the accented upbeat on *Four* to prepare the fanfare in the brass.

VERDI, *Aïda*

Remember this handy rule:

When there are several rests in the accompaniment, keep with or a trifle ahead of the tempo, but always allow yourself one beat at the end for a good preparation. If necessary, wait just before giving this preparatory beat.

Additional examples for the study of beating rests:

Barber: Overture to *The School for Scandal,* bars 6 and 7.

Beethoven: Symphony No. 8, 1st movement—15 bars from the end.

Dukas: *L'Apprenti Sorcier,* beginning of *Vif,* 3/8.

Haydn: Symphony No. 102, 4th movement, (Coda).

Kodály: *Háry János* (Suite), 1st movement, bars 73-76.

Mahler: Symphony No. 1, 1st movement—last 10 bars.

Nielsen: Symphony No. 3, 1st movement, beginning (1-beat).

Rossini: Overture to *Semiramide,* last bars of *Andantino,* 6/8; bars 63-65 of *Allegro.*

Shostakovitch: Symphony No. 1, 1st movement—bars 8 and 9.

Sibelius: Symphony No. 5—last 9 bars.

Wagner: Prelude to *Parsifal,* passage in 6/4.

Rests at the beginning of a piece:

Bach: Mass in B minor, *Et resurrexit.*

Bizet: *L'Arlésienne Suite No. 1,* 1st and 2nd movements.

Dvořák: Symphony No. 8, 2nd movement.

Haydn: Symphony No. 86, 4th movement.

Saint-Saëns: Symphony No. 3, 2nd movement.

Sibelius: Symphony No. 2, 1st movement.

Verdi: *Aïda,* Prelude to the 1st act.

Rests in accompaniment:

Beethoven: Violin Concerto, 1st movement.

Bizet: *Carmen,* all recitatives.

Grieg: Piano Concerto, 1st and 3rd movements.

Haydn: *The Creation*, No. 12—Recitative.

Mozart: *Die Zauberflöte*, 1st act, No. 8 (Finale)—Recitative.

Rachmaninoff: Piano Concerto No. 2, 3rd movement.

The Recitative from Mozart's "Die Zauberflöte" included in the list is a dialogue between tenor and bass extending over 120 measures. It lends itself to practice in class, with two students singing the vocal lines, another student playing the piano (from the full score!), and all students taking turns conducting the accompaniment. For perfect coordination, the conductor must make a clear distinction between neutral and preparatory beats.

Chapter 16

RITARDANDO AND ACCELERANDO

JUST AS GRADUAL CHANGES in dynamics require well-controlled gestures, so do gradations in the speed of music. In order to obtain the desired results in speeding up and slowing down, the conductor's mind must be ahead of his hand. The way you *lead into* the count on which the change starts should prepare the players. If you do not think of the change until you are *on* the count, it will be sudden and awkward instead of gradual and smooth. However, this preparation must not start the change prematurely; it only warns the players that one is coming. *It is helpful to use a slightly larger beat before a ritardando and a slightly smaller beat before an accelerando.*

A quick change in the size of the beat is also very effective in indicating "a tempo." For "a tempo" after ritardando, use a smaller beat; after accelerando, use a larger beat.

Once a tempo change has been started, it gains a certain momentum of its own, and the conductor must be careful that he does not cause exaggeration by indicating too much on the subsequent beats. A tempo change must be planned, just as a dynamic change must be. Know exactly how fast or how slow you want to be when the change is completed, and you will achieve a smooth and continuous gradation.

Practice ritardando and accelerando, with return to tempo, on all counts and in different rhythms. Have your friend at the piano improvise simple chords while following your beat. Practice the changes in varying degrees from poco ritard. to molto ritard. and similarly with accelerando. The following should be remembered:

For more ritard. on the   wait longer before moving

1st beat		to the left
2nd "		" " right
3rd "	in 4-beat	" " left
4th "		up
1st "		to the right
2nd "	in 3-beat	" " left
3rd "		up

138

1st "	} in 2-beat	up (rebound)
2nd "	}	up
"	in 1-beat	up

By practicing ritardando and accelerando according to these suggestions, you avoid the spasmodic gestures that mar the conducting of inexperienced leaders and disturb the security of the players.

Ex. 203: (1) No preparation is required for poco rit. within an entire bar. (2) Since you have only 2 beats for the ritard., prepare it. (3) Prepare; subdivide for eighth-notes. (4) Very gradual. (5) Small exact beat on *Three* in bar 2 (a tempo).

Ex. 204: (5) Be sure to return to the exact tempo — no faster!

Ex. 205: (5) The 2 last chords are "a tempo"; wait on *One* in bar 4, then beat the eighth-rest and the 2 chords strictly in time.

Exx. 206 and 207: Only by following the markings painstakingly can you get the full benefit of these exercises.

Ex. 208: Subdivide in the 4th measure; "lento" is twice as slow as the 1st tempo. In bar 5 a beat on *Two* is superfluous; cut off with a small gesture to the right (see p. 133).

Ex. 209: Gradual ritard. in bars 2–5; "a tempo" immediately in the 6th bar; for the "meno" in the 8th, stop the beat on *One* and use the 2nd beat to prepare *Three* in the new tempo.

Ex. 210: In the 4th measure, wait on *Two* and use *Three* to prepare the "a tempo." For this type of preparation, see Ex. 32.

Ex. 211: 2 bars strictly in tempo (conductors who prefer a tempo slower than ♩ = 50 subdivide this passage); well-planned gradual stringendo with complete stop on the *ff*; subdivide *One* (bar 7), using the rest for an eighth-note preparation in the original tempo.

Ex. 130: Despite the large orchestration, a heavy and large beat is not required. On the contrary, a small energetic beat for *animando* keeps the brass instruments well under control. Do not do much for the rit. or the orchestra will overdo it.

Ex. 212: Start subdividing in bar 6, using the rest in bar 7 for preparation, as in Ex. 211.

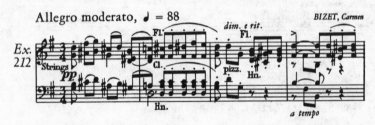

Ex. 213: You get the full advantage of this example by following a singer in his individual rendering of Pagliaccio's lament. Subdivide in bars 9–13. In this case, subdivision is used to control the sustained chords of the accompaniment, but the subdivisions should be unobtrusive.

Ex. 214: 2-beat, full-staccato. For the 1st bar, the gesture must not be too large, to allow for larger beats in bars 2 and 3 in order to lead the ritard. Subdivide in bar 4, with incisive beats on *Three* and *Four* for slowing down the eighth-notes. Return to 2-beat (Tempo I°) with a vigorous downbeat.

Ex. 215: Subdivide for the first ritenuto. After the stringendo use a larger beat to start "ritenuto" (the composer undoubtedly meant rallentando) and slow down, first by subdividing, then changing to 3-beat (see p. 176).

Ex. 216: The accelerando in bar 3 is rather marked. A clear beat on *Two* in the 6th measure brings the basses in with the harp, which plays very slowly. The notes marked "rubando" are quite fast; wait on *Six*, then give an eighth-note preparation, as though the 6th count were subdivided.

Additional examples for the study of ritardando and accelerando:

4-beat:

Barber: Overture to *The School for Scandal*, 9th bar after F.

Brahms: *Variations on a Theme by Haydn*, 9 bars from the end.

Prokofiev: *Peter and the Wolf*, passage starting at No. 54.

Prokofiev: Symphony No. 5, 2nd movement—No. 50–51.

Tchaikovsky: *Overture 1812, poco a poco rallentando* (bar 340).

3-beat:

Bizet: *Carmen*, 2nd act, No. 12—Gypsy song.

Brahms: Symphony No. 2, 1st movement, passage starting 15 bars after M.

Tchaikovsky: Symphony No. 4, 1st movement—*Ritardando*, 4th bar after E.

2-beat

Bartók: *Dance Suite*, 2nd movement—bars 23, 26, 59.

Berlioz:*Symphonie Fantastique*, 1st movement, *Allegro agitato e appasionato assai.*

Copland: *Tender Land Suite*, 1st movement.

Dvořák: *Slavonic Dance in A-flat major, Op. 46, No. 3.*

Liszt: *Les Préludes*, passage starting at E.

Mendelssohn: Overture to *A Midsummer Night's Dream*, end of the development section.

1-beat

Bartók: Concerto for Orchestra, 1st movement—bars 470-488, with subdivision (3/8 and 4/8) in bars 474 and 475 (see Appendix A, No. 5).

Beethoven: Symphony No. 9, 2nd movement—8 bars before *Presto* (see p. 347).

Dukas: *L'Apprenti Sorcier, Vif* 3/8, several passages.

Mahler: Symphony No. 1, end of 2nd movement.

Mahler: Symphony No. 6, 2nd movement—No. 84-85.

Sibelius: Symphony No. 5, 1st movement, beginning at *Allegro moderato* after N—tempo increases from ♩. = 80 to ♩. = 138.

Tempo Transitions by Changing the Number of Beats in a Measure

When a ritardando or accelerando is not temporary—that is to say, when it leads to a slower or faster section—it is often necessary to change the number of beats in a bar. If you are using 2-beat, a slower section may require 4-beat or 6-beat, while a faster section may find 1-beat useful. Subdivision is very helpful as an intermediate step. The conductor, however, must be sure that a change of the number of beats in a measure is clearly understood by the players—even when it is marked in the parts, and especially when it is not.

First indicate the change of tempo by slowing down or speeding up for a few counts, without changing the number of beats; then switch to the new rhythmic pattern.

Ex. 217 (1): A smooth transition can be achieved by emphasizing *One* and *Three* in the 3rd bar, changing to subdivision in the 4th or 5th bar. *Two* and *Four* become weaker and almost disappear, which makes for a smooth transition to the 2-beat in bar 6. (For this change of beat, 4/4 to ₵, Diag. 42b is best suited.)

(2): Start subdividing in bar 5 to lead easily into 4/4. Diag. 42a or b will work.

(3): The changes are more sudden and require a more concentrated beat.

Ex. 218: (1) For the accelerando first weaken *Two*, then *Three*, until they disappear. (2) *Three* reappears first in the ritardando, then *Two*.

Ex. 219: Subdivide in the 3rd measure and change to 2-beat.

Ex. 220: You have 9 bars for accelerando with change from 2-beat to 1-beat. Beat *Two* with less and less emphasis until it disappears altogether, but without losing control over the rhythm, and arrive at Presto without any last-second readjustment.

Ex. 221: Do not subdivide until bar 4; subdivision in the 3rd bar would exaggerate the ritardando.

OFFENBACH, *Orphée aux Enfers—Overture*

Additional examples for the study of tempo transitions which involve a change of the number of beats in a measure:

Changing from 4-beat to 2-beat:

Grieg: *Peer Gynt Suite No. 1*, 4th movement.

Liszt: Piano Concerto No. 1 1st movement, use 2-beat at *animato* after B.

Strauss: *Also sprach Zarathustra*—after No. 11 and after No. 17.

Strauss: *Tod und Verklärung*—at F (or 2 bars earlier).

Changing from 2-beat to 4-beat:

Schoenberg: Kammersymphonie, bars 79–84.

Tchaikovsky: *Romeo and Juliet*, after the 2-beat at *Allegro* (5 bars after C) return to 4-beat at *Molto meno mosso*.

Changing from 3-beat to 1-beat:

Strauss: *Also sprach Zarathustra*, at No. 26 (*etwas zurückhaltend* requires a subdivided 3-beat).

Stravinsky: *L'Oiseau de Feu* (Suite), *Danse infernale*, at No. 29 or earlier.

Changing from 1-beat to 3-beat:

Barber: *Essay for Orchestra*, 6th bar after No. 21.

Puccini: *Madama Butterfly*, 2nd act, 10 bars after No. 35 and 5 bars after No. 36.

Strauss, Johann: *Emperor Waltz*—Coda, several bars before *Tempo di Valse*.

Changing from 2-beat to 1-beat:

Falla: *Three-Cornered Hat* Suite No. 2, 2nd movement, at No. 10

Tchaikovsky: *Capriccio Italien*, the 1-beat begins at *Presto* before F; the preceding 2-beat (*stringendo molto*) follows a 6-beat.

Changing from 1-beat to 2-beat:

Bartók: *Dance Suite*, Finale, bars 100–110.

Sibelius: Violin Concerto, 1st movement—after the 1-beat (which usually begins 15 bars before No. 11), return to 2-beat 4 bars before No. 11 in preparation for the *Allegro molto vivace*, whose attack needs an incisive upbeat to coordinate the solo violin with the orchestra.

Ritenuto

A special technique is used for a sudden, marked slowing down of the tempo. In ritenuto there is no gradual change; one beat is in tempo and the very next is much slower. The beat used for this is in effect a wait on the count without stopping the motion.

This technique is especially useful in accompaniment, where the more or less unpredictable changes on the part of the soloist force the conductor to wait on a certain count. A sudden complete stop would confuse the players, but the flexible ritenuto beat keeps the orchestra under control.

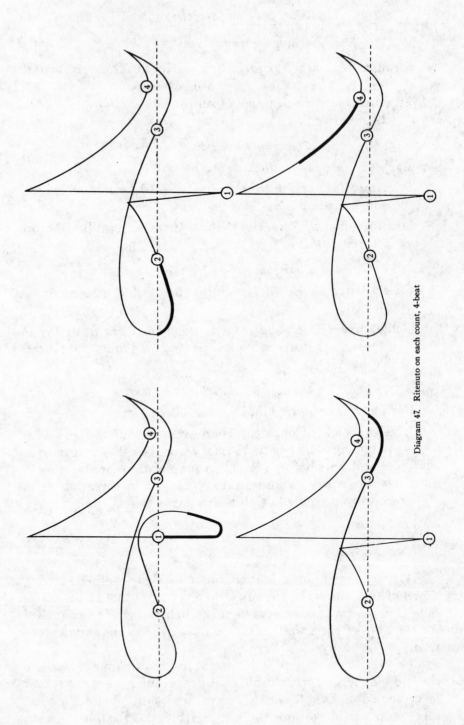

Diagram 47. Ritenuto on each count, 4-beat

Diagram 47. The heavy black line indicates an extremely slow and very intense movement, as though the baton were being drawn through a strongly resisting substance. The length of time you can keep moving the baton while still on the count will surprise you. The point where the heavy line changes back to the medium line (normal speed) must be distinct in the beat, for the release at this point leads to the next count. Practice first on all counts without music.

Ex. 222: The solo part may be either sung or played. Practice first with the conductor indicating the ritenuto and "a tempo." Then have the soloist take his own liberty in rhythm and lead the accompaniment only.

Chapter 17

THE TENUTO PATTERN

The tenuto beat is a smooth motion with a stop on each count. It resembles the marcato, but lacks the aggressive impetus of that beat. Each beat is sustained with or without intensity, depending on the music. The size varies from small to large.

Diagram 48. The connecting gesture between two counts serves as release and preparation. It should not be hurried (as in staccato) or leisurely (as in legato). Diagram 48a allows a more expressive connection. This expressive form of tenuto is characterized by a "holding on" to the count, as though you were loath to let go of it. This is still more evident in the pattern of 48b, which gives strong emphasis to single counts, especially when marked ===== or ===== =====. The technique is similar to the ritenuto (p. 149), but with great intensity—coming from the forearm—on the very slow part of the pattern (heavy line).

The tenuto beat is used for chords that are detached but held and for melodic passages of portamento character. The preliminary beat for tenuto is legato. The piano is not the ideal instrument for music of tenuto character. The exercises should therefore be played by a small ensemble.

Diagram 49 is useful for those not too frequent occasions when you want to limit yourself to a very academic time-beating. This "dry" tenuto lacks the strong holding quality of the expressive form.

Since there are no new problems in 3-beat tenuto, apply the principles of Diagram 48. The 2-beat tenuto is shown on Diagram 50 and 50a; the "dry" pattern (Diag. 51) is recommended for legato passages in very fast tempo, the stops on *One* and *Two* being very short. For 1-beat, apply Diagram 33.

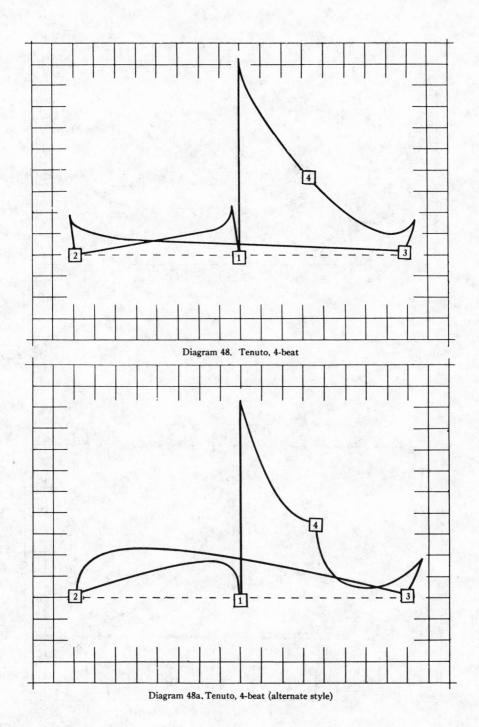

Diagram 48. Tenuto, 4-beat

Diagram 48a. Tenuto, 4-beat (alternate style)

153

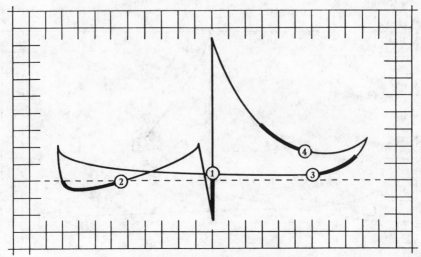

Diagram 48b. Tenuto, 4-beat (alternate style)

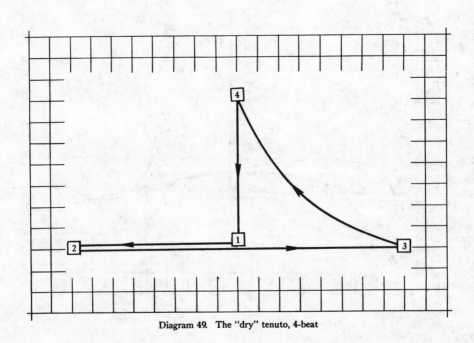

Diagram 49. The "dry" tenuto, 4-beat

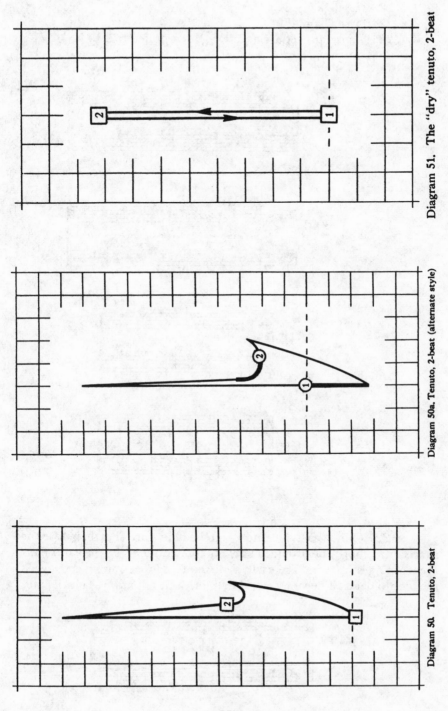

Diagram 50. Tenuto, 2-beat

Diagram 50a. Tenuto, 2-beat (alternate style)

Diagram 51. The "dry" tenuto, 2-beat

Ex. 223: Use Diag. 48 or 48a.

Ex. 224: Use Diag. 48b.

Ex. 225: Same procedure as in Diag. 48 applied to 3-beat.

Ex. 226: Diag. 50

Ex. 227: Since each half-note is to be held until shortly before the succeeding chord, beat tenuto only on *One* and *Three*. *Two* and *Four* are legato gestures and are easily reduced to connecting links between the tenuto beats. They may even be slightly out of tempo—a little late.

Ex. 228: The sustained chords require the tenuto beat.

Ex. 229: Use the tenuto beat for the *pp* accents in the first bars; for the *ff* chords use the more emphatic pattern of Diag. 50a. For the triplets in bars 5 and 6, the tempo is more relaxed; use subdivision (see p. 162).

Ex. 230: The brass chords in bars 5 and 6 need the tenuto for the intense sustained quality. Support with left hand.

Ex. 231: At the "rit." the accompaniment should be carefully synchronized with the solo. Subdivide the triplet if necessary. If 2 pianos are available, the practice will be more realistic. The ending in the 3rd and 4th bars is of a type found in many pieces: repetition of the same chord detached. This is best controlled with the tenuto beat (see p. 162).

Ex. 232: The tenuto pattern, which by means of its connecting gestures gives emphasis to the main counts, is more effective here than regular subdivision.

Ex. 233: Indicate the crescendo in the 2nd measure by increasing the expressiveness in the tenuto beat.

Ex. 234: Same technique as in Ex. 227.

Ex. 84: For the 3rd counts in bars 3 and 4, use a tenuto beat to sustain these chords within a continuous crescendo.

Ex. 200: Tenuto beat will insure the full value of the closing *ff* eighth-note chords.

Chapter 18

HOLDS (I)

CONTROL OF HOLDS and interruptions is one of the hardest problems confronting the student conductor. Although it is hardly possible to establish simple general rules, some degree of systematization can be achieved. This is done by dividing holds into those that occur at the end of a piece; those during a piece, and either followed or not followed by rests; and holds followed or not followed by breaks.

Concluding Holds

Many pieces have a fermata on the last played note. Regardless of the note value, beat only one count and sustain it as long as you feel the music requires. The manner of execution depends upon the orchestration and the dynamics.

The effectiveness of a *f* is greatly increased by raising the baton for the fermata. Merely stopping the motion of the baton is not sufficient to sustain a *f* or *ff*; only a diminuendo would result. Maintain the volume by indicating intensity with either the right or left hand. The left-hand gesture was explained on page 22. The right hand may make a similar gesture by shaking the baton, but do not exaggerate. Some conductors indicate a continued *f* by moving the baton very slowly, the same way as in the ritenuto beat (Diag. 47). In *p*, simply stopping the baton on the fermata is sufficient. In *pp*, the left hand keeps the orchestra subdued.

The end of the hold is indicated by a cut-off. The gestures are similar to those for a general cut-off, described on page 133. Because of the indefinite length of the hold, however, the cut-off must be especially decisive in order to insure the simultaneous stopping of all the players. Although the gesture is sudden and quick, it must still avoid any suggestion of an accent at the very end unless an accent is marked by the composer.

Ex. 235: Do not beat *Four* in the last bar; sustain a moderate *f* with the left hand.

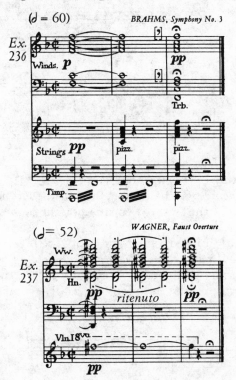

Ex. 230: The hold actually starts on the 2nd beat of bar 7; it is not necessary to beat for the last measure.

Exx. 236 and 237: While in 236 the last pizzicato chord will take care of itself, the 1st violins in 237 need an extra gesture of the left hand for a cut-off. This gesture should be unobtrusive and clearly directed toward the violins, so that none of the wind players will mistake it for the concluding cut-off (see p. 214).

Exx. 238 and 239: Both examples illustrate diminuendo on the fermata. The first starts *fff* and is played by the winds (the last string chord again takes care of itself), while the second starts softly and dies away in the strings. Indicate the diminuendo in 238 by gradually lowering both hands, if the right hand was in a raised position; if not, use the left hand alone. A wind chord, no matter how soft, always requires a cut-off. The "morendo" in 239 may be expressed by a "dying-away" gesture which is very effective for strings: both arms slowly fall to the side with no definite cut-off.

Ex. 238 — Allegro — DVOŘÁK, Symphony No. 9

Ex. 239 — Andante, (♩ = 72) — GRIEG, Last Spring

Exx. 229 and 231: Two endings with $<\ >$, expressed by raising and lowering both hands together, or the left hand alone. The size and intensity of the gesture depend upon the orchestra's response.

Ex. 240: The uplifted left hand sustains the *ff* tutti while the right hand directs the kettledrum. The baton waits on *One* and cuts the drum-roll on *Three*, then joins the left hand for the tutti cut-off. The gesture directing the kettledrum must be relatively small.

Ex. 240 — Allegro

BEETHOVEN, *Die Weihe des Hauses—Overture*

Ex. 241: Beat the first 3 counts in the last bar. The 4th beat is superfluous since the pizzicato needs no cut-off. Sustain the violins throughout with the left hand.

Ex. 242: Since only part of the orchestra has a fermata on the last chord, and the other part holds the 4th and 5th counts, you must beat all 6 counts. The 6th beat is small, so that it cuts off part of the orchestra and does not look like the concluding cut-off.

Holds During a Piece, Not Followed by a Rest

Such holds may or may not require a cut-off. If they do, there may be only a short break for "breathing," or there may be a longer pause. The length of the pause often depends upon the individual interpretation. Consider how differently the fermata in *The Star-Spangled Banner* is treated by conductors! Only the techniques are discussed here. Their application to the following examples may vary, depending on the personal taste of the conductor.

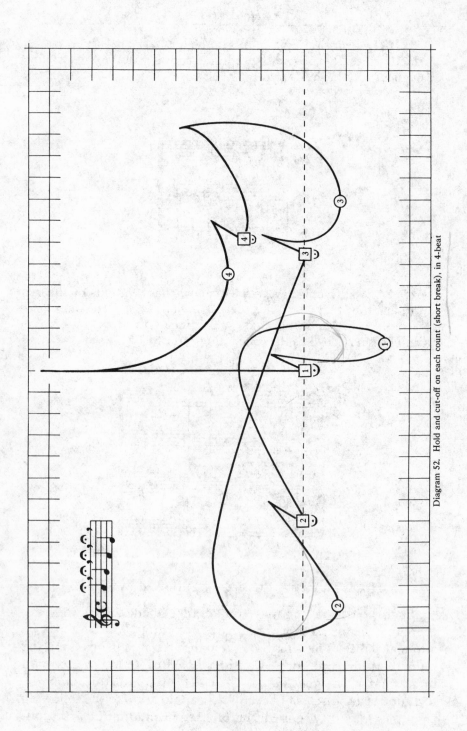

Diagram 52. Hold and cut-off on each count (short break), in 4-beat

164

(1) If there is only a slight interruption after the hold, the cut-off gesture is also the preparation for the next count.

Diagram 52 shows the technique of making a hold and cut-off on any count in 4-beat. On each count *the beat is repeated:* 1 is for the hold, ① is for the cut-off and also serves as preliminary to 2 . In most cases, click on the repeated count for a clear release.

The principle of repeating the beat after the hold is applied to 3-beat, 2-beat, and 1-beat in Diagrams 53–55. It can easily be applied to all other patterns.

When the note under the fermata is of greater value than one count, it is not necessary to repeat any beats, as will be seen in the following examples.

Ex. 243: The hold in bar 2 is treated according to Diag. 52. The fermata in the 4th measure, however, includes several counts; stop on 1 for the hold, then (skipping *Two*) beat ③ , which serves the double purpose of cutting off the hold and preparing ④ . Thus, only 3 gestures are used in this measure.

Chorale Setting by J. S. Bach

In this context, the chorale settings are used as exercises for the handling of fermatas, although in Bach's time their main purpose was to mark the phrase groups.

Ex. 244: For the hold in the 2nd bar, stop on 1 and use ② for cut-off and preparation.

Chorale Setting by J. S. Bach

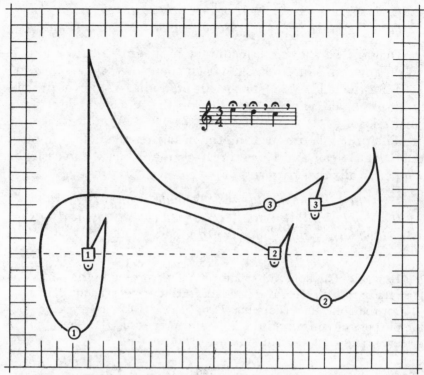

Diagram 53. Hold and cut-off on each count (short break), in 3-beat

Ex. 245: In bar 4 stop on ☐3 ; cut off and prepare with ④

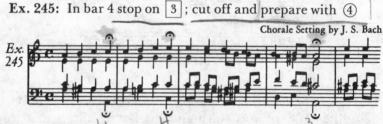

Chorale Setting by J. S. Bach

Ex. 246: Since the cut-off also serves as preparation, it must have all the different expressions of the preliminary beat. In bar 2 it is full-staccato. In the last measure the orchestra has a half-bar rest. After a sharp cut-off of the second fermata, use a neutral downbeat (synchronized with the first chord of the piano) and prepare the staccato chord with *Two*.

Allegro maestoso, (♩ = 112)

LISZT, *Piano Concerto No. 1*

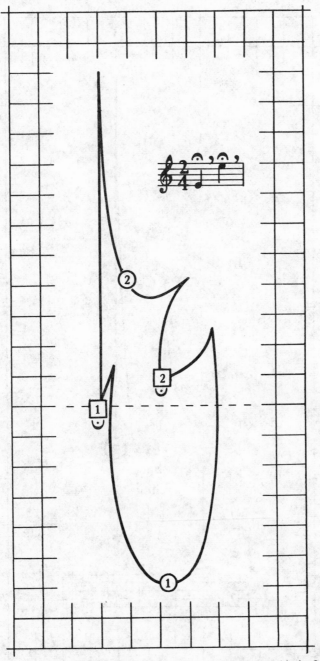

Diagram 54. Hold and cut-off on each count (short break), in 2-beat

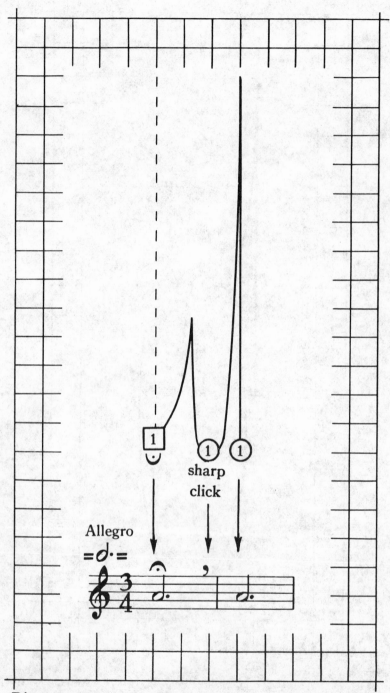

Diagram 55. Hold and cut-off (short break), in 1-beat

Ex. 247: In bar 2 use a full staccato cut-off, which prepares the tutti attack (see p. 172).

Ex. 248: Stop on ⬚1⬚ in the 4th bar. Following the usual procedure—beating the cut-off ③ strictly in tempo—results in a whole-beat pause. Considering the very slow tempo, the conductor may prefer to shorten the pause, perhaps by as much as half, using an eighth-note beat.

Exx. 249–251: Use Diag. 54. For Ex. 249 see Ex. 311. In Ex. 251 change from *f* to *p* with a definite but small cut-off.

HAYDN, *The Creation*

Ex. 252: Apply Diag. 55. Though the held note comes after the beat, just stop on *One* and wait for the orchestra to finish the bar.

BEETHOVEN, *Symphony No. 9*

Ex. 253: When a fractional value occurs after a fermata, do not change the regular procedure (see Ch. 12, Start After the Count). Thus the 3rd fermata is treated just as the first two are.

BORODIN, *Symphony No. 2*

Ex. 254: The two types of combined cut-off and preparation, one with and one without repeated beat, are illustrated in 254a and b. In the 3rd measure of 254a, only two gestures are used: the hold is on *One*, while *Two* cuts off the winds and also prepares the string entrance (staccato gesture!). This way of beating does not follow the notation, for the dotted quarter should be held until after *Two*. However, *it is not unusual for the beat to contradict the notation under a fermata, provided the beat is convenient and will not confuse the players.* In Ex. 254b, the hold for the 1st violins is on D, and not Eb as in some older editions. The cut-off gesture (2nd beat repeated!) should be rather gentle and smooth, so as to have a very slight break.

Ex. 255: All counts are subdivided except the very first. The 1st eighth-beat on *Two* has two functions: it cuts off the fermata and prepares the entrance of oboes and bassoons. For the start, see Ex. 141.

The following two examples have rests after the holds. They are discussed here because the technique involved is the same as in the previous examples, owing to the fact that the rest actually includes only part of the count.

Ex. 256a: Beat 1 in bar 2 and wait for the lower instruments with their fermata, then beat ② for cut-off and preparation.

Ex. 256b: Wait on $\boxed{2}$; a sharp downbeat on *One* in the following bar cuts off the fermata and prepares the next attack (see p. 380).

Ex. 247 (bar 4): While the second fermata may be executed without repeating the 3rd beat, most conductors desire a longer break and therefore repeat *Three*. But if this is done, beat the repeated *Three* downward so that the players will not confuse it with *Four*.

Additional examples for the study of fermatas followed by a short break:

Beethoven: Symphony No. 6, 1st movement—bar 4.

Copland: *A Lincoln Portrait*, bar 211.

Franck: Symphony in D minor, 2nd movement—bar 100.

Haydn: Symphony No. 104, 1st movement—bars 1 and 2; 2nd movement—bars 25, 115, 117.

Rimsky-Korsakov: *Scheherazade*, 4th movement—11 bars from the end.

Schoenberg: Kammersymphonie—bar 4.

(2) If the interruption after the hold is longer than one count, a different technique is used. There are two separate gestures, one for the cut-off and one for the preparation.

The nature of this cut-off is similar to that at the end of a piece. The execution, however, is now determined by the fact that the music continues after the pause. Consequently, the cut-off gesture carries the baton from one complete stop ($\frown$) to another ($\boxed{\text{ATT}}$) in the most simple and direct manner. To prepare the attack after the pause, use the position of attention and the regular preparatory beat just as at the start.

There can be no hard and fast rule for the application of these gestures. The procedure depends on the position of the baton at the fermata and on where you want the baton to be at attention. Diagram 56 shows some of the more useful of the many possibilities. Whenever an upward or sideways cut-off could be mistaken for a direction to continue, use a downward cut-off.

Ex. 257a: Depending on interpretation, the fermatas can be done in three different ways (see p. 97).

(1) Without pause. Cut-off and preparation are done with the same downbeat. This works best if the baton, while sustaining the fermata, moves up slowly before sweeping down for the *One*, all in one continuous gesture.

(2) Separate gestures for cut-off and preparation, strictly in time, as indicated after the first fermata in Ex. 257b (Diag. 55).

(3) Separate gestures, but with a freely timed pause between, as indicated after the second fermata in Ex. 257b. Most conductors treat the first 5 bars as an introduction to the movement, taking the cut-off and the downbeat after the first fermata in tempo, but waiting longer after the second fermata. The cut-off after the second hold must carry the baton to where it can start the 2nd violins in the clearest and most comfortable way.

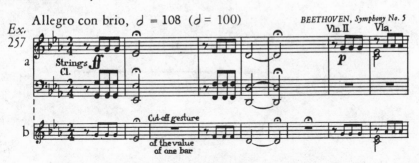

Exx. 258 and 259: In these examples a definite break is made after the slow introduction before starting the fast movement. The conductor must feel for himself how long to wait on the pause. For the 1st bar of Ex. 258, see what was said about Ex. 170. After the fermata in Ex. 259, the music continues with a start after the count, since the "vivace" goes alla breve.

ROSSINI, *Il Barbiere di Siviglia—Overture*

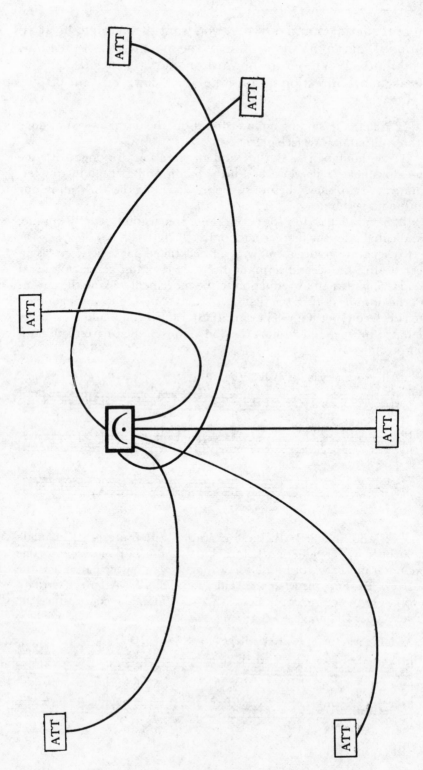

Diagram 56. Fermata, cut-off and pause

Ex. 259

Ex. 260: The first *ff* is a kind of introduction in itself and is followed by a short silence. Raise the baton for the fermata and use a strong downbeat for the cut-off. The *p* subito in bar 5 needs the sudden appearance of the left hand. Be careful not to have the baton too high in cutting off the second hold, so as to be in a convenient position for the allegro attack (see p. 220).

Ex. 260

BEETHOVEN, *Symphony No. 1*

Exx. 261 and 262: Pauses indicated by the composers: in Ex. 261 by using the sign //, in Ex. 262 by inserting a fractional rest with a fermata (for Ex. 261, see p. 182).

Ex. 261

MENDELSSOHN, *Midsummer Night's Dream—Nocturne*

Ex. 262

WILLIAM SCHUMAN, *Symphony No. 3*

Additional examples for the study of fermatas followed by a longer pause:

Bartók: *Dance Suite*, Finale, bar 17.

Beethoven: Symphony No. 3, 4th movement—bar 348 (before *Poco Andante*).

Brahms: Symphony No. 1, 4th movement—before the beginning of the *Allegro* section.

Haydn: Symphony No. 103, 1st movement—before the beginning of the *Allegro* section.

Rossini: Overture to *Tancredi*, bar 121 (beginnning of the recapitulation).

Sibelius: Symphony No. 3, 1st movement—3 bars from the end.

Smetana: *Dance of the Comedians* from *The Bartered Bride*, 2nd bar.

(3) Even if there is no interruption after the hold and no cut-off is required, a gesture is needed to resume the progress of the music.

The type of gesture to be used depends on the notation, and the different possibilities are illustrated in the examples.

Exx. 215 and 263: Since the note under the fermata has a greater value than one count, wait on the 1st beat of the held note and use the 2nd, or, in general, the last, for preparation with no cut-off. While this gesture leads unequivocally into the next count in strict tempo, it must be smooth rather than sharp, so that players cannot mistake it for a cut-off.

MENDELSSOHN, *Midsummer Night's Dream—Overture*

Ex. 264: Stop the beat on *Two*, releasing the horn with a left-hand gesture. Soon after the flute reaches the fermata, the singer releases her sustained note. Wait for her to take a breath and, with a smooth connecting gesture, coordinate the attack of her next phrase

with the flute going into *Three* while the strings continue their pizzicato.

Ex. 265: Sometimes the method of skipping beats on a fermata
can lead to misunderstanding about the release and the continuation
of the music. Whenever this may occur, it is necessary to beat all the
counts. In the present example, the bass instruments may enter prematurely unless the 4 counts in bar 3 are clearly indicated. Wait on
Two for the hold; the preparatory 3rd beat should not be too large,
while *Four* is done with an incisive motion. In the 1st measure, do not
neglect the correct indication of the rests; *Two* and *Three* are neutral
but distinct beats; *Four* is preparatory.

Ex. 266: When the same notes are tied over to the next count,
with no new instruments entering, no additional gesture is required;
just continue beating after the hold according to the notation. In the
4th bar, release the winds with the left hand (see pp. 198, 213, and
214).

In the concluding measure, the winds end with a quarter-note
while the strings finish pizzicato. A literal interpretation would sustain
the full value of the wind chord. In Brahms's time, however, it was

customary to shorten such a chord slightly to coordinate it with the fading pizzicato sound.

In the following nine examples, the beat used for the hold is repeated. However, this is done differently from the cut-off and preparation discussed under (1) and (2). As you see in Diagram 57, the baton leaves the hold without any special gesture and merely resumes the motion with which it entered the hold. The smoothness of this motion precludes the possibility of clicking.

A number of conductors use the pattern of Diag. 57 even to direct fermatas which are followed by a short break, making the motion after the hold more emphatic to indicate the release. But this gesture lacks the incisiveness of Diag. 52, and the student conductor will do well to adhere to the method taught in section (1).

Ex. 267: Stop on the 3rd beat in bar 2; the repeated *Three* will tell the clarinetist to continue with the triplet.

Ex. 268: In 268a the beat after the hold can have the value of either a quarter or an eighth. By beating a quarter you will make the sixteenth-note a little calmer. In slow passages like 268b, subdivision of the last beat gives more control at the fermata. Lead into the next bar with either an eighth- or a quarter-beat.

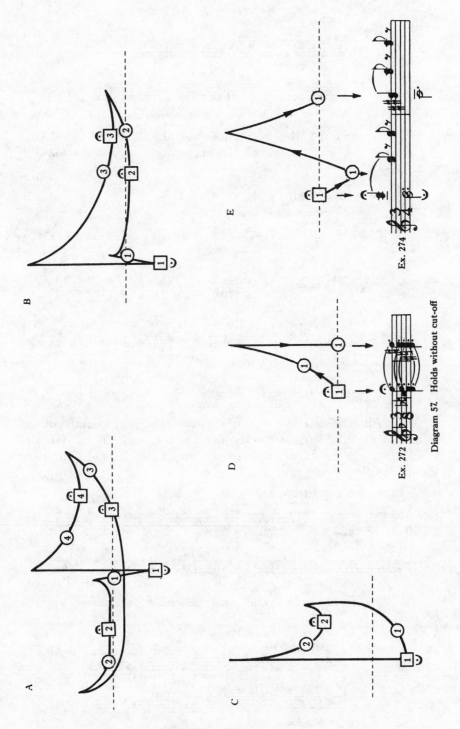

B

A

C

D

Ex. 272

Diagram 57. Holds without cut-off

E

Ex. 274

179

OFFENBACH, *Orphée aux Enfers—Overture*

Ex. 269: In bar 2, the repeated *Two* is a small gesture to indicate the change to *p* and to release the accompanying instruments (see p. 327).

MOZART, *Die Entführung aus dem Serail-Overture*

Ex. 270: The first two fermatas need an especially smooth continuation so that the various entries blend into one another. After the third, however, use a sharp staccato gesture to cut off, and to prepare the sudden *ff*.

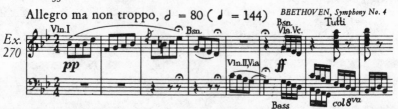

BEETHOVEN, *Symphony No. 4*

Ex. 271: Hold on *Two* and continue with a preliminary eighth-beat.

MASCAGNI, *Cavalleria Rusticana*

Ex. 272: Use Diag. 57d, noting the difference between this technique and that used for Ex. 252 (Diag. 55).

BERLIOZ, *Roméo et Juliette*

Ex. 273: Allow sufficient time for the G after the hold, without rushing the repeated 5th beat.

RIMSKY-KORSAKOV, *Scheherazade*

Ex. 274: The beat after the hold (upbeat quality) must express the change of tempo and dynamics. Use Diag. 57e.

J. STRAUSS, *Vienna Blood*

Ex. 275: While the cellos and basses hold the B, give a small but well-timed preliminary beat for the Allegro, with no break.

BEETHOVEN, *Leonore Overture No. 3*

Sometimes, especially in accompaniment, there is no time for a regular preparatory beat. A short smooth gesture is needed which, without being in tempo, leads convincingly into the next count. The pattern for this is identical with the tenuto of Diags. 48 and 48a.

Ex. 276: Use this technique for connecting the two fermatas in bar 2; a small 3rd beat serves as cut-off (see p. 189).

Ex. 277: Stop on the 3rd beat and, using the short connecting motion, pick up *Four* with the singer.

Ex. 213: The 13th measure calls for the same procedure in 2-beat.

Ex. 261: An application for this smooth connecting gesture (from *One* to *Two*) to purely instrumental music.

Additional examples for the study of fermatas without cut-off:

Without using an extra beat:

Beethoven: Symphony No. 6, 3rd movement, end of the section in 2/4-bar 203 (the fermata in bar 204 requires a cut-off followed by a preparatory beat).

Borodin: Symphony No. 2, 3rd movement — last bar.

Gershwin: *Rhapsody in Blue*, 1st and 15th bars.

Haydn: Symphony No. 97, 4th movement — 27 bars from the end (a similar passage occurs earlier in this movement).

Mahler: Symphony No. 1, 4th movement, 2 bars before No. 40 (in the 8/8 measure, stop on the last beat and use the release gesture to prepare the rhythm for the following slow 4/4 while the basses sustain their note).

Mahler: Symphony No. 6, 1st movement — bars 359–361.

Mussorgsky-Ravel: *Pictures at an Exhibition*, No. 8 — *Catacombae*.

Rimsky-Korsakov: *Scheherazade*, 2nd movement, bars 415 and 417 (in bar 419, an extra gesture is required: *Two* is repeated!).

Sibelius: Violin Concerto, 1st movement, 11 bars before No. 4, 6-beat with a fermata on the first count (the connecting gesture leading to the next count must be coordinated with the soloist, at the same time bringing in basses and timpani; the beat must be flexible to allow for the increase of speed in the solo part, resulting in a 2-beat two measures later).

Using an extra beat:

Berlioz: *Symphonie Fantastique*, 1st movement, 46th bar of the *Allegro* section (*Two* must be repeated to lead the violas and cellos which play different notes on the downbeat after the fermata!)

Borodin: Symphony No. 2, 3rd movement — 2nd and 3rd bars after B. (*Three* must be prepared because of the change of harmony.)

Delius: *Brigg Fair* — passages after Nos. 3 and 6.

Franck: Symphony in D minor, 1st movement — bar 186 (in bars 188 and 190, no extra beat is required!).

Sibelius: Symphony No. 2, 1st movement — 4 bars before P.

Strauss, Johann: *Voices of Spring* — 82nd bar of the Coda.

Chapter 19

HOLDS (II)

Holds Followed by Rests

Ex. 278: The beat on the *preparatory one* rest serves to cut off the hold and prepare the following count.

no double 4

Chorale Setting by J. S. Bach

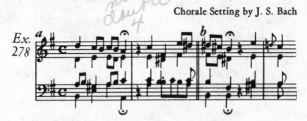

Ex. 279: For the 1st measure use Diag. 57c. In bar 2, an incisive downbeat secures a clear release and prepares *Two*.

Ex. 280: In the 2nd bar, wait on *One*, skip *Two*, and cut off on *Three*. Then wait for the singer, who traditionally starts after the cut-off. Synchronize your 4th beat (*p* staccato!) with "waste-."

Additional examples for the study of
fermatas followed by rests:

Borodin: Symphony No. 2, 3rd movement — 1 bar before **A**.

Franck: Symphony in D minor, 2nd movement — bar 96.

Kodály: *Háry János* (Suite), 4th movement — 3rd bar after No. 2.

Rimsky-Korsakov: *Scheherazade,* 2nd movement — bars 111 and 121.

Rossini: Overture to *Semiramide,* 62nd bar of the *Allegro* 4/4.

Holds on Rests

Ex. 191, 208, and 350: In cases like these, neglect the rests. Just keep the baton up during the interruption in readiness for the next attack.

Ex. 281: The stop for the fermata carries the baton to the left for "attention." *Three* is the gesture for a start after the count (in a footnote, the composer asks for two different tempi: ♩ = 84–92 is the main tempo, but the passages in the low strings are to be played at ♩ = 144. Therefore, *Four* in bars 1 and 3 prepares the faster speed, but the main tempo is resumed on *Three* in bar 2).

Ex. 282: The fermata is on a whole-rest. Beat a neutral *One* for cut-off, and wait; *Two* serves as preparation.

FRANCK, *Symphony in D minor*

Ex. 141: The fermatas are directed in a similar manner.

Ex. 283: The notation is not followed literally. In bar 2 the stop is on *One*, because the orchestra needs no further beat to play the three chords. After the pause, prepare on *Two*. Although the time signature is **C**, the composer's metronome indication asks for a 2-beat.

Ex. 284: There are two ways to conduct this passage. You may cut the first chord with *One* in the 2nd bar and then wait; a sharp upbeat on *Two* starts the violins. Alternatively, the chord may be cut with the baton in high position (no downbeat!); after the pause, beat *One-Two*, but remember that *One* must not be too emphatic or it may be mistaken for the attack. (The second method is similar to using an extra beat for the beginning of a piece, see p. 98.)

Ex. 285: The players start counting at the double bar; therefore beat *One-Two* at the beginning of the *Presto*, thus establishing the new tempo. To be ready for this, beat the *sf* in bar 2 with a vigorous rebound and keep the baton high during the pause (see the 1st movement of Tchaikovsky's Sixth Symphony, in which a similar transition occurs at the end of the introduction).

Ex. 286: In the 1st measure beat *Four* to cut off, raising the baton only slightly; pause and repeat *Four* to prepare. The 3rd beat in bar 2 and the 4th in bar 3 are treated similarly. Use the pattern of Diag. 57a.

Ex. 287a: Stop on *Three* in the 1st bar, cutting off with the left hand; repeat *Three* after the pause (Diag. 57b). Use the left hand again when you stop on *Three* in the 3rd measure, and resume the tempo on *Four* (preparation).

Ex. 287b: Since the notes before the first hold are pizzicato, just stop on *Four*, which is repeated.

Ex. 288: The 4th beat in both bars is repeated.

Ex. 289a: Use the pattern of Diag. 23a. In the 2nd bar, stop on *Two* by moving the baton to the left with a short turn of the wrist. The

clarinet now plays the cadenza without being directed until it comes to the last B♭ (⌢). Beat *Two* again, this time as an upbeat leading into bar 3, using a gesture which prepares *f* legato. The stop on *Two* and repeated beat are done in a similar manner in the 4th measure, but the upbeat is now *p* staccato. (Note that the sideways motion used here on *Two* for the stop is much more convenient than carrying the 2nd beat to the top of the field.

Ex. 289b: Subdivide into bars 1–3 for good rhythmic control. After the pause at the end of bar 2, beat *One* directly in the 3rd bar without preparation.

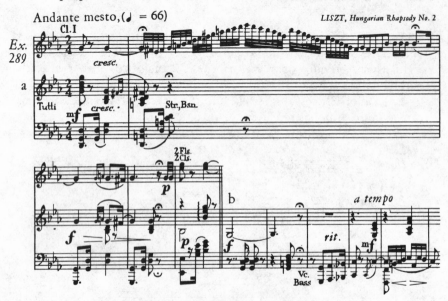

Ex. 290: *One* in the 2nd measure is repeated. Inexperienced conductors sometimes try to prepare the repeated beat with an extra gesture, instead of following the regular procedure, in the erroneous belief that this increases their control. By beating the *pp* chords light-staccato at about shoulder level, you have plenty of space for the second downbeat after the pause. This downbeat is a vigorous full-staccato.

Ex. 291: Stop and wait on the downbeat in the 4th measure, then continue as shown in Diag. 57d. Bring in the strings with a gentle but definite upward movement of the baton. A similar upward movement, but slower (Meno presto!) leads the winds after the second fermata.

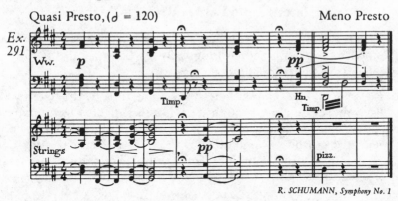

R. SCHUMANN, *Symphony No. 1*

Ex. 292: The same technique is here applied to accompaniment. Cut the chord in bar 2 by beating *Three* and wait for the singer; then repeat *Three* as preparation.

HAYDN, *The Creation*

Ex. 276: The 3rd beat in bar 2 is repeated.

Additional examples for the study of fermatas on rests:

Bizet: *Carmen*, 2nd act, *Toreador Song* — bar 24.

Copland: *Orchestral Variations* — Theme.

Haydn: Symphony No. 103, 1st movement (development section), and 4th movement.

Hindemith: *Mathis der Maler*, 3rd movement — 1 bar before No. 10.

Kodály: *Háry János* (Suite), 5th movement — upbeat.

Tchaikovsky: Symphony No. 6, 4th movement—11th, 14th, and 16th bars after F.

Weber: Overture to *Oberon*, bar 9.

Different Note Values Under a Fermata

When some instruments have a different note value under a fermata than others, the conductor must be careful not to omit any necessary beats (see Exx. 240–242).

Ex. 293: While the left hand sustains the tutti *ff*, the baton waits on *Two*, moves quickly through *Three*, and cuts off the timpani on *Four*. This *Four* is done with a small gesture; a larger one is used for the repeated 4th beat which cuts off the tutti and prepares the next bar. In bar 2, the first wait is on *One*, and the second wait occurs on the 3rd beat which also ends the timpani roll.

BEETHOVEN, *Die Weihe des Hauses—Overture*

Ex. 294: The 3rd beat must be given very clearly to start the double-tonguing in the trumpets, the tremolo in the strings, and the percussion. Save the left hand for the crescendo.

COPLAND, *A Lincoln Portrait*

Ex. 295: While the baton sustains the strings (on the 6th beat), cut off the flute quietly with the left hand.

BRAHMS, *Symphony No. 4*

Ex. 296: In the 3rd bar, indicate the entrance of horns, trumpets, and timpani after the count with an extra downbeat (small!) or with a gesture of the left hand. *One* in the next bar cuts the hold (see p. 200).

R. SCHUMANN, *Symphony No. 1*

Additional examples for the study of different note values under a fermata:

Beethoven: Symphony No. 8, 1st movement—42 bars from the end.

Berlioz: *Marche Hongroise (Rakóczy March)* from *La Damnation de Faust*, last bar.

Enesco: *Roumanian Rhapsody No. 1,* 2nd bar.

Haydn: Symphony No. 102, 1st movement—last bar of the introduction.

Liszt: *Les Préludes*, before the double bar after D.

Schuman, William: Symphony No. 3—Part 2, bar 141 (contrabass!).

Interruptions

Most interruptions are executed by stopping the beat, if necessary with cut-off. After the pause, which may be short or long, prepare the next attack. Since the players may overlook an interruption, especially if it is not clearly marked, it is sometimes advisable to use a sudden warning gesture of the left hand.

Exx. 297–299: The regular preparation follows the break. Use no rebound in bar 4 of Ex. 298, since you need the upward gesture for preparation. In Ex. 299, use the left hand for cut-off; after the interruption, beat clearly the 4th eighth in preparation for the next phrase.

Ex. 300: The traditional interruption is very slight. Do not bounce the baton in bar 3, but keep it down as in a tenuto beat. Immediately after the 3rd quarter-note, begin the legato preparation, which is somewhat shorter than the regular whole-beat; otherwise the interruption would be unduly prolonged.

Ex. 301: The most practical way of indicating the interruption is to use an extra *quarter*-beat at the end of bar 2, which virtually becomes a 5/4 bar (♩♩♩). The extra beat serves as cut-off and is followed by the downbeat of bar 3.

After a very short interruption between two bars, the music can be resumed by moving the baton downward immediately after a stop at the top of the field of beating. This use of the down-stroke is the only exception to the rule that the baton must change direction in order to lead the orchestra into an attack. The forearm always participates in the downward gesture with a motion that is gentle in *p*, forceful in *f*. This procedure for attacking the 1st count in a bar is applied occasionally to directing certain other entries (see "Free preparatory gestures," p. 245). However, it requires considerable skill and does not lend itself to general use; the student should use this technique only for interruptions of the type discussed in the following three examples.

Ex. 302: An extra quarter-beat (♩ ♩ ♩ ♩) may be used to indicate the pause and to prepare the next measure. For a very short interruption, however, the following procedure is preferable. Subdivide the 3rd count, the last quarter-beat being a somewhat sudden upward gesture which, after a very short stop at the top of the field, is succeeded by a gentle downbeat. The latter starts the next bar without preparation. The motion of the baton may be supported by a smooth gesture of the left hand.

Reprinted by permission of the copyright owners,
Stainer & Bell, Ltd., London

Ex. 303: Subdivide the second half of bar 1, using an accented upbeat on the last eighth. Hesitate on this beat and proceed directly into the new tempo. Since this leaves no time for preparation, the first 2 beats in "molto più mosso" must be sharp and determined. In bar 3, use the accented upbeat again on *Four* and continue with the downbeat after a momentary break.

MAHLER, *Symphony No. 2*

Ex. 173: Cut the tutti fermata, wait, and beat *One* (bar 5) as preparation; hesitate briefly after a small but snappy *Two.* (In bar 4, do not forget to cut off the percussion instruments, which is best done with the left hand.)

Additional examples for the study of interruptions:

Bartók: Concerto for Orchestra, 5th movement — bar 572.

Bartók: *Music for Strings, Percussion, and Celesta*, 4th movement — bars 25 and 51.

Berg: *Lulu Suite, Variations* — last 6 bars.

Brahms: *Variations on a Theme by Haydn*, after each Variation.

Britten: *Four Sea Interludes*, No. 4 (*Storm*) — between nos. 7 and 8.

Gershwin: *Rhapsody in Blue*, 7th bar after No. 15, 3 bars before No. 37, 1 bar before No. 39.

Hindemith: *Mathis der Maler,* 1st movement — double bar before No. 12; 3rd movement — double bar after No. 34.

Mahler: Symphony No. 1, 4th movement — between nos. 12 and 14.

Mussorgsky: *A Night on Bald Mountain*, 4 bars after F.

Sibelius: Symphony No. 2, 1st movement — double bar after N, and at O.

Chapter 20

ACCENTS AND SYNCOPATION

Accents

FOR THE INDICATION of an accent, the beat that precedes the accent is always used for preparation. The preparatory gesture is similar to that at the beginning of a piece, its size and character depending on the degree of the accent to follow. The accented count itself is indicated by the strength of the beat. The emphasis that is put on the accented beat can be varied widely. For a subtle accent in legato, either a larger beat or clicking on the accent may be employed. Tenuto, marcato, or even staccato may be used for stronger accents. In staccato passages, emphasis is obtained by the increased sharpness of the beat.

An especially strong accent requires a particularly effective preparation, because an unusual amount of space and energy is needed to coordinate the players in a powerful attack. If the accent is on the 1st count of a measure, the accented upbeat of Diagram 21 is used. To accent the last count of a measure, prepare with a backward thrust of the arm as described in Example 32. For a strong accent on *Two*, in 4- or 3-beat, the regular patterns do not allow enough space for adequate preparation. Therefore, in 4-beat carry the baton to the *right* on the rebound of the 1st beat with a quick curved motion, then sweep to the left for the accented *Two*. In 3-beat this procedure is reversed.

The object of the combined preparation and emphasis is to secure a unified attack on the part of the players. Conductors sometimes try to get this result by hesitating just before the accent, a procedure that often fails in its purpose because the players do not coordinate properly. The method given above is an aggressive one in the sense that it actually carries the players into the accented count. In soft music, of course, in order to avoid overemphasis, the aggressiveness should not be made too obvious. This can be accomplished by beating the unaccented counts with a minimum of gesture. In that case, a small preparation will still suffice.

The left hand may also be used to indicate an accent, either together with the right hand, or by itself. This is a matter of personal preference. The left-hand gesture includes the preparation on the preceding count and the indication of the accent itself. The preparation is made by an upward motion of the left arm (while the right hand continues its motion undisturbed!). The accent may be indicated in several ways. For example: in *p*, a sharp motion toward the players, the tip of thumb and index finger together; in *f*, a strong downward movement with the hand or the fist, the gesture varying from very small to very large.

Exx. 304a and 305a: The accents are indicated by > and *sf*. Naturally a stronger gesture is needed for an accent in a *f* passage than in a *p* passage. Practice each of these exercises with different degrees of force and with several techniques.

Ex. 306: The composer's time signature is ₵, but many editions print C, an error which may have led conductors to take the introduction to this symphony more slowly than intended by Schubert (see p. 353). Lift the baton slightly higher on *Four* in bars 1 and 2 to prepare the accents in *piano*. The accent in *ff* (306b) can be prepared with an accented upbeat.

Ex. 196 (bar 3): A staccato gesture cuts off on *Three* and also provides the preparation for the accented cello attack; beat *Four* legato and somewhat larger than the following *One*.

Ex. 307: For these accents, use very incisive gestures.

Ex. 308: For the accented 4th counts, use a curved preparation on *Three*. *Four* is done with a sharp staccato gesture. Observe that in Ex. 308a the accent is followed by a neutral beat. In Ex. 308b, bar 3, beat *One* with a snappy rebound and *Two* in a *down*-left direction and stop, skipping *Three*; prepare the new tempo on *Four*. This means that here the preparatory beat starts from down-left instead of from the right, as is customary.

VERDI, *Aida*

Exx. 142 (bar 3) and 199 (bars 2 and 3): For a sudden tutti staccato chord, use the same technique as for an accent.

Exx. 266, 309, and 310: Various accents in 3-beat. In fast tempo, the gesture indicating accents must be made with very little arm motion; the necessary quick turns of the baton should be made with a flexible wrist (for Ex. 310, see p. 215).

Ex. 311a: Only a very slight beat is needed on *One* in the 4th bar, so as to use a minimum of gesture for the accent.

Ex. 311b: Raise the baton only slightly to prepare the accents on *One*.

Ex. 312: Use larger beats on *Two* to prepare the accents; use small gestures elsewhere so that the accents are more prominent.

Ex. 313: Because of the accents, carry the 2nd beat to the left and use a smaller gesture than usual for the 4th beat.

Ex. 314: The beat in the 2nd measure is a preliminary beat, just as if the piece started in bar 3. Beat staccato for the *sf*.

Ex. 296: The accents in bars 1 and 5 are made with a slightly emphasized staccato. The rebound in the 2nd measure must be vigorous.

Ex. 127: Because the right hand indicates *f* in the 5th measure with a large gesture, the left hand is needed for the accent in bar 6.

Ex. 156: The accent in *ff* can be expressed by marcato, the one in *p* by tenuto.

Additional examples for the study of accents:

Beethoven: Symphony No. 4, 2nd movement.

Beethoven: Piano Concerto No. 5, 1st movement.

Borodin: *Polovtsian Dances* from *Prince Igor*.

Brahms: *Academic Festival Overture*.

Gershwin: *Rhapsody in Blue*.

Haydn: Symphony No. 92, 1st movement (development section).

Haydn: Symphony No. 97, 1st movement (*Vivace*).

Mahler: Symphony No. 6, 1st and 2nd movements.

Tchaikovsky: *Nutcracker Suite, Ouverture miniature; Danse russe (Trepak)*.

Verdi: *Messa da Requiem, Dies Irae* (the time-signature is ₵ , but subdivide for *sf*).

Wagner: Overture to *Tannhäuser*.

Syncopation

(1) *Syncopated passages without accents* require no special beat. The gestures must be very definite and the rhythm steady.

You must beat, so to speak, between the notes, not on them. Discipline yourself to keep strictly in tempo, neither rushing nor dragging. Occasionally, it is better to beat tenuto or staccato even in legato phrases to give the orchestra a solid feeling for the rhythm.

Exx. 315–318, and 133: Syncopations in various rhythms. Ex. 318 requires special concentration and a beat that is very precise without becoming stiff. If two pianos are available, practice this entire section of the concerto; have the solo part played on one piano and the orchestra part on the other. Conducting this accompaniment is a very challenging problem for any young conductor.

(2) *Syncopated notes with accents* are indicated on the preceding beat, which is staccato. The sharpness of the beat increases with the degree of the accent. In contrast with an ordinary accent, which is on the count, this staccato beat is not prepared. The beat itself is the preparation for the syncopated note that comes after the count. Again, never beat the syncopation, beat the rhythm! Be especially careful not to beat the count after the syncopated note too soon.

Ex. 267: 4-beat. This demonstrates a staccato accent in a legato passage; in bar 1, beat staccato on *One* and *Three*, legato on *Two* and *Four.*

Exx. 319 and 320: 3-beat. In Ex. 320, bars 2 and 4, do not accent the 2nd beat or you will weaken the strong accent on the 3rd.

Exx. 152 and 321: 2-beat.

Ex. 322: Though this can be done in free style (p. 303), practice with the syncopation beat, a vigorous staccato.

Allegro energico, ($\textit{d}$. = 84)   SMETANA, *The Bartered Bride*

Additional examples for the study of syncopations:

Without accents:

Beethoven: Symphony No. 4, 1st movement—*Allegro vivace* (also with accents).

Debussy: *Nuages*, 5 bars from the end; also strings pizzicato in the next bar.

Mascagni: *Cavalleria Rusticana*, Arrival of Alfio (*Allegretto* 2/4).

Mozart: *Die Zauberflöte*, 2nd act. No. 17—Aria, 3 bars from the end.

Sibelius: Symphony No. 4, 1st movement.

Verdi: *La Traviata*, 1st act, No. 2, *Allegro vivo* C—passage beginning in bar 38.

With accents:

Bartók: *Music for Strings, Percussion, and Celesta*, 4th movement—bar 235.

Brahms: Symphony No. 2, 4th movement—at F.

Dvořák: Symphony No. 7, 3rd movement.

Gershwin: *Rhapsody in Blue*

Prokofiev: *Classical Symphony*, 1st movement at No. 17.

Puccini: *Tosca*, 1st act, bar 4.

Respighi: *Feste Romane*, 2nd movement—after No. 12.

Rimsky-Korsakov: *Capriccio Espagnol*—at M.

Weber: Overture to *Der Freischütz*-at bar 53.

Accents on Off-Beats

Accents on off-beats are indicated in the same way as syncopated notes with accents, i.e., by a sharp staccato on the preceding beat.

Exx. 187b and 304b: These exercises, directed in 2-beat, are very instructive for accents both on and off the beat. Remember that the rests not used for preparation are neutral. In Ex. 187b, the short *f* chords on the off-beats are treated as though they were accented. Use a neutral beat for *Two* in bars 1 and 2, and for *One* in bars 4 and 5.

Ex. 305b: In music directed in 1-beat with the accent on an off-count, use a sharper staccato with a larger and very quick rebound.

Exx. 197 and 323: While the indication of the accented off-beats in Ex. 197 offers no problems, the staccato chords in Ex. 323 require much concentration on the part of the conductor. The beat should be primarily concerned with the chords and not the string passage. In the 1st bar, *One* is *f* staccato, *Two*, light-staccato, and *Three* is the preparation for *Four*. In the 2nd bar, *One* is a sharp downbeat for the off-beat chord, *Two* again is light-staccato, and so on. Use rather small gestures and keep strict time.

Ex. 324: 2-beat (see Ex. 384). The *f* chords that end the phrases are treated like syncopations with accents.

Exx. 325 and 326: For the beats that are followed by accents, use a clear staccato with a quick rebound on *Two*.

Ex. 123 (bars 6 and 7): The Same for 1-beat.

Ex. 180 (bar 2): Accented off-beat in a subdivided pattern.

Ex. 327: The off-beat accent is combined with sustained notes, but the technique remains the same. This is also true for the syncopated entry on *One* in the 2nd measure.

Ex. 328: The serenade from the 2nd act of *Die Meistersinger* is difficult to conduct, because of the continually changing fermatas (with and without repeated beat) and accents (both on and off the beat). Repeat the beat on the fermata in the 1st and 3rd bars, but not in the 2nd bar in which *Three* (preparatory!) follows the hold directly. The accents in the 2nd bar are on the beat, those in the 1st and 3rd bars are after *Three* and *Four* respectively. The entire serenade should be studied and practiced.

Additional examples for the study of accented off-beats:

Barber: Symphony No. 1, 2nd and 3rd bars after No. 50.

Beethoven: Symphony No. 4, 3rd movement.

Beethoven: Symphony No. 6, 4th movement.

Brahms: *Variations on a Theme by Haydn*, Variation No. 5.

Brahms: Violin Concerto, 3rd movement.

Dvořák: String Serenade, Op. 22 — Finale.

Mozart: Overture to *Die Zauberflöte, Allegro.*

Schuman, William: Symphony for Strings, 3rd movement — passage starting at bar 58.

Tchaikovsky: *Romeo and Juliet* (Overture-Fantasia), 3 bars from the end.

Verdi: *Messa da Requiem*, No. 3 — at No. 61, *Quam olim Abrahae* (although marked C, this passage is directed with a 2-beat by most conductors).

Wagner: Overture to *Tannhäuser, Allegro.*

Fp

Fp is executed in much the same manner as an accent. It requires a staccato or marcato beat, and the left hand is used often to secure a unified and sudden drop in the dynamics. This warning gesture (palm facing the players) comes almost together with the *fp* beat.

Exx. 42, 210, 220, and 239: *fp* on sustained chords. In anticipation of the *p*, the bounce of the baton is reduced to a minimum. The left hand should be used in Exx. 42 and 239.

Ex. 329: *fp* in strings, tremolo, requires a very definite and unhesitating preparation. You get the best results with a clear sweep of the *point* of the baton. In the 1st measure, the beats on *One* and *Two* indicate both the tutti chords and the timpani *ffz* on the off-beats; *Three* is non-espressivo, giving the timpani enough time to fade away; *Four* is the precise preparation for the sharp downbeat (not too large) indicating the *fpp*.

Ex. 330: Control of the *fp* is especially important for the operatic conductor, because of the frequent occurrence of a soft accompaniment immediately after a sharply attacked chord.

Exx. 331 and 332: The same technique is used for a change from *f* to *p* within one beat. Since the baton cannot indicate both *f* and *p* with one gesture, the left hand is needed.

It sometimes happens that there is a change from *p* to *f* within a single beat. This is not, strictly speaking, an accent, but it is convenient to discuss in this chapter the technique for directing such a change. The gesture used must bring out the element of surprise inherent in the music. Hence, in contrast to an accent, no preparation should be felt on the preceding beat. The effect is achieved by suddenly enlarging the beat on which the *f* enters.

Ex. 333: Start to beat the 4th measure as though the *p* would continue uninterrupted, but extend the downbeat sharply with the baton tipped downward. Use the left hand for the *p* subito in bar 5.

Ex. 334: The 2nd beat in bars 3 and 7 is larger, but the 1st beat must not give away the change prematurely. Left hand in the 5th measure.

Additional examples for the study of *fp*:

Barber: *Essay for Orchestra*, 4th bar after No. 19.

Beethoven: *Fidelio*, No. 7 (*Arie mit Chor*).

Beethoven: Symphony No. 2, 1st movement—Introduction.

Franck: Symphony in D minor, 3rd movement—bar 5; also bar 53.

Mahler: Symphony No. 1, 4th movement—passage between Nos. 36 and 37 (regardless of the sustained *f* in the horns, the beat must reflect the *fp*).

Prokofiev: *Classical Symphony*, 1st movement—1 bar before No. 9.

Rossini: Overture to *Guillaume Tell, Allegro vivace* 2/4.

Smetana: *The Moldau*, bar 126.

Wagner: *Lohengrin*, 1st act—1st scene.

Chapter 21

PHRASING

To INDICATE PHRASING, several different techniques are used. They will be explained in connection with the examples. Although the methods of phrasing differ, they have this in common: there is a decreased intensity at the end of a phrase, and by contrast a fresh motion at the beginning of a new one. A slight break results but with no delay in the rhythm, which remains steady. Thus the players shorten slightly the last note before the break.

Ex. 335: In the 1st bar, beat tenuto (the "dry" tenuto) on *Two*, not leaving it until just before *Three*, so that the 3rd beat is somewhat hurried. In the 2nd measure, go only halfway to the right for *Three*, and immediately start *Four* with an espressivo gesture. In the 3rd bar, beat tenuto on *Three* in the manner described in Ex. 227. Refer to Diag. 58a for details of the gestures.

The following six examples show different phrase endings after the 1st beat; the method of directing them varies. Notice the difference between the techniques used here and those used for interruptions (p. 192). In the latter case, the rhythmic structure of certain bars had to be altered; in phrasing, however, the rhythmic continuity is not affected.

Ex. 336: Beat *One* in bar 4 with a vigorous staccato and a large rebound, just as if the piece started on *Two*.

210

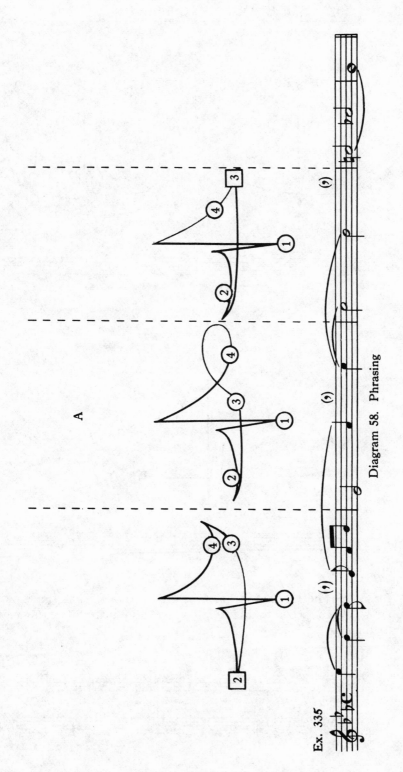

Diagram 58. Phrasing

211

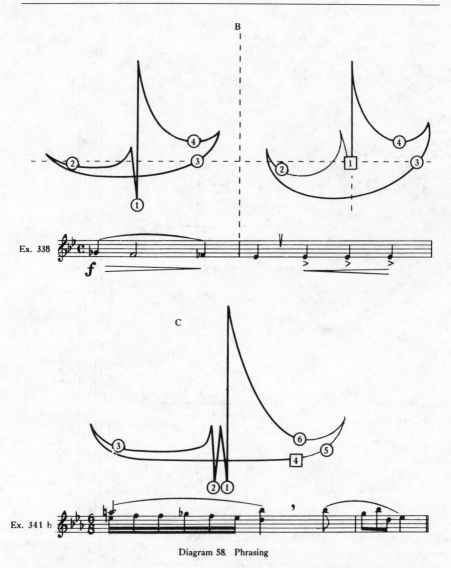

Diagram 58. Phrasing

Ex. 337: The 1st beat in bar 5 is given with a fairly large legato rebound, which provides breathing space and introduces the new phrase on *Two*.

Ex. 338: In the 3rd measure, the composer indicates the phrasing. Beat tenuto on *One*, then swiftly prepare the accented *Two* (Diag. 58b).

Ex. 339: The 2nd beat in bar 3 is very small. Continue the 1st beat in the next bar below the left-right line with an espressivo gesture, thus gaining an animated start for the new phrase. Use the same technique for the next phrase, which begins after a rest.

Ex. 97: Stop on *One* in the 4th measure, and prepare a new start on *Two* with a very soft and gentle gesture.

Ex. 266: In bar 5 there is a break because of the rest, and a calm legato beat would be sufficient. If a pronounced break is desired, beat tenuto on *One*.

Ex. 340: The phrasing in the 2nd measure is marked by the composer. Lead the horns by interrupting the legato line with a tenuto beat on *Three* (Diag. 58a, bar 3).

Ex. 139: Beat tenuto on *Three* in the 2nd measure and resume the staccato on *Four*. A straight gesture is used to reach 3 . After the staccato beats in bars 1 and 2, the holding quality of the tenuto brings out the structure of the musical phrase.

Ex. 341a: For the 2nd measure, apply a technique similar to that used in Ex. 335, bar 2.

Ex. 341b: Beat tenuto on *Four*, prepare with *Five* (Diag. 58c).

There are other cases of phrasing in which the object is not to build the melody, but to achieve clear separation between successive chords or to secure a sharp release after a sustained note. These are illustrated in the remaining examples of this section.

Ex. 342: In the 2nd and 3rd bars, beat tenuto on *One* and *Three*, using *Two* and *Four* for preparation (staccato).

Ex. 236: In this typical symphonic ending, a separation must be made before the last chord is attacked. Stop on *One* in bar 2 and use a delayed *Two* to prepare the final chord.

Ex. 266 (bars 6 and 7): To separate the chords, beat *One* with a gentle staccato beat, followed immediately by a small preparatory gesture which leads into the next chord.

Ex. 343: A rhythmic figure following a sustained note gains clarity if an energetic beat is used to cut the long note. Thus, *Three* in bars 1 and 2 of Ex. 343a is a sharp staccato. The same thing occurs in the 2nd measure of Ex. 343b; both *Two* (accent) and *Three* (cut) are given sharply.

Ex. 344: While *Three* in the 1st bar is neutral, *Three* in the next bar is preparation, as is *Two* in bar 3. Cut the phrase with a sharp downbeat in bar 4.

Ex. 345: A sharp beat on *Four* in the 3rd bar. (A short break after the sustained note assures a clean attack of the staccato passage; for this the violin players must lift the bow for a split second.)

Ex. 310: A sharp staccato beat on *Three* in bar 2 secures a unified ending of the trill in the woodwinds and trumpets, and indicates a slight pause.

Exx. 126 (bar 13) and 215 (bar 6): The same technique in 1-beat.

Additional examples for the study of phrasing:

Brahms: Symphony No. 3, 3rd movement at I.

Copland: *The Tender Land Suite*, 1st movement—the last 7 bars.

Gluck: Overture to *Iphigénie en Aulide*, bar 20.

Liszt: *Hungarian Rhapsody No. 2, Andante mesto.*

Mahler: Symphony No. 5, 4th movement (*Adagietto*).

Prokofiev: *Classical Symphony*, 2nd movement.

Tchaikovsky: Symphony No. 5, 1st movement—Introduction.

Wagner: *Siegfried Idyll.*

Sustained Notes

After a sustained note has been attacked, the remaining counts are very often treated as though they were rests. To beat during soft held notes with anything more than a small neutral beat is meanlingless. In *f*, sustained notes are held most effectively with the left hand.

Exx. 131 (bars 5 and 7) and 233 (bar 3): *Two* and *Three* are neutral, while *Four* is preparation. In each of these the left hand maintains the dynamic intensity.

Ex. 346: This music is a combination of sustained notes and accents, and its adequate direction requires a well-controlled baton technique. The left hand maintains the intensity, while the function of the baton is limited to a sharp indication of the accents on and off the beats; neutral beats are used for the unaccented counts. Use 4 strokes (subdivision) for the accents in bar 14 (see p. 265).

Molto agitato ed energico, ♩. = 76   WILLIAM SCHUMAN. *Symphony for Strings*

Ex. 346   Strings *ff*

Crescendo and diminuendo on a sustained note are not usually directed in the same way as in a melodic line. The change is expressed chiefly by the left hand, while the intensity of the beat increases or decreases. In other words, the size of the beat is not as important as the change in tension revealed by the general attitude of the conductor.

Ex. 347: If the forearm has sufficient tension and the facial expression is convincing, you can indicate the crescendo with small baton gestures even without using the left hand. (The tempo must not drag by "milking" the crescendo; even though the strings divide the bow, beginning with an up-bow, there is a limit to the increase in volume.)

Ex. 259: The diminuendos may be expressed with the left hand while the baton, on the 2nd and 3rd counts, simply marks time and stops on the fermata. Subdivide *Four* in each of the first 3 bars and use the last eighth for preparation in order to avoid interfering with the diminuendo.

Ex. 348: Diminuendo with the left hand, fairly small beats with the baton. After the eighth-note preparation (staccato) for bar 1, you need not subdivide on *One* and *Two*. Subdivide *Three* to bring the strings in because, in this slow tempo, a quarter-beat would not indicate the attack clearly. Continue subdividing so as to lead the descending octaves securely.

Ex. 349: Staccato eighth-note preparation and staccato down-beat (*fp!*). The following 2 eighth-beats are neutral, the next leads into the new chord. This beat, the 4th eighth, also prepares a unified pizzicato attack. Hence, it is somewhat larger than the neutral eighth-beats and is very precise. The left hand, which had been raised in the *fp*, helps to lead the change of harmony and the pizzicato. The 6th eighth is used for an unobtrusive cut-off (winds). It is not necessary to beat on the 7th eighth, but keep in time so that the preparation on the last eighth is strictly in tempo. The 2nd bar is done like the 1st, except that the preparatory last eighth indicates *p* and legato (the tempo is well established and the pizzicato will work without staccato beat). Because of the crescendo in the 3rd measure, the beats are no longer neutral. You may use tenuto on the 5th and 7th eighths to build the crescendo. In bar 4, the left hand sustains the 1st violins, the right cuts off the rest of the orchestra by clicking on the 3rd eighth. On the 4th eighth the baton picks up the legato, while the palm of the left hand turns quickly toward the violins, indicating the sudden *p*.

Ex. 350: Cut off the violins, cellos, and basses on the 2nd eighth in bar 3, then count to yourself, but do not beat until the last eighth, which prepares the tutti chord. Beating out this measure would weaken the tension among the players. The brilliance and dramatic tension of the sudden *ff* are increased by beating the preparation a trifle late rather than strictly in tempo. Do not forget that the bounce after the downbeat carries the baton into the position of attention for the violin attack (Allegro).

Additional examples for the study of sustained notes:

Beethoven: Symphony No. 3, 2nd movement—bars 158 and 159.

Beethoven: Symphony No. 5, 2nd movement—bars 149-153.

Brahms: Symphony No. 4, 3rd movement at I.

Gounod: *Faust*, 1st act—Introduction.

Prokofiev: Symphony No. 5, 1st movement—passage beginning at No. 24.

Sibelius: *Finlandia, Andante sostenuto.*

Strauss: *Till Eulenspiegel*, fermata bars after No. 38.

Wagner: Prelude to *Lohengrin*, passage starting at tne entrance of the trumpets.

Wagner: *Götterdämmerung*, 1st act—Prelude.

Shaping the Melodic Line

The manner of interpreting a melody is one of the most individual characteristics of a musician. Just as a melody played by different soloists may produce varying impressions, so a melody played by an orchestra under different conductors may not affect the listener in the same way. In the case of the orchestra, the gestures by which the conductor conveys his intentions to the players are at least as important as verbal explanations during rehearsal. In fact, a competent conductor, at the first rehearsal with an unfamiliar orchestra, can lead a melody according to his intentions by means of his gestures alone.

In short, the shaping of a melodic line is achieved by means of a purposeful combination of the basic techniques that have been discussed. The use of legato, staccato, and tenuto beat for indicating articulation has been taken up previously. It has been shown that changes in the size of the beat affect not only the dynamics but also the phrasing. In addition, subtle variations in the size of the beat, even from count to count, can express the inflections in the melody that are not indicated by interpretation marks but are "behind the notes." The value of variations in the intensity of the beat, from very intense to completely neutral, has also been treated.

Only by a vital and natural combination of all these elements can the conductor's beat present his conception of the melody to the players. The manner of doing this cannot be put into any formula. Yet, the conductor's feeling for the music will be reflected in the size, intensity, and shape of his beat.

Now that you have all these techniques at your disposal, it will be helpful to review some of the melodic passages among the examples. You will find that you now have more flexibility and freedom in conveying your intentions.

Ex. 27: Beating this music espressivo with the same size and intensity on all counts would not get much personal reaction from the players. Personal reaction means that each player, in this case in the string section, has the same feeling of initiative he would have in a solo performance. To inspire the musicians, the beat needs variety of size and intensity, corresponding to the musical expression. The student should try several ways of expressing the melodic contour, to find which of them best suits his own musical personality. One way is suggested, but it is not the only possible way, nor the "right" one.

Use a fairly large, incisive beat in the 1st measure, decreasing size and intensity in the 2nd, but with an expressive preparatory gesture on *Four*. A smaller beat on *Four* in bar 3 and more relaxed beats on *One* and *Two* in bar 4 make for a good contrast before the crescendo, which is rendered more effective by the sudden increase in intensity. The first 2 beats in bar 5 are large, *Three* is very incisive. The 2nd beat in bar 6 is small, the 3rd an expressive preparation. In the 8th bar, the beat becomes smaller and more relaxed.

Ex. 260: It is impossible to express the whimsical charm of the music by academic time-beating. Every aspect of the conductor's appearance is important — the way he stands, his facial expression, and the variety in his beat. Here again, every player must be inspired to feel like a soloist and to put himself completely into the music. One way of using contrasting beats to bring out the life of the whole passage follows.

Remain motionless after the cut-off of the first fermata. With the small staccato preparation (*Three* in bar 1), relax your manner and facial expression. In bars 2–4, use a legato downbeat and a small "dry" tenuto on *Two* for cut-off; then staccato on *Three* and *Four*, the preparation becoming a little more animated each time. The downbeat in the 5th bar is hardly noticeable because of the sudden appearance of the left hand (*p* subito), which remains lifted during the rests and is used for the cut-off on the second fermata. The right hand gives a delicate staccato beat on *Three* (bar 5), changing into legato on *Four*.

In 1-beat, the continued up-and-down motion of the baton may easily become monotonous, which would have a fatal effect on a melodic passage. This may be avoided in two ways—either by using a graceful curved motion of the baton rather than a straight up-and-down motion, or by changing the size of the beat. A good passage on which to try these methods is the second theme of the first movement of Beethoven's Fifth Symphony.

Ex. 351: Direct the first 4 bars with small forceful gestures, indicating the secco character of the 5th and 7th bars with an incisive downward gesture of both arms (bar 6 is preparatory). The gesture in bar 8, to lead the entry of the French horns, should have an upbeat character. The three *sf* notes are marcato. Immediately after the third, the gesture changes to prepare the entry of the *p* legato melody. The rise and fall of the melody is brought out by the size of the beat; in the unstressed measures the beat is very small. An alternative method is to use small gestures throughout and lead the melody with the left hand. If the cellos and basses tend to enter late in bars 14 and 18, let the beat in these bars have a slight staccato quality.

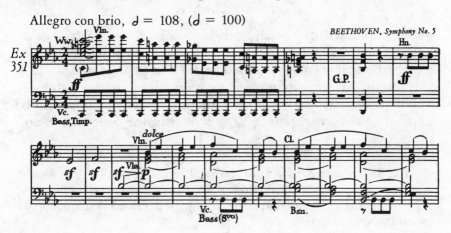

Chapter 22

DIFFERENT USES FOR BASIC PATTERNS

THE TREATMENT OF THE SIX basic patterns has so far had for its object the mastery of each of the individual patterns. Consequently, in most of the examples the beat has followed the notation, so that when legato was marked a legato beat was used, and similarly for staccato. There have been a few exceptions. In actual conducting, however, it is often necessary to use a beat which does not conform to the notation. While there can be no specific formula for the application of the patterns, the following discussion will cover the most frequent cases.

Non-Espressivo

As explained previously, this beat is used for soft and emotionally neutral passages. It is also used to mark time when nothing rhythmical occurs (sustained notes) and to indicate rests. It is very useful in accompaniment to keep the orchestra subdued. While primarily used for legato, the non-espressivo may also be applied to detached passages, as shown in the following example.

Ex. 352: A staccato beat in leading the strings would be pedantic. Non-espressivo lets the music flow in a simple and natural way without preventing the players from articulating: detached eighth-notes followed by portato (see Ex. 488).

Similarly, when the conductor does not want the orchestra to play a very detached staccato, he may use non-espressivo instead of staccato. This principle can be applied to the beginning of

Exx. 16 and 166. Here, and in the following discussion of choice of beat, the pattern chosen should often depend upon the way the orchestra responds to your gesture. The beat may assume a corrective function. If the orchestra's playing is too detached, the non-espressivo will tell the players to decrease the sharpness of the staccato; if the music is not played sharply enough, the staccato beat will bring out the desired articulation.

Espressivo-Legato

This beat has such a definite character that it is applied only when the music is both legato and espressivo.

Light- and Full-Staccato

The appearance of single staccato beats in legato passages has already been discussed; they are used for phrasing, for accents, and as preliminary beats to strengthen a start in *f*. To attack a sustained note in *f*, a full-staccato preparation is always used.

Slurred passages do not necessarily require a legato beat. Often, especially in fast tempo, clear direction needs a staccato gesture.

Ex. 353: In bar 3ff., use light-staccato.

Exx. 148, 354, and 355: Full-staccato is used despite the phrase markings. Try to beat legato and you will see how inadequate it is.

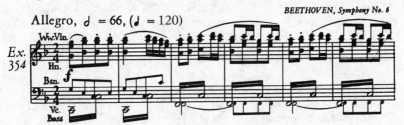

Ex. 355 Allegro, (♩.= 104)   BRAHMS, Symphony No. 1.

A staccato beat may be used in passages where no staccato is marked but where you wish to concentrate the players' attention on the rhythm.

Ex. 356: Light-staccato beats starting on *Two* in the 2nd measure help to emphasize the rhythm and assure unified playing by the strings on *Four*. Be sure not to slow down in your anxiety to stress the rhythm—it would upset the ensemble (see p. 365).

Ex. 356 Poco sostenuto, ♩ = 69   BEETHOVEN, Symphony No. 7

The use of a *gentle staccato*, between non-espressivo and staccato, has already been suggested several times. This beat uses a quick motion before the counts, but there is no stop. Apply it where the detached quality is not felt very strongly but where legato would be inappropriate.

Ex. 357: Gentle staccato is applied to this music because of the rather slow tempo. Staccato with full stop on the count would be too jerky, and the legato beat would not express the rhythmic vitality.

Marcato

The aggressive character of this pattern makes it applicable only to strong and forceful music. Sometimes a marcato beat may be used in espressivo-legato on *One*, or on *Four* and *One*, to emphasize the rhythm strongly, but this procedure causes monotony if repeated too often.

Tenuto

The use of the expressive form of the tenuto beat has already been discussed. The "dry" form used on single counts for purposes of phrasing has also been treated. When employed for whole bars, the "dry" form (Diags. 49 and 51) indicates the rhythm in an academic manner. Use it chiefly as a corrective measure to maintain the ensemble, or when for other reasons the rhythm must be stressed in a completely neutral way. It is helpful in accompaniment to point out the counts clearly and avoid misunderstanding. In the first few bars of Ex. 131, this beat prevents the brasses from dragging; be sure to keep strictly in time and do not delay the beat by waiting for the sixteenth-notes.

Strangely, the "dry" tenuto beat is sometimes taught as the standard pattern. The lifeless nature of this beat, however, prevents adequate musical expression and results in mere time-beating. This undesirable effect does not occur in rapid tempo, especially in 2-beat; here the "dry" tenuto is convenient as a substitute for legato. In this case, the legato rebound on *One* would make the quick gestures confusing. In the first bars of Ex. 270, the "dry" tenuto beat, done by the wrist alone, is easily seen to be the most convenient gesture.

Legato and Staccato Simultaneously

When legato and staccato are played simultaneously by the orchestra, the beat usually has the character of the leading melody.

Ex. 358: Beat legato; the moderate staccato needs no special attention.

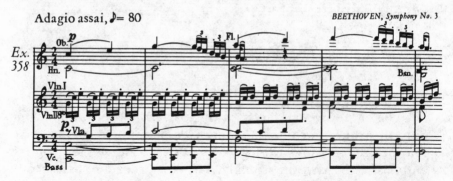

Ex. 359: The staccato beat changes to legato with the entrance of the main theme in viola and bassoon. You may use an occasional gentle staccato beat to express both melody and counterpoint.

Ex. 360: The woodwind passage in bar 3ff (2-beat) would be conducted legato if it stood alone. The staccato beat is used, however, for two reasons: the brisk viola figure requires more attention, and the winds would naturally play legato. Furthermore, the staccato beat insures a good attack on the triplet figures in the violins and bass instruments.

There are passages where several important but different melodies occur and to which the same pattern cannot be applied for any length of time. Sometimes the gentle staccato is useful as a compromise beat. Often it is necessary to change quickly from one pattern to another to get the best results.

Ex. 361: Use a gentle staccato motion (1-beat).

Ex. 362: Beat non-espressivo, changing to poco espressivo in the 2nd measure. Return to neutral beats in bar 3; in the next bar, add some staccato quality to the beat, for the release of the sustained brass chord and to lead the detached notes. Then change back to non-espressivo.

Additional examples for the study of passages in which legato and staccato are played simultaneously:

Berlioz: Overture *Le Carnaval Romain*, passage starting at the 35th bar of the *Andante sostenuto* 3/4.

Debussy: *La Mer*, 3rd movement.

Haydn: Symphony No. 101, 2nd movement.

Mahler: Symphony No. 4, 1st movement.

Mendelssohn: Symphony No. 4, 2nd movement.

Prokofiev: Symphony No. 5, 4th movement.

Tchaikovsky: Symphony No. 5, 4th movement—bar 414.

Verdi: *Otello*, 3rd act, beginning.

Wagner: Prelude to *Die Meistersinger*, 38 bars before *Sehr gewichtig*.

Simultaneous Different Dynamics

An orchestral score often has different dynamic markings occurring simultaneously. The timpani or brass may enter softly while the rest of the orchestra is playing a loud passage, or a solo instrument may play *f* while the rest of the orchestra plays *p*. In most cases the baton directs the larger group of instruments and the left hand takes care of the others if needed. Thus, the left hand may give the warning *p* gesture while the right has a large espressivo beat, or a non-espressivo with the baton may be combined with a stimulating gesture of the left hand.

Ex. 363: The right hand beats *fp* in bar 3, as it did in bar 1. The left hand addresses the violins and indicates their sudden *p* (see p. 96).

When crescendo and dimuendo occur at the same time, both hands are needed. The baton again is concerned with the larger group and the left hand leads the others.

Ex. 364a: The left hand cues in the *p* entrance of 1st violins and cellos, while the baton indicates *f*. In the second half of the measure the size of the beats decreases. The left hand takes over the diminuendo of the woodwinds in bar 3, while the right directs the crescendo in the other instruments.

Ex. 364b: The left hand leads the instruments on the top staff and the baton leads the others.

Gustav Mahler and Richard Strauss were among the first composers who, in the interest of a well-balanced over-all sound, applied contrasting dynamics to various instrumental groups. Their scores provide ample material for study. Since then, careful dynamic markings have become common practice. The conductor must insist that they are meticulously observed by all players, although his gesture may occasionally contradict the dynamic indications in their parts.

Additional examples for the study of passages with simultaneous different dynamics:

Barber: *Second Essay for Orchestra*, passage starting 2 bars before No. 11.

Berlioz: *Symphonie Fantastique*, 4th movement — 39 bars from the end.

Brahms: Symphony No. 2, 4th movement — 12 bars after C (109th bar of the movement).

Debussy: *La Mer*, end of 1st movement.

Dvořák: Symphony No. 9, 1st movement—passage starting at No. 9.

Mahler: Symphony No. 5, No. 3, *Scherzo* (in the revised edition of the score the composer changed many dynamic markings).

Mendelssohn: *Fingal's Cave Overture*—several passages.

Sibelius: Symphony No. 2, 2nd movement—several passages.

Strauss: *Tod und Verklärung*.

Problems of Orchestration

Generally speaking, the nature of the instrumental groups is such that the winds need an especially clear and precise beat while the strings call for a warmer gesture. The combination of both requires an intelligent mean, the nature of which is an essential part of the relationship between the conductor and his players. This will be discussed in greater detail in Chapter 24.

Similarly, the extent to which the conductor should indicate articulation and dynamics is closely connected with the response of the different instruments and groups. Certain results are obtained rather easily from the strings, but you must work harder to get them from the winds, and vice versa. A crescendo in the woodwinds requires a larger gesture than in the brass. It is an erroneous notion that the massive effects of the brass need a huge gesture. On the contrary, a small and very definite beat controls the brass instruments most effectively and prevents them from dragging.

How to beat pizzicato depends entirely on the musical context. Lack of unity in pizzicato is a very common mistake, but the young conductor must not assume that he is always to blame. Even a correct beat does not secure a unified attack if the players are not attentive. Generally, string players tend to anticipate pizzicato entrances, and the conductor must be especially careful when such an entrance occurs in combination with other instruments. The preparatory gesture must be distinct and incisive.

When pizzicato occurs alone, it is directed like staccato.

Ex. 365: The last chord requires a sharp full-staccato, but not too large.

Exx. 142, 198, and 366: The soft pizzicato needs a small staccato beat and may be assisted by the left hand. The left-hand gesture uses the preceding count for preparation and imitates the action of plucking the string. Some conductors use this so effectively that they rely on it alone for the pizzicato.

When some strings play pizzicato while others play arco, or play pizzicato in combination with wind instruments, there are two possibilities. If the rhythm is established and steady, a special gesture would disturb the players rather than help them. But when the rhythmic pulsation is not continuous and often after rests, a staccato preparation helps secure a unified attack.

Exx. 62, 163a, and 367: Beat legato, with no special gesture for the pizzicato.

Ex. 190: In bars 17 and 19 the same instrumental combination is used, but the strings play arco the first time, and pizzicato the second. Consequently the preparation for the second chord has staccato quality.

Additional examples for the study of passages in which pizzicato occurs alone or in combination with various instruments:

Beethoven: Symphony No. 4, 1st movement — Introduction.

Beethoven: Overture to *Coriolanus*, last few bars.

Franck: Symphony in D minor, 2nd movement.

Haydn: *The Seasons,* No. 18 — Recitative.

Mendelssohn: Symphony No. 3 (*Scotch*), 3rd movement.

Prokofiev: *Peter and the Wolf*, several passages.

Schuman, William: Symphony for Strings — 3rd movement.

Strauss, Johann: *Pizzicato Polka.*

Tchaikovsky: Symphony No. 4, 3rd movement.

Tchaikovsky: Piano Concerto No. 1, 2nd movement.

Chapter 23

ACHIEVING COMPLETE PHYSICAL CONTROL

General Appearance

CONTROL OF PHYSICAL GESTURES and movements, necessary to everyone who appears on a public platform, is especially important for the artist, because his poise and ease of movement not only impress the public, but—and this is far more significant—also affect his own performance. The conductor needs freedom of motion more than any musician, because his work consists of communicating musical expression directly by gestures. Like other performers, he must find a happy medium between tension and relaxation; he will show this in the way he mounts the podium and faces the players—and indeed in every gesture he makes.

Authority over the players, knowing what you want musically, and confidence in your technique enable you to overcome gradually personal idiosyncrasies such as stamping the feet, wandering about the podium, moving the body unnecessarily, and making grimaces. The two extremes to be avoided are shyness and exhibitionism. Every gesture the conductor makes should say something to the players. The genuinely inspired musical leader concentrates upon meeting the demands of the music and of the orchestra; he has no time or energy for superficial gestures having only audience appeal. Nevertheless, there must be a harmonious continuity of gesture, each movement blending with the next, resulting in an appearance of smoothness and security.

The conductor must not be carried away by his emotions. Despite the intensity and passion of his feeling for the music, some part of his mind must act as a control mechanism and prevent him from losing himself in the music to the extent that his ears no longer bring him an objective perception of what the musicians are doing. In this way, the conductor is able to think ahead and is alert for any emergency, and the players feel that they can rely on him in any situation.

233

Field of Beating

It is important to remember that the field of beating is described by the *point of the baton,* and it is here that the attention of the orchestra must be focused. This object cannot be achieved if the center of motion is the hand, with the baton carried along as a lifeless appendage. With the point of the baton as the center of motion, it is easy to coordinate the playing of groups seated relatively far apart. Then the conductor does not feel the necessity of "going to the orchestra with his gestures," but rather draws the players toward himself, strengthening his feeling of security and authority.

The center of the field of beating in the standard form (as used for the diagrams) is directly in front of the conductor, about midway between the shoulder and the waist levels. Therefore it is important that the conductor's desk, just high enough for the score to be read easily, should not interfere with the beat.

Moving the field of beating slightly up or down may bring variety into the beat, but the student is cautioned against the continual use of an abnormally high or low field. Moving the center of the field sideways, either by carrying the arm over or by turning the body, should be done only when it accomplishes a definite purpose, such as addressing one particular group very strongly. The players on the opposite side of the orchestra must never be allowed to lose sight of the baton. Too-frequent change of the field of beating disrupts the continuity of gesture and confuses the players. This is also true for moving the field toward or away from the body.

Much has been said in previous chapters about the relation of the size of the beat to the dynamics. It has also been pointed out that the intensity of the gesture is at least as important as the size. For this reason, loud music does not always require a large beat, and a conductor can use small but intense motions most effectively. Several prominent conductors, in fact, have achieved magnificent results by keeping their field of beating always quite limited in size. But this technique is effective only when serving a particular type of personality, otherwise it lacks expression and tension.

There are situations in which, for reasons other than dynamics, the size of the field must not be too large. In fast tempo, large gestures are easily blurred and lose their effectiveness. In leading a small group, the gestures can be smaller than those used in leading a large group. Also, an operatic conductor, directing in a darkened orchestra pit, must be certain that his gestures are within the lighted area of his desk.

Use of the Eyes

The eyes are an invaluable means of establishing personal contact between the conductor and the players. Therefore, they should be used as much as possible, and a minimum amount of time should be spent in looking at the score. If you cannot entirely memorize the music, you must still be able to keep your attention on the orchestra most of the time, referring to the score only at intervals of several bars. This ability can be built up by training. Learn to see a number of bars at once, so that by glancing down at the score you know what is coming. Of course, you must know the score so well that you will have no fear of losing the place while you are looking away. Without this knowledge, you are apt to turn your eyes toward the players too late, with a resulting feeling of discomfort. Not only the preparatory gesture but the way you look at a player can tell him in advance what kind of expression you expect. However, don't stare at a player before a tricky solo passage—it might make him nervous.

Independence and Use of the Left Hand

That the left arm must be independent of the right is generally taken for granted. The conductor must be able to beat steadily with the right arm and feel no muscular tension in the left. The achievement of this independence, however, is a problem for the student, who will often automatically make some kind of rhythmic movement in sympathy with the right arm.

There are many exercises that are useful for training the arms to perform different gestures simultaneously. Some of the best follow.

Describe a circle with one arm while moving the other up and down. Practice first with the forearm, then with the entire arm. Alternate arms suddenly.

Beat time steadily with the right hand while the left independently makes typical conductor's gestures, such as indications for dynamics, accents, and warnings. Use various rhythms in the right hand and be sure to include 12 beats in a measure.

Practice beating different rhythms in both hands. Start by tapping the edge of a table, since hearing the rhythm makes it easier to coordinate. Tap 3 against 2, and 3 against 4. It helps to think of the fractional values within the bar:

one hand	3/4	
other hand	3/4	
one hand	4/4	
other hand	4/4	

It is a good rule to avoid doubling the baton gestures with the left arm because it is a wasted motion. Nevertheless, even the best conductors do it occasionally, but only at moments of great climax. To double continually is a sign of lack of control.

In general, the function of the left hand is to indicate details of interpretation, while the baton focuses attention on the rhythm. The ability of the left hand to express the most subtle nuances as well as the most dramatic accents is one of the characteristics of fine conducting. When and how to use the left hand are matters of individual taste, but it should always tell the orchestra something essential. If the conductor uses the left hand continually, the players will ignore it.

In earlier chapters the use of the left hand has been discussed in connection with dynamics, articulation, cuing, accents, and so on. These gestures may reinforce the indications of the baton, or express details that the baton cannot bring out adequately, or even, in some cases, express the opposite of the baton gestures. The rest of this chapter will deal with other typical functions of the left hand.

The left hand is used often to bring out a particular group of instruments (see the instruments on the top staff in Ex. 364b). When you want to cue in a group without disturbing the general line of the baton, use the left hand. In Ex. 355 it can indicate the entry of the strings in bar 3, or the trumpets and timpani in bar 4. In Ex. 324 use the left hand for emphasizing the off-beat chords in bars 2 and 9. Apply a sharp downward gesture with the fist. This must not interfere with the smooth progress of the baton to the following neutral beat. (Note that in bar 9 the left hand is lifted simultaneously with the downbeat of the baton!)

The left-hand gesture may differ from that of the right in regard to phrasing, dynamics, and articulation. In Ex. 364, for instance, each hand indicates a different degree of dynamics.

Ex. 368: In bars 3 and 4, the baton indicates non-espressivo while the left hand builds the expressive $<\;>$.

Ex. 369: The right hand beats staccato throughout, while the left may indicate tenuto for the 1st violins in bar 3, and the cellos and basses in bar 4.

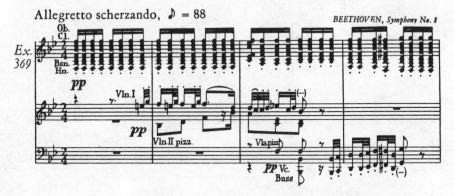

Another helpful gesture of the left hand is the raised finger for attention, e.g., when an instrument is about to enter after a long rest. Also, a number of fingers may be raised to warn the orchestra that you will change the number of beats in a measure. For instance, if you are beating all the counts in 4-time and at a più mosso want to beat alla breve, raise 2 fingers one bar before the change. This is an emergency gesture, not necessary when the change is marked in the parts or has been sufficiently rehearsed.

When not in use, the left hand should be in a neutral position. It is best to hold it on or near the lapel, whence it can move easily for the various gestures. Occasionally, you may keep the hand at the side, though this sometimes looks stiff or gives the conductor an appearance of indifference if used too often. Resting the hand on the desk, on the hip, or in the pocket is not recommended.

Turning a page must not interrupt a left-hand gesture; it is better not to begin a motion than to stop it in the middle. Better still, know the score so well that turning a page can wait a few bars.

The most rigid way to test brachial independence is the ability to perform all conducting patterns with the left arm, not in reverse motion, but in strict conformance to the movements which are normally assigned to the right arm. Aside from the possibility that an accident may put a conductor's right arm out of action, the skill derived from such practice will make the effort worthwhile.

Chapter 24

ON PREPARATION IN GENERAL

Techniques of Starting

THE FIRST THING TO DO after reaching the conductor's stand is to make sure that all the players are present. The manner in which you pick up the baton must be authoritative, and fussy gestures should be avoided. A well-disciplined orchestra does not require a noisy tap on the stand to call it to attention. With one motion take the position of attention, which can in itself set the mood, and face the group of instruments that plays first. Do not look at the score before the playing begins! The left hand need not be used for every start. The baton is usually raised to about shoulder level; if it is held too high, the preliminary beat may be awkward.

Securing a good opening attack can be a problem which is not always solved successfully—even with the best orchestras. While part of this problem has to be worked out in rehearsal, and consequently is not discussed here, a good beat is still necessary for clean execution. The first requirement is that all the players be ready and alert; do not give the preliminary beat until all eyes are on you. It is also indispensable that conductor and players be in agreement on the number of beats in a measure.

In a large majority of cases the regular preliminary beat will secure a unified attack. However, certain instrumental combinations present difficulties that require special consideration. The inexperienced conductor may find it difficult, especially in soft entrances, to bring in wind instruments simultaneously, or winds combined with harp, or high strings. The problem is caused by the purely physical difference in the way each instrument "speaks." For instance, the oboe player reacts differently at the attack than the trumpet player, and various other instruments respond differently in very high or very low registers. Despite these differences, a good ensemble must be achieved, or the entrance will be "arpeggiated." This difficulty occurs not only at the beginning but also in the course of a piece, especially after rests.

The solution of the problem depends to a certain extent upon the understanding between the conductor and his players. As far as the beat is concerned, two extremes are possible—a dry beat or a flexible one. Some conductors use an anticipatory beat. The played attack does not coincide with the baton movement but follows it by as much as half a second or longer. The conductor uses a rather dry beat (tenuto, or, for *f* attacks, marcato), stops on the opening count and *waits* for the orchestra, then proceeds as usual. Thus the first beat (but not the count!) takes a little longer than the subsequent beats. Some orchestras are accustomed to the use of this technique, either for the entire group or only for certain soft entrances in the winds; the conductor visiting these orchestras will do well to adapt his beat to this well-established habit, for it would take a great deal of training to replace it.

The reason that such an anticipatory beat works is that the players are accustomed to adjusting their attacks so that they follow immediately after the beat. Many conductors, however, adhere to the principle of always beating *with* the orchestra. A flexible and more rounded beat is needed to secure a good ensemble at these difficult attacks. With this beat, you "breathe" with the players and almost "put the notes in their mouths." After the preparation, the beat curves down and up with a very plastic gesture, while the attitude and facial expression say to the players: Now—start! Every conductor must find the method that is most effective for him.

Ex. 370: The difficulty here is caused by the oboe, 2nd bassoon, trumpets in the low register, and trombones, all of whom start *ppp* and must be synchronized with the rest of the orchestra. The anticipatory beat may be used here; a small, clear downbeat anticipates the played attack. If the flexible gesture is used, the left hand can help express the inviting quality with a smooth, gentle motion toward the orchestra.

Largo, ♩ = 60   *VERDI, Il Trovatore*

Ex. 8: In a well-trained orchestra, the strings will listen to the solo English horn and adjust their playing in case of a slight delay in the attack. No special beat is needed.

Ex. 352: For a perfect start, no amount of rehearsal will do the trick unless the beat is clear and helps the players to concentrate on a unified attack.

Entries

It is not mandatory to indicate every cue; in fact, there are cases where cuing can even be harmful. When the players know the music very well and you give an unnecessary cue with an emphasized gesture, it may be interpreted as an indication to play loudly. In fast tempo, it is often impossible to give many cues within a few bars; do not let your gestures become too involved or confusion will result. Still, the conductor should not spare himself in giving cues, as they constitute one of the chief means by which he maintains contact between himself and his players, giving the latter a feeling of security, and identifying himself with them.

Cues are given for three purposes:

(1) You may simply remind the players to enter after a number of rests. This depends partly on the reliability of the individual players, but certain entrances are so difficult for the musicians that cues must be given in any case. Besides, there are cues which are expected as a matter of habit, and their omission may cause uncertainty.

Ex. 371: There is nothing particularly difficult about the oboe entrance since it occurs after a rest of only 5 bars. The player, however, may be surprised if the cue is not given and may not enter in time.

(2) A cue may be given to insure precision of attack.

Ex. 372: The eye is sufficient for the woodwind entrance in the 5th bar, and a gesture would be superfluous. However, the strings in the next bar do need some gesture, not because they would get lost after only the 1-bar rest, but to insure a clean and precise attack. A staccato motion on *Two* strengthens the rhythmic feeling of the players; it should be small and delicate. At the same time, the left hand takes care of the *p* in the winds.

Ex. 373: A gentle staccato gesture on the 2nd quarter in bar 3 helps the violins to enter precisely—an assistance especially needed here, because the fast passage starts after the count. Most conductors subdivide this count. It should be done unobtrusively, resuming the legato line by the 3rd quarter.

There are certain cases where there is danger of a delayed entrance: for instance, heavy brass entrances in fast tempo. This can be avoided by beating the preceding count slightly ahead of time. Thus, in Ex. 111, *Two* in the next to the last bar is somewhat hurried, and *One* in the last bar is actually an anticipatory beat. While this is a matter of individual preference, a conductor with good control may execute such an entry without using an anticipatory beat, especially with the help of the left hand. There are certain passages in accompaniment, however, that can hardly be done without this type of beat.

Ex. 374: Beat the preparation for the tutti entrance a little ahead of time, to avoid a delayed attack. Just how much in advance to beat depends partly upon the soloist's playing and partly upon the conductor's experience with the orchestra. If the soloist hurries the passage, it may be necessary to apply subdivision in order to reestablish a firm rhythm (subdivided 2-beat).

Allegro molto vivace, (♩ = 80)   MENDELSSOHN, *Violin Concerto*

Ex. 374

(3) Often the conductor wants to lead an entry in a particular way: loud or soft, expressive or emphatic, lyric or dramatic. His purpose is not just to give a cue, but to convey to the orchestra his detailed intentions concerning the interpretation of the music. This use of the preparatory gesture to lead an attack in which the cuing *per se* is unimportant is so fundamental that it is treated under a separate heading.

Preparation in Its Broader Aspects

It is entirely erroneous to think that preparatory gestures are used only to start a piece. On the contrary, they are used continually and constitute one of the most effective tools by means of which the conductor brings life and variety into the performance. In a sense, all conducting is preparation — indicating in advance what is to happen. With the preparatory gestures, the conductor not only brings in the instruments with a particular shading and expression, but also emphasizes the salient points of the melody and underlines the phrase groups.

Mere time-beating would never be enough to accomplish musically significant results. If you did not use preliminary gestures in Ex. 179, the players would still play the notes correctly. But to bring out the tenderness of the string entry on *Three* in the 1st measure and the strong, noble staccato chord in the 2nd, preparatory gestures are needed; in fact, they are more important than the beats themselves. The more the conductor can express in these gestures, the more response he will get from the players in the way of shading, articulation, and expression.

Ex. 375: The purpose of a stimulating 2nd beat in bar 2 is not so much cuing as expression; a strong gesture secures a brilliant entry in the violins. Use the same kind of preparation on the 4th beat for the cellos and basses. Lead the energetic cello passage in the 1st measure with small gestures, so as not to confuse the violas, who are playing *p*.

Often it is necessary to use one or more smaller and less intense beats before the preparation, so that the larger and stronger preparatory gesture may be more effective. If you were to use large beats for the crescendo in Ex. 173, it would be difficult to find a more powerful motion for the preparatory downbeat in the 2nd bar which is needed for a rhythmic *ff* attack of the motive ♪♪♪. Therefore, indicate the crescendo with the left hand and save the larger baton gestures for this preparation.

Ex. 376: Use forceful beats for the chords and the preparations on *Three,* and very small beats for the violin passages. This treatment is not only helpful technically but also conforms to the structure of the music.

Ex. 377: The beats in the 2nd and 4th bars should be sharp but without too much intensity, so that the downbeat preparation and accented *Two* in the 3rd and 5th bars will be more effective. In the 6th measure, however, *Two* is used to prepare the important entrance in the bass instruments.

Free Preparatory Gestures

The rule that preliminary beats must be given in strict time cannot always be observed. Some exceptions have been discussed in the chapter on holds and interruptions. There are other cases in which the rule may be neglected. Often it is not possible to give a strict preparation in an emergency, especially when following a soloist. It may be necessary to cut the preparation short, so that the orchestra will not enter late. A typical example is the beginning of Beethoven's Piano Concerto No. 5. In the first movement, bars 3 and 5, the coordination of the tutti attacks with the end of the piano cadenzas can present a problem. Only skillfully timed, free preparations will bring about the desired effect. Even in the absence of an emergency, it may be more convenient to dispense with a strict preparation, namely, when a correctly timed gesture may be either too long or too short.

Ex. 378: The tempo marking is disregarded in the preparations for the fermatas. The preliminary beats are free and take into consideration the quiet feeling of the opening. In fact, the first beat that needs strict timing is the preparation for the violin entrance.

Allegro di molto, ($\downarrow$ = 144) MENDELSSOHN, *Midsummer Night's Dream—Overture*

Freely timed preparatory gestures are justified only if the results are satisfactory. The student should first master the strict technique; he will then find it an interesting experiment to try other methods. It is quite possible that very dramatic or very delicate attacks may be executed in an extremely effective way by ignoring the pulse of the music in the preparation.

Preparation with Subdivision

In slow tempo, a full-beat preparation may be too long and it might be necessary to subdivide the count preceding the entry. This would result in a clearer gesture and establish closer contact with the musicians.

Ex. 379: While quarter-beats are adequate in the 1st bar, a good attack on the *f* in the 2nd requires a vigorous eighth-note preparation, both in the interest of clarity and to express the sudden change in the music. Therefore, subdivide on the 3rd count (see p. 268).

Ex. 380: The 4th counts in bars 1 and 2 are subdivided by some conductors to obtain a precise sixteenth-note (see the comments in connection with Ex. 141). The same subdivision is helpful in the 3rd bar, because without a clear indication of *Four-and*, the violins would not feel secure in their triplet.

Exx. 141 and 170: Even at the very start of a piece, subdivision may be useful to facilitate the playing of a short anacrusis. Beating *Four-and* at the beginning leaves no doubt about the tempo. For the first eighth-beat use a small sidewise motion; the upbeat on the second eighth is the actual preparation and requires a larger gesture. This type of subdivision is a special case of the use of an extra beat for a start after the count. (see p. 98).

Study and practice scores No. 5 and 6 discussed in the Appendix.

Chapter 25

NUMBER OF BEATS IN A MEASURE (I)

General Considerations

THE CONDUCTOR CANNOT rely upon the time-signature to tell him how many beats he should use in a measure, because composers do not always think of beat patterns when setting the rhythm. Nowadays, composers are more apt to consider conducting problems when marking their scores, but the indications in many older compositions can be confusing. Metronome markings can also be misleading: one would not use 1-beat for the 4th movement of Beethoven's First Symphony, although the metronome refers to the whole bar as the rhythmic unit (see Ex. 260). Regardless of the music's meter, clear direction may demand that priority be given to technical considerations.

The following examples will show how the beat patterns that have been discussed in previous chapters are best applied to music of various styles. Additional beat patterns, including techniques needed for the performance of twentieth-century music, will come up for discussion in Chapter 27.

In general, you may use for 12 units in a measure:				12 or 4 beats
"	9	" " "	" :	9 or 3 "
"	8	" " "	" :	8 or 4 "
"	6	" " "	" :	6, 2, or 1 "
"	4	" " "	" :	12, 8, 4, 2, or 1 "
"	3	" " "	" :	9, 6, 3, or 1 "
"	2	" " "	" :	6, 4, 2, or 1 "

Three main factors are to be taken into consideration: the tempo of the music, the players' need for rhythmic security, and the degree of intensity you desire on the weak counts or in the smaller rhythmic values. The last is more a question of style and interpretation than of technique.

The speed of the music sets a limit to the number of possible beats in a measure. Thus, in Presto or Allegro molto in 4/4, a 4-beat would often be uncomfortable for the conductor and confusing to the players. The musical pulsation, moreover, may demand an alla breve beat rather than a stroke on every written count, as in Mendelssohn's *Wedding March* (see Ex. 134) or the Allegro vivo in Rossini's Overture to *Il Barbiere di Siviglia* (see Ex. 258). On the same principle, Exx. 155 and 156 need 1-beat, although marked 2/4.

On the other hand, many slow movements written in 2/4 or ₵ have to be directed in 4, for otherwise so much time would elapse between beats that the rhythm would no longer be clear (see Exx. 16, 25, 37, and 306). In these movements, even though the musical pulse may be felt in two, a 4-beat pattern serves a better definition of the rhythm, giving the musicians the security they expect from the beat.

Ex. 381: In spite of the metronome marking and the composer's indication "very moderate quarter-notes" the players would feel uneasy unless the conductor used subdivision.

A subdivided 2-beat is often practical for music to which neither 4-beat nor 2-beat can be applied continuously, but which requires changes in the beat, as in the second movement of Schubert's Symphony No. 9 (see Ex. 229) or the Andante più tosto Allegretto of Haydn's Symphony No. 103 (*Drum-roll*). In these movements, the alternating use of the regular and subdivided 2-beat allows the conductor to adjust his gesture to the pulsation of the music. If the transition from one pattern to the other is performed with ease and flexibility, the change, sometimes even from bar to bar, will not upset the clarity of the beat.

Similarly, subdivision is often applied to slow movements in 4/4 time.

Ex. 382: If you try to beat 4, you will find that the first half of bar 1 may turn out satisfactorily, but both the continuation of the melody and the triplets in the accompaniment demand 8 beats in a measure.

Ex. 42: At a pace slower than ♩ = 50, a 4-beat might be impractical. Subdivision helps to coordinate double bassoon and low strings.

The problems which arise in triple time are treated similarly. 1-beat in its straight or subdivided form is often used for fast movements in 3-time (see pp. 79 and 124). In slow 3-time, use subdivision with 6 beats or, when triplets occur on each count, 9 beats in a measure. 2 beats in a bar may be used for fast 6-time, 3 beats for 9-time, and 4 beats for 12-time.

Ex. 383: The metronome marking suggests 2 beats in a measure, but it would be difficult for the flutists to coordinate their playing unless the conductor indicates the eighth-notes. Use a subtle subdivision (Diag. 46).

In all cases, the choice of beats must not affect the choice of tempo. Do not drag when using more beats than indicated in the time-signature; do not hurry when using fewer beats.

In addition to the tempo of the music, there are considerations other than technique that determine the number of beats in a measure. It may happen that there is a choice between two ways of beating, both technically correct, but having different effects on the musical interpretation. The rule, sometimes taught, that no more beats should be used than are absolutely necessary to mark the time, may be good for time-beaters but is never followed in artistic conducting. It is obvious that if one beats the smaller rhythmic values even though this may not be "absolutely necessary," the weak beats are played with more intensity. On the other hand, the indication of fewer strokes can result in a broader flow of the music. Thus, the mode of beating may have a marked influence on the meter of the music, which in turn can affect the interpretation of a whole piece. It is self-evident that Exx. 95 and 167 require a different number of beats, though both are marked 6/8 and are played in about the same tempo. 2-beat is adequate for the lilting melody of the Barcarolle, while 6-beat is needed to bring out the polyphonic interweaving in the example from Bach.

Ex. 384: This music is usually directed in 2-beat. It has been conducted in 4-beat without altering the tempo significantly. The shape of the theme, however, is quite different in the two cases, because of the sub-accent on the third quarter in 4-beat. The *tenuto* signs must be observed by the players, but are not reflected in the beat. A special gesture would be fussy and might lead to an accent.

Allegro con brio, ($\downarrow$ = 84)

BEETHOVEN, *Coriolanus Overture*

There are other cases in which stylistic considerations determine the number of beats in a measure. A particular feeling for rhythm may be an essential characteristic of a composer's style,

and failure to do justice to this feeling may result in a performance which either lacks intensity or is overemphatic.

Ex. 385: This music has been conducted with 4 beats in a bar and
with 12. Aside from the question of tempo, the difference is that in the
latter case the eighth-note values receive more stress. Such emphasis
does not conform to the best traditions of performing Bach (see
p. 335).

Ex. 499: This passage (as in fact the entire first movement of the
Jupiter Symphony) is conducted with a 2-beat. 4-beat would be possi-
ble from a purely technical point of view, but would not convey the
Mozartean flow of melody.

That the baton technique can be closely related to the musical language of different composers may be seen by comparing
certain passages from the works of Verdi and Wagner. Verdi's
music often demands a beat that gives to the smaller time values
that intensity that is so characteristic of Italian rhythmic feeling.
For Wagner, on the other hand, an alla breve beat is often used
to bring out the broad line of the music, although the time-signature is 4/4.

Ex. 386: Outside of Italy this may be heard conducted alla breve.
Such treatment loses the dramatic effect of the music and makes the
melody sound rather banal.

Ex. 387: In these two passages, typical of Verdi's style, the composer's metronome markings indicate half-beats; but most Italian conductors use 4 strokes, generally with the subdivided pattern. This results in a more exciting performance and at the same time secures better rhythmic control. Thus the violins will play the descending figure in Ex. 387a clearly, whereas the passage is apt to be muddy when directed alla breve. In Ex. 387b, the syncopated rhythm will hardly come out distinctly unless the conductor indicates 4 beats in a bar.

Ex. 388: The section marked C requires an alla breve beat, although the string passages look as though they need 4-beat. The latter, however, would not bring out the grandeur of the melody (see p. 358).

WAGNER, *Die Walküre*

Simultaneous Different Rhythms

Another case in which the conductor must determine how many beats he will use in a measure occurs when different rhythms are played simultaneously by various groups of the orchestra. The principle to be followed is this: avoid gestures that would disturb the rhythm of any group. This is best done by weakening or omitting such disruptive beats.

Ex. 389: The melody is in triplet quarter-notes against the 4/4 rhythm of the accompaniment. A change to alla breve is not recommended; it is not difficult to play the triplets against the regular 4-beat, provided *Two* and *Four* are somewhat weakened. This will help the triplet figure without confusing the accompanying instruments.

TCHAIKOVSKY, *Capriccio Italien*

Ex. 390: In the 1st measure, 6 beats are needed for clear direction of the various groups. In the next bar only slight subdivision is recommended, so as not to interfere with the smooth execution of the triplet. Do not subdivide at all for the triplet in bar 3; then you may return to subdivision.

Ex. 391: Since the rhythmic figures in the woodwinds and trumpets are predominant, continue beating 2 in the 3rd bar. Violins and horns thus play their 3/4 rhythm as a syncopation.

Ex. 392: In spite of the composer's metronome formula ($\quarternote = 132$) for the quadruplet in bar 2, the 3-beat ($\quarternote = 100$) continues. The players carrying the melody must coordinate the four notes with the 3-beat. Changing the pattern would confuse the ensemble.

Ex. 177: Because of the very slow tempo, 4-beat in bar 2 would make the players feel insecure. Use 12 beats in a measure, so that the violas and cellos play their duplets against the rhythm in the timpani. You can help the string players by slightly emphasizing the 2nd, 5th, 8th, and 11th eighth-beats.

Ex. 393: For the quintuplet in bar 3 use 1-beat; in bars 6 and 7 use 2-beat with weakened *Two.* For the entrance of the first violins (bar 6) it is advisable to indicate a sharp *Two* with the left hand, a gesture that does not interfere with the brass figure. Be sure that the 1-beat is strictly in time, $\quad = 63$.

Ex. 394: Mentioned in the composer's *Traité d'Instrumentation,* this passage has become a classic example of simultaneous different rhythms. As Berlioz points out, the Allegro movement in the violas is maintained in the Allegretto by subdividing bar 3. The 4th bar, however, is not subdivided, for this would disturb the rhythmic feeling of the solo melody.

Ex. 395: The 8/8 and 7/8 against 3/4 cannot both be included in the beat. Use 3-beat, but with weakened 2nd and 3rd beats, which facilitates the synchronizing of the odd rhythms with the beat. Apply a similar technique to bars 3 and 4.

In many instances, the choice of beat takes into consideration which players are most in need of direction, while others can coordinate their divergent rhythmic patterns without difficulty.

Ex. 396: The flute and clarinet players calculate for themselves where their notes coincide with the 4-beat. Their triplets will be sufficiently well established and will allow a smooth execution in the 2nd measure, even though the rhythmic figures do not always coincide with the beat. However, the conductor may find it necessary to help the flutes and clarinets by indicating 6 beats in a measure with the left hand while beating 4 with the baton. (This procedure is recommended as an interesting exercise to achieve independence of the two hands!)

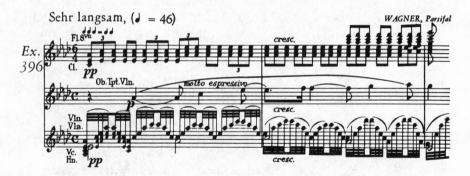

Additional examples for the study of passages in which different rhythms occur simultaneously:

Barber: *Second Essay for Orchestra*, passage starting at No. 19.

Brahms: *Variations on a Theme by Haydn*, Finale.

Bruckner, Symphony No. 5, 2nd movement.

Debussy: *La Mer,* 1st movement — passage beginning 2 bars before No. 1.

Debussy: *Nuages,* passage starting at the 7th bar after No. 2.

Hindemith: *Mathis der Maler*, 3rd movement — passage starting 5 bars before No. 25.

Rimsky-Korsakov: *Scheherazade*, 4th movement — at *Vivo* 2/8 (6/16, 3/8).

Schoenberg: *Five Pieces for Orchestra*, No. 1

Sibelius: Violin Concerto, 1st movement — passage beginning 6 bars after No. 3 (*Largamente*); 4-beat and 6-beat alternate, because the conductor's main concern is with clarinet and bassoons. It is practical to change to 2-beat 10 bars after No. 3.

Tchaikovsky: *Overture 1812*, passage starting at bar 188.

Irregular Measures

There are occasions when the composer includes more counts in a measure than are allowed by the time-signature. The treatment of such measures depends on the musical context.

Ex. 397: Beat the first 3 counts distinctly, stopping at *Three* while the strings continue playing. Listen to the solo clarinet and synchronize the preparatory gesture so that the attack on the 2nd bar will not interfere with the steady pizzicato. Whether to use a free or an eighth-beat preparation depends on individual experience.

RIMSKY-KORSAKOV, *Scheherazade*

Ex. 398: Use *Two* for the cut-off and preparation, with the strings playing the G on the off-beat. Direct the remaining notes of the figure with two or three small extra strokes on the left side of the field of beating. (The third can be omitted, if this results in a smoother flow of the *rubato*.)

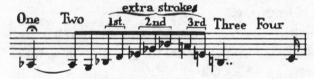

Beat the regular *Three* on the B

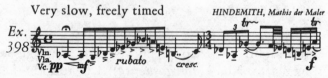

From *Symphonie Mathis der Maler* by Paul Hindemith,
Copyright 1934 by B.Schott's Söhne, Mainz
Copyright renewed 1962. Used by permission of European American Music
Distributors Corporation, sole representative
of all rights in the U.S.A. and Mexico.

Additional examples of irregular measures:

Bartók: Concerto for Orchestra, 4th movement — bar 143.

Copland: *A Lincoln Portrait* — bar 183.

Ravel: *Rapsodie Espagnole,* 1st movement, at Nos. 6 and 8.

Respighi: *The Pines of Rome,* Part II (*Lento* 4/4) — 5th and 9th bars.

Verdi: *La Traviata,* 2nd act — Germont's aria (*Di Provenza il mar*), 4th bar.

Verdi: *Otello,* 3rd act — 1 bar before Q.

Chapter 26

NUMBER OF BEATS IN A MEASURE (II)

Changing the Number of Beats
for One or More Bars

IT SOMETIMES BECOMES NECESSARY in the middle of a piece to change the number of beats in a measure. This situation can be caused by a change in the rhythmic structure of the music, as, for instance, by the appearance of triplets in duple or quadruple time. Another cause is the occurrence of intricate rhythms or rapid passages that may be played indistinctly unless the conductor has the added control over the players gained by beating the smaller values. This technique may be compared to the routine of counting "one-and, two-and," familiar to all instrumentalists as an aid in the precise performance of rhythmically difficult passages. Whether to beat the smaller values or not may also depend upon the ability of the particular orchestral group; experienced and technically superior musicians may not need such help. Furthermore, a change of beats may be desirable, not for technical reasons, but for the sake of expression. In slow or moderate tempo, the regular strokes often will not allow sufficient indication of intensity. The conductor then feels that his gestures are becoming purely mechanical instead of "being with the orchestra," and that only by adding more beats to the bar can he regain close contact with the players. Or else, in lively tempo, he may sense that there is too much excitement in his gestures, and that only by reducing the number of beats can he make the music flow more calmly.

As far as baton technique is concerned, such changes require an especially clear beat that leaves no doubt about the conductor's intention. This is particularly true when the change is not marked in the players' parts. A change from 4 to 2 beats or vice-versa can be the cause of trouble if it is not executed properly. It is dangerous to use curved espressivo gestures during such a change because the orchestra may be unable to see "where the conductor is." The main counts should be easy to recognize, while smaller gestures should be used for the weak beats. The subdivided patterns lend themselves readily to temporary changes. They are also used to achieve a gradual transition, applying the technique discussed on pp. 146 ff., except that now the tempo is not changed.

Ex. 399: The triplets in the 5th bar may require a change from 4-beat to 2-beat. The change should be marked in the parts.

PUCCINI, *Madama Butterfly*

Ex. 400: Change to 1-beat in the 3rd bar and return to 2-beat at rallentando.

PUCCINI, *Tosca*

Ex. 401: Because of the slow tempo, the triplet in the 6th measure ("breit") is directed with 3 strokes, applying a regular 3-beat.

BRUCKNER, *Symphony No. 4*

Ex. 402: The structure of the music calls for a change of beat. The 3rd and 4th bars are directed with 4 strokes; subdivide in the second half of bar 2 to get an effective preparation for the *ff*. Return to 2-beat in the 5th measure, at the same time giving a clear indication of the sudden *p*.

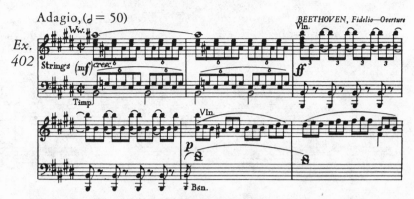

Ex. 403: The 4th bar requires 3-beat if the traditional ritenuto is made.

Ex. 404: In bar 5, sustain *One* with the baton. Release the singers with an unobtrusive left-hand motion, then cut off the orchestra with a decisive gesture. Right after this, bring in the singers with your left hand. They should begin their crescendo without hesitation. The baton, which has remained "in attention," is then used to attack bar 6 with a 1-beat preparation, just like a start after the count.

Ex. 405: Because of the slow pace (ritardando), the syncopated passage in bar 3 must be directed with 8 beats in a measure, or the violins will lose the feeling of security.

Ex. 406: The first 3 sixteenth-notes of the "precipitando" are held back slightly; the others are played quickly and violently. Hence, subdivide the first half of the 3rd measure with sharp gestures, but use only one stroke for the second half. The following bar is legato.

Ex. 407: Here the conductor must know to what extent the orchestra needs his help for a flawless rhythmic execution. Subdivision may not be necessary when the players are thoroughly familiar with the music and have strong rhythmic feeling of their own. If this is not the case, the conductor will prefer to subdivide for the triplet figure in Ex. 407a, bar 3 ff., either by using 6 small beats (Diag. 46), or by beating *One-Three-Four-Six* with downward gestures for *One* and *Three*, upward gestures for *Four* and *Six*. Beat legato in the first two bars and then change to staccato. In Ex. 407b, bar 2, use 6-beat with neutral gestures but with staccato on *Six*; return to 2-beat in the 3rd measure. Bars 4 and 5 need no subdivision.

Ex. 408: Direct the opening (which is a start on the 3rd count) with a very calm 3-beat. In bar 2, however, change to subdivision to lead the flute passage and the harp chords. In the next bar return smoothly to the calm 3-beat.

Ex. 409: Although this music is marked alla breve, 4-beat is advisable, even for the best orchestras, to secure precision in the violin and viola passages. Change to 2-beat in the 5th measure.

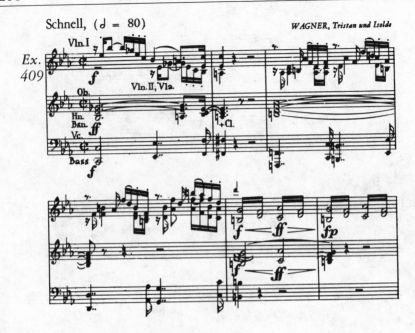

Ex. 410: Though conductors differ in the way they lead the 12/8 section of this movement (4 or 12 beats in a measure), there is no doubt that, starting from the last quarter of the 1st bar, the beat must be subdivided.

Ex. 411: In many orchestras, the violin run in bar 3 will be muddy unless directed with 6 beats (Diag. 46), light-staccato. Return to 2-beat legato in the next measure.

Ex. 412: The rhythmic figure requires 8 beats in a measure. In the 4th bar, change to a calm 4-beat, but return to subdivision on the 4th count in bar 5.

Ex. 413: As the metronome marking indicates, this music is directed with 1-beat. However, the first violin section may need your help to coordinate the 32nd-notes; subdivide the 1st bar (Diag. 30b).

Ex. 414: Although the metronome marking suggests 8 beats in a measure, most conductors find that continual subdivision would upset the calmness of the line. Use a sixteenth-beat as preparation and subdivide for the beginning, then only when needed, as for the staccato chords. Subdivision is essential for the horn entry (in older scores this entry is printed 1 count too late).

Ex. 346: In case the off-beat accents (bars 3, 6, etc.) lack precision, skillful subdivision on the preceding counts may give a satisfactory result.

Ex. 415: Mozart's time-signature is C, but 2-beat is recommended for most of the movement. Some passages fare better when conducted with subdivision, as the rhythmic figure in bars 3 and 4. Resume the alla breve in bar 5 for the natural flow of the music.

Allegro con spirito, ($\,\lhook = 72$-76)

MOZART, *Symphony No. 35*

Ex. 416: Here, again, subdivision is not mandatory, but the use of 6 beats in bars 2 and 4 underlines the expression of the melody.

PUCCINI, *La Bohème*

Ex. 417: The entire movement from which this passage is taken requires frequent change from regular to subdivided 3-beat, partly for technical reasons, partly for the sake of expressiveness. In the 4th measure, the eighth-note values must be indicated to secure a smooth execution of the dotted rhythm. Start to subdivide unobtrusively on the 1st count in that measure. In bar 6, the subdivision is hardly noticeable since the rhythm is now established. In the next bar, however, subdivision helps greatly to give intensity to the lyric passage.

Andante sostenuto, ($\,\lhook = 56$)

BRAHMS, *Symphony No. 1*

Ex. 418: The last part of this theme (bars 1–4), the second theme of the movement, is done with 3-beat. Some conductors continue to beat 3 at "a tempo." However, this *pp* section achieves its quality of lightness and suspense when directed with a small 1-beat. This entire movement demands flexibility on the part of the conductor; he brings life into his interpretation with a skillful mixture of 3-beat, 1-beat, and the subdivided pattern *One-(two-) Three.*

Ex. 418

BEETHOVEN, *Symphony No. 8*

Additional examples for the study of passages in which the conductor usually changes the number of beats for one or more bars:

Berlioz: Overture *Le Carnaval Romain, Andante sostenuto* 3/4; whether and where to subdivide the 3-beat depends on interpretation. Most conductors subdivide at No. 3 for clear definition of the rhythm—*Allegro vivace* 6/8; 1-beat is recommended for the *pp* passage with three-measure phrase groups, which begins 2 bars after No. 14, but 2-beat should be resumed at No. 15.

Brahms: Symphony No. 1, 4th movement; for the Introduction see Ex. 42 (including the comment on p. 249) and Ex. 211. Subdivision is applied to the passages with 32nd-notes. Whether to return to 4-beat 3 bars before letter B is a matter of interpretation. Some conductors increase the tempo in these measures noticeably, although such a change of speed is not indicated by the composer and might make it difficult for violins and violas to execute the sextuplets correctly. Brahms's careful notation of the timpani rhythm before and after letter B seems to mark a tempo relation between the *Adagio* and the *Più Andante*, usually disregarded in performances (see the composer's remark on "free artistic interpretation" quoted on p. 358). In the *Allegro non troppo*, several passages require a 2-beat, for instance at *animato* (8 measures after E), but a 4-beat must be resumed whenever necessitated by the musical context.

Dvořák: Symphony No. 9, 4th movement. Use 4-beat at the start but change to 2-beat (marcato) in bar 10; resume the 4-beat at No. 2. Similar changes are applied to the rest of this movement.

Puccini: *La Bohème*, 1st act, Rodolfo's aria. In the *Andante lento*, subdivision is applied to the measure before the 2/4 bar.

Strauss: *Also sprach Zarathustra*; passage beginning at No. 31. Subdivide whenever the rhythm needs clear definition and should be emphasized.

Tchaikovsky: Symphony No. 6, 3rd movement; change to 2-beat for the concluding section. With "virtuoso" orchestras, the entire movement may be directed with 2-beat, using subdivision for passages that require rhythmic emphasis. In the 4th movement, the beat changes frequently from regular to subdivided 3-beat.

Verdi: *Aïda*, 1st act, 1st scene. In Aïda's aria (*Ritorna vincitor*) 2-beat is used at *Cantabile*, with subdivision for the triplet at *tremendo*. Return to 4-beat after the fermata.

Wagner: Overture to *Der Fliegende Holländer*. In the *Andante*, change from 6-beat to 2-beat at *Animando un poco*.

Subdividing a Single Count

Subdivision of single counts has been discussed as a means of directing ritardando. It may be used occasionally, even though the tempo does not change, either for secure playing or for the sake of intensity. The skillful application of this technique adds vitality and expression to the interpretation. Indeed, to use it without interrupting the flow of the musical line or upsetting the clarity of the beat is the mark of a master. However, young conductors are warned against too frequent subdivision of this kind, especially in espressivo; many curved gestures in a bar are hard to follow if they are not used in a completely convincing way. Perfect control of the baton is required for the application of such intermediate strokes.

On the other hand, subdividing single counts can be very useful in slow passages with dotted rhythm when a small note-value follows a larger one, as in Ex. 379. Beginning on *Four* in the 2nd bar, use subdivision to secure correct playing of the 32nd-notes; subdivide only on the counts on which the dotted rhythm occurs.

Ex. 419: Subdivide on *Four* in bars 2 and 3; subdivision can also be applied to the first 2 counts in bar 4, to control the triplets.

Ex. 420: Should there be any difficulty with the after-beat of the trill in flutes and violins, a skillful subdivision of the 3rd count in bar 2 will keep the instruments together. The gesture must be small and precise, without any delay.

MENDELSSOHN, *Midsummer Night's Dream—Nocturne*

Ex. 421: Subdivision on *Two* in bar 5 leads the violins (C and D♭ played with two up-bows!) to indicate the tender expression of the phrase.

Ex. 422: The triplet in bar 2 is subdivided (composer's note "Die Triole ausschlagen"). It is advisable to subdivide also on the 3rd count for the accented D♯. The singers enter on the 3rd triplet note, which should be conducted as an accented upbeat for the *Luftpause* (see Ex. 303).

Chapter 27

5-TIME, 7-TIME, AND OTHER ASYMMETRIC TIME PATTERNS

THERE ARE TWO WAYS of beating these odd counts. If the tempo is not too fast, each count receives one beat. When the tempo is so rapid that this cannot be done distinctly, several counts are included in one gesture. The techniques to be applied depend on the rhythmic structure of the music.

5-Time with Beats on Each Count

Several patterns may be used, depending on the way the groups of notes fall within the bar. A 5/4 signature may stand for continual alternation of 2/4 and 3/4, in which case Diagram 59a or 59c is applicable (the diagrams indicate staccato; other types of gestures can easily be deduced from them). Some conductors actually alternate 2-beat and 3-beat in the same size, but the 5-beat pattern shown in Diagram 59a has this advantage: since the second group (*Three-Four-Five*) is kept smaller and toward the top of the field of beating, the downbeat on *One* stands out and the orchestra has a definite point of orientation.

Ex. 423: Apply Diag. 59a. The entire third movement of the symphony follows this beat.

Ex. 424: The notation indicates 3/4 + 2/4; apply Diag. 59b or 59d.

271

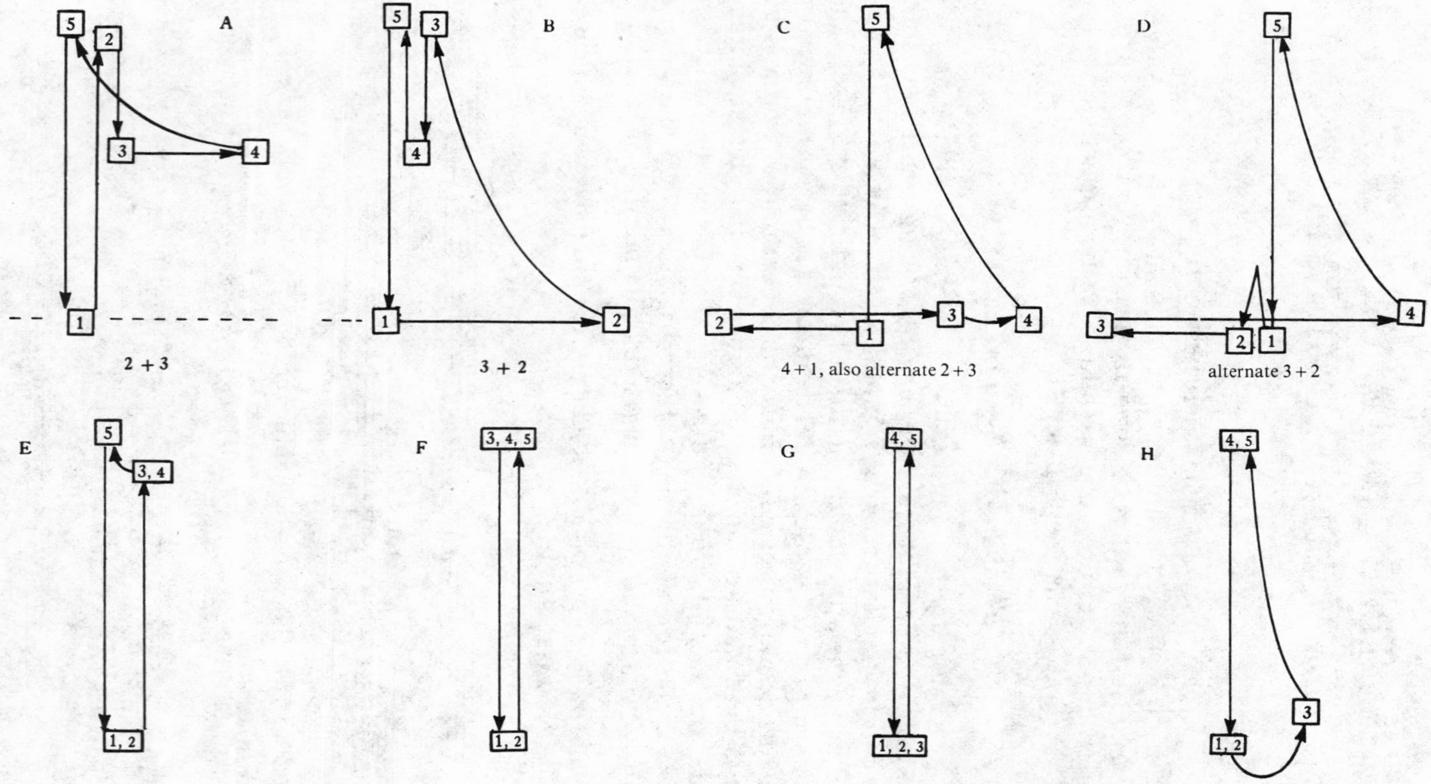

A

B

3 + 2

C

4 + 1, also alternate 2 + 3

D

alternate 3 + 2

E

F

G

H

2 + 3

Diagram 59. 5-time

272

Ex. 425: No division of the 5-group is apparent. The pattern of Diag. 59c is the best (4/4 + 1/4), because it is close to the 4-beat of the preceding and following bars.

Ex. 426: In bar 3, the rapid pace necessitates a modification of the 3 + 2 pattern. The first 3 counts are directed with a subdivided 1-beat, while *Four* and *Five* are done with a small 2-beat at the top of the field of beating. (A subdivided 1-beat also applies to bars 1 and 2; see Ex. 448.)

Additional examples for the study of the 5-beat patterns:

2 + 3 beats:

Barber: *Second Essay for Orchestra*, 3rd bar after No. 25.

Bartók: *Music for Strings, Percussion, and Celesta*, 3rd movement — bars 54–58.

Britten: *War Requiem, Agnus Dei*, 5/16, ♪ = 80 (2 + 3 alternating with 3 + 2).

Griffes: *The White Peacock*, passage starting at bar 7 (alternating patterns; apply Diag. 59a, b, or c, according to the rhythmic structure).

Mahler: Symphony No. 8, 1st movement—No. 23 to No. 28.

Mussorgsky-Ravel: *Pictures at an Exhibition*, all *Promenade* passages.

Rimsky-Korsakov: Overture *Russian Easter*, beginning, 5/2 with subdivision, ♩ = 84 (for each bar, combine Diag. 42 and 45 with relatively small gestures except for a fairly large downbeat).

3 + 2 beats:

Bartók: *The Wonderful Mandarin*, passage beginning at No. 26 (alternating with 2 + 3).

Berg: *Lulu Suite, Variations*—Variation No. 3.

Copland: *Orchestral Variations*—Variations IV and VI.

Ravel: *Daphnis et Chloé*, Suite No. 2, passages beginning at No. 194 and No. 198.

Respighi: *The Pines of Rome*, Part II—bar 13; also at *Ancora più mosso* (here the pattern 4 + 1 can be applied).

Strauss: *Salome*, passage starting at No. 15.

Strauss: *Salome—Salome's Dance*, from F to K.

Stravinsky: *Agon, Four Duos*, beginning with bar 521.

4 + 1 beats:

Bartók: *The Wonderful Mandarin*—2 bars before No. 31.

Mahler: Symphony No. 7, 2nd movement—1 bar before No. 72.

Shostakovitch: Symphony No. 1, 2nd movement—bar 2.

5-Time with 1, 2, or 3 Beats in a Measure

When the tempo is too fast to beat clearly and easily on each count, fewer beats are used in a measure. In Diagram 59e there are 3 beats: the 1st includes *One* and *Two*, the 2nd *Three* and *Four*, and the 3rd, with a small turn of the wrist, indicates *Five*, which has a preparatory quality. There are only 2 beats in Diagrams 59f and g, resulting in a lopsided pattern. Which pattern to use depends on the rhythmic stress of the music and, to a certain extent, upon what turns out to be most practical in any given situation. Using a wrist motion on *Three*, you may prefer Diagram 59h for bars in which *Four* is accented.

Ex. 427: Execute the 4th measure according to Diag. 59e, since the feeling is $2/4 + 1/8$.

Ex. 428: The 5/8 rhythm in bars 4–7 seems to conform to Diag. 59e or f.

Ex. 429 (bars 2, 3, and 5): Diagrams 59f or g could be used; if pattern f is used, the *ff* figure ♪♪♪ is felt as a syncopation, while with pattern g the upbeat coincides with the attack of that figure (see pp. 281, 285, and 291).

If the music moves very quickly, it becomes necessary to use 1-beat. This requires a definite feeling on the part of the conductor for the 5 small note-values within each beat. The following exercises are recommended.

STRAVINSKY, *Le Sacre du Printemps*

Ex. 429

(1) Set the metronome at 50. Count aloud, starting with *One* for each tick, and repeat several times. Then double the count, with *One, Two* on every tick. Continue to increase the count, one at a time, up to 5 counts for each tick. The sequence of counts within each tick must be kept smooth and continuous. In this way you learn to alter the rhythmic unit while the beat for the measure remains fixed.

(2) The next exercise trains the rhythmic control by changing the measure and keeping the unit. Set the metronome at 208 and beat 1-beat. Start with 2 ticks per beat, then use 3, 4, and 5. You will find that with 5 ticks per beat the metronome is not fast enough for a convenient 1-beat. Hence, use one of the Diagrams, 59e-h. Next dispense with the metronome and increase the tempo until 1-beat becomes convenient in 5-time.

Exx. 430a and b: These exercises serve the practice of (a) maintaining a steady beat in spite of changing units, or (b) adjusting the beat to an even flow of constant units.

Ex. 430

Ex. 431: The 5/8 bars are conducted with 1-beat (see p. 291).

Ex. 432: Beginning with bar 2, the sixteenth-note unit ($\flat$ = 252), which is derived from the metronome $\flat$ = 126, remains constant. The preparation after the fermata is timed as a whole measure (2/16). The 2/8 bars are directed with a regular 2-beat, but the 5/8 bar requires a lopsided beat (Diag. 59g). The downbeat in bar 12 (timpani) must be very incisive for the syncopated tutti *ff* entry.

Additional examples for the study of 5-time with 1, 2, or 3 beats in a measure:

1-beat:

Bartók: *Music for Strings, Percussion, and Celesta,* 2nd movement, bars 260–290 (there may be a choice between 1- beat and lopsided 2-bĕat; most of the time a 1-beat is more practical).

Britten: *War Requiem, Requiem Aeternam.* (Each quarter-beat is a quintuplet within slow 4/4 time, $\quarternote = 42–46$. The players must maintain an even distribution of 5 units on each count with the pattern.

Stravinsky: *Variations,* bars 11, 68, 75, 76 (5/16).

lopsided 2-beat:
3 + 2 (Diag. 59f)

Bartók: Concerto for Orchestra, 4th movement (also 2 + 3).

Copland: *Appalachian Spring,* between Nos. 31 and 33.

Prokofiev: Violin Concerto No. 2, 3rd movement—at No. 77.

Stravinsky: *Le Sacre du Printemps*—numerous places (also 2 + 3).

2 + 3 (Diag. 59g)

Barber: *Medea's Meditation and Dance of Vengeance*—starting at No. 20.

Bartók: *Dance Suite,* 2nd and 3rd movements (also 3 + 2).

Copland: *Music for the Theatre,* No. 2 *Dance.*

Stravinsky: *Variations,* bars 41–43, 66.

lopsided 3-beat:

Stravinsky: *Dumbarton Oaks Concerto,* 3rd movement—at No. 57 and after No. 58 (Diag. 59e).

Stravinsky: *Variations,* bar 7, $\eighthnote = 160$ in 5/8 (Diag. 59h).

7-Time with Beats on Each Count

Diagrams 60a–d show different methods of execution depending on the grouping within the measure. Diagram 60a combines 4-beat with 3-beat. In Diagram 60b the 3-beat precedes

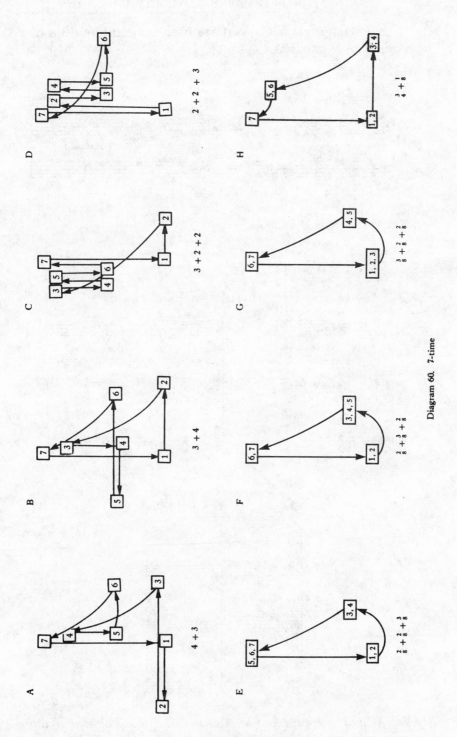

Diagram 60. 7-time

279

the 4-beat. Diagrams 60c and d are used for combinations of 2-beat and 3-beat patterns.

Ex. 433: Apply Diag. 60a.

Ex. 434: Apply Diag. 60b.

Ex. 435: The composer has indicated the grouping by two alternating patterns, $3 + 2 + 2$ and $2 + 2 + 3$. Use Diag. 60c and d.

Additional examples for the study of the 7-beat patterns:

4 + 3 beats:

Barber: *Medea's Meditation and Dance of Vengeance,* passage before No. 13.

Barber: *Second Essay for Orchestra,* 11th bar after No. 21.

Britten: *War Requiem, Dies Irae,* at No. 17 (in spite of the rapid pace, ♩ = 160, use Diag. 60a at least for the start; once the rhythm is firmly established, Diag. 60e may be applied).

Delius: *A Song of Summer,* the first 15 bars.

Griffes: *The White Peacock,* 2 bars before A.

Mussorgsky-Ravel: *Pictures at an Exhibition—Promenade* before No. 5.

3 + 4 beats:

Barber: *Medea's Meditation and Dance of Vengeance,* at No. 12.

Berg: *Lulu Suite, Variationen*—Variation No. 4 (3 + 4 and 4 + 3 alternate).

Stravinsky: *Le Sacre du Printemps,* 2nd movement—2nd bar after No. 106 (the 3 + 4 pattern is recommended because of the *sf* in the horns).

7-Time with 3 or 4 Beats in a Measure

Diagrams 60e–h show various patterns. Their application is guided by considerations similar to the ones discussed in connection with 5-time patterns.

Ex. 429: The 4th bar is best executed with Diag. 60e.

Ex. 436: For bars 2 and 5, use Diag. 60e; for the 6th measure use Diag. 60f. Bar 4 (5/8) is best done with Diag. 59f.

Ex. 437: Although the metronome refers to eighth-notes, the 2nd measure is best directed with a 2/8 + 2/8 + 3/8 pattern. Use Diagram 60e at the speed of ♩ = 80. Diagram 60h is an alternate.

Additional examples for the study of 7-time with 3 or 4 beats in a measure:

2 + 2 + 3 (Diag. 60e)

Bartók: *Dance Suite*, 2nd movement—passage between Nos. 17 and 18 (changing patterns).

Bartók: *Music for Strings, Percussion, and Celesta*, 1st movement (the tempo allows for marking all the counts in the several 7/8 bars; the patterns in Diag. 60 to be used for subdivision are e and g).

Copland: *Orchestral Variations*—Variation XV

Stravinsky: *Agon*, bars 452-462 (sequence of 6/16, 5/16, and 7/16).

Stravinsky: *Variations*, bar 95 (7/16, ♪ = 160).

2 + 3 + 2 (Diag. 60f)

Bartók: Concerto for Orchestra, 4th movement, bars 47 and 55).

Prokofiev: Violin Concerto No. 2, 3rd movement—at no. 52.

3 + 2 + 2 (Diag. 60g)

Bartók: Concerto for Orchestra, 4th movement, bar 59.

Bartók: *Divertimento for String Orchestra,* 1st movement, bar 30.

Dallapiccola: *Variazioni,* Variation No. 6, bars 5 and 10 (bars 2 and 7 are done with Diag. 60e).

$$2 + 2 + 2 + 1 \ (3/4 + 1/8, \ Diag. \ 60h)$$

Dallapiccola: *Variazioni,* Variation No. 8 — bar 33.

Stravinsky: *Dumbarton Oaks Concerto,* 3rd movement — 3 bars after No. 55 (as indicated by the composer).

Various Asymmetric Time Patterns

Asymmetrical grouping of counts within a measure is part of the contemporary musical idiom. For the conductor, it means that time-signatures now refer to a greater variety of beat patterns than found in scores written before the turn of the century. Depending on the number of rhythmic units, beats are shortened or lengthened, thus producing lopsided conducting patterns, similar to the diagrams which were discussed in this chapter.

8-Time with Lopsided 3-Beat

In 8-time, three asymmetrical patterns are possible: $3 + 3 + 2$, $2 + 3 + 3$, or $3 + 2 + 3$. Practice these three forms of a lopsided 3-beat, first by counting the units. Practice at various speeds, alternating legato, staccato, and tenuto gestures. When you have gained a firm feeling for the rhythm, dispense with counting.

Ex. 438: The metronome speed (an equivalent of ♪ = ca. 200) precludes subdivision. A graceful, yet clear, beat is needed to bring out the lilt of the music. If a small string group is available, the first movement of Bartók's *Divertimento* should be conducted in class.

Additional examples:

Bartók: *Dance Suite,* 4th movement.

Bartók: *Music for Strings, Percussion, and Celesta,* 1st movement.

Copland: *Orchestral Variations* — Variation XVI.

Copland: Symphony No. 1 — passages beginning at Nos. 18 and 27.

Dallapiccola: *Variazioni* — Variation No. 4.

Stravinsky: *Agon, Gailliarde* 8/4.

9-Time with Lopsided 4-Beat

Four patterns are possible: $3 + 2 + 2 + 2$, $2 + 3 + 2 + 2$, $2 + 2 + 3 + 2$, or $2 + 2 + 2 + 3$. Two of them are shown in the following examples.

Exx. 439a and b: The pattern for bar 3 in a is $2 + 3 + 2 + 2$, which means that the second beat is extended to 3/8. Subdivide the preceding alla breve and conduct the 9/8 measure with a lopsided 4-beat at ♩ = ca. 138. In 439b, the extended beat falls on *Four*: $2 + 2 + 2 + 3$.

Ex. 429: In the context of this passage, the 9/8 measure can be directed either with a regular 3-beat, or with a lopsided 4-beat $(2 + 2 + 2 + 3)$. In the first instance, each of the 3 strokes must conform to ♩. = 96, the equivalent of the composer's marking ♩♩ = 144.

In the 1st movement of Britten's *Spring Symphony* (*The driving boy*, 4 bars before No. 16), the composer requests that measures with the time-signature 9/8 be conducted with 4-beat, $2 + 2 + 2 + 3$.

10-Time with Lopsided 4-Beat

Out of six possible patterns in 10-time, four are found in the 1st movement of Bartók's *Music for Strings, Percussion, and Celesta*: $3 + 3 + 2 + 2$, $3 + 2 + 3 + 2$, $3 + 2 + 2 + 3$, and $2 + 2 + 3 + 3$.

An extended passage based on the pattern $3 + 3 + 2 + 2$ occurs in Roussel's *Bacchus et Ariane*, Suite No. 2, beginning 4 bars before No. 111.

11-Time

The best known and, technically speaking, simplest example is the 11/4 measure that introduces the section *Glorification de l'élue* in Stravinsky's *Le Sacre du Printemps* (No. 104). The tempo allows a stroke on each of the 11 counts, using any beat pattern that suits the conductor.

The 11/8 measure in Bartók's *Music for Strings, Percussion, and Celesta* (7 bars before the end of the 1st movement) calls for a 4-beat, $3 + 3 + 3 + 2$. It is followed by an 8/8 measure with the 3-beat pattern $3 + 3 + 2$.

In Dallapiccola's *Variazioni*, an 11/16 measure occurs (Variation No. 1) that requires a lopsided 5-beat with an extended *One* at the speed of ♪ = 84: $3/16 + 4/8$.

13-Time

The 2nd movement of Janáček's *Sinfonietta* contains several measures with the time-signature 13/8. A 6-beat is used with the pattern $2 + 2 + 2 + 2 + 2 + 3$. Asymmetrical rhythms of this kind present no problem to a conductor who has trained himself to apply precise gestures to a rapid succession of beats, whether each beat stands for two or three constant units.

Chapter 28

CHANGES OF RHYTHM AND TEMPO

CHANGES OF TIME-SIGNATURE and of tempo are not found frequently in the music of the classic composers, but occur quite often in scores by Wagner and later composers. When they are found in the older music it is usually at the beginning of a new section, while in modern scores they occur from phrase to phrase and even from one bar to another. In all cases, these changes require clear gestures and, for change of time-signature, the new rhythmic pattern must be unmistakable.

Change of Time-Signature Without
Change of Tempo

While change of time-signature in itself involves no new technical problems, a rapid succession of changes requires a clear mind and a flexible hand. Exx. 440–443 contain, in the form of exercises, typical rhythmic changes such as occur in modern music. As in all music of this sort, the conductor must study carefully the rhythmic arrangement of the measures before he even lifts his baton.

There are two types of changes. (1) Most often, the *rhythmic unit remains constant* although the time-signature changes. In this case the conductor must be certain that, for instance, ♩ equals ♩ exactly. Exceptions to this rule are usually specifically indicated by the composer. (2) Sometimes, although the rhythm (time-signature) changes, the tempo (pulse) is maintained by keeping the *bar length constant*. This is usually indicated in the score.

Ex. 440: 1-beat in bar 5, 3-beat in bar 10.

Ex 441: Resist the temptation to slow down in the 7th and 15th measures! 1-beat in bars 9, 10, and 16, 2-beat in bar 17.

Ex. 442: Keep the rhythmic value of the beat constant in bar 4. The change in the 7th measure makes one old bar equal to half of a new bar. *In bar 10, the 2-beat remains constant.* According to tradition the special indication ($o = o \cdot$) is omitted; in fast tempo when 2-beat is used throughout, it is customary that at the change to 6-time, bar equals bar. On the other hand, it is taken for granted that at the change from ₵ to 3/2 (bar 14), d equals d. As a result of these traditions, which contradict strict logic, bars 10 and 14 are of different length.

Ex. 443: 1-beat in bars 3–7. Use Diag. 59e for bar 15. Be sure that the sixteenth-note values remain constant in bars 3, and 10–13, and beat accordingly with unmistakable down-strokes.

Ex. 444: This shows clearly the difference in applying 6-beat for the time-signature 6/4 (Ex. 444a), and subdivided 3-beat for the time-signature 3/2 (Ex. 444b). (Unfortunately, composers do not always indicate this correctly; they may mark double time, 6/4, in passages which actually are in triple time, 3/2; in such cases the conductor must use his own judgment.) Note that in the following two passages the value of the quarter-note remains constant.

SHOSTAKOVITCH, Symphony No. 5

Review the following examples in which the rhythmic value of the beat remains the same, although the pattern of the beat changes with the time-signature: Exx. 213, 230, 279, 368, 393, 395, 425, 427 (bar 2), and 435.

Ex. 445: The 3/4 bar offers no particular problem, because the quarter-beat was present in the subdivision of the previous measures.

COPLAND, A Lincoln Portrait

Ex. 446: At the Alla breve the composer indicates that the bar length is unchanged.

BEETHOVEN, Symphony No. 3

Additional examples for the study of passages in which the time-signature changes while the beat remains constant:

Barber: Symphony No. 1, from the beginning until No. 4 (study score pages 1–10).

Berlioz: *Roméo et Juliette*, 4th part (Scherzo) — transition to *Allegretto* 3/4.

Brahms: *Tragic Overture*, double bar at K, *Molto più moderato* 4/4.

Liszt: Piano Concerto No. 2, *L'istesso tempo* 6/8 (12 bars after K).

Mahler: Symphony No. 6, 2nd movement — passage from No. 88 to No. 95).

Puccini: *La Bohème*, 1st act, passage between Nos. 9 and 10.

Rimsky-Korsakov: *Scheherazade*, 2nd movement, transitions at H and N.

Sibelius: Symphony No. 2, 2nd movement.

Tchaikovsky: Symphony No. 4, 4th movement — *Andante* 3/4.

Wagner: *Siegfried*, 1st act — 1st scene.

In the above examples, the beat was constant regardless of the change of time-signature. In the examples that follow, the rhythmic value of the beat changes with the time-signature. Hence the conductor must "think" the rhythmic unit, just as in the handling of asymmetrical time patterns. The slightest uncertainty in the beat may jeopardize the ensemble.

Ex. 447: The ♪ remains constant throughout; therefore the 1-beat starting in the 4th bar must be very precise and sure, securing a steady sixteenth-note movement. Be especially careful of the return to 2/4 and do not delay *Two!* (An ambitious student will do well to practice the entire 3rd scene of the 3rd act of *Die Meistersinger*.)

Ex. 448: 3/4 is done with 1-beat (straight, or subdivided *One-Three*). The 4/4 bars are beaten alla breve with the quarter-unit remaining constant. The first 76 measures of the 2nd scene in the 3rd act of *Tristan und Isolde*, from which this example is taken, are notable for being the first instance of frequent rhythmic changes of this type. The full score should be studied and used for practice (see Ex. 426).

Ex. 449: The use of two time-signatures within one measure is rare. In effect, bar 2 is a 9/16 measure to be directed with a lopsided 4-beat, $2 + 3 + 2 + 2$ (see p. 284), as indicated by the composer's "battre à 4." The metronome marking points to subdivision in bar 1. Even if the conductor does not subdivide each count, he must make sure that the continuity of the sixteenth-unit is preserved.

Ex. 428: Be sure to keep the tempo steady when returning to 2-beat in the last measure; do not rush!

Ex. 429: When conducting this passage as a whole, set the metronome at 144, which gives the quarter-beat and thereby establishes the eighth-unit. Double tempo in bar 6 results in $\quarter = 144$ (composer's mark: $\eighth = \quarter$).

Ex. 431: This passage begins at a speed of $\dottedquarter . \quarter = 46$, which actually means $\quarter = 160$. With the *stringendo,* the tempo increases to about $\quarter = 178$ in bar 8. A definite feeling for the eighth-unit is best maintained by counting to yourself and using sharp downbeats in bars 1-12. Counting the small units to yourself is useful in conducting passages of this kind.

Ex. 432: Review this music by conducting the entire passage in continuity. Consult the full score.

Ex. 436: Apply the techniques described above. Study the entire score.

Additional examples for the study of passages in which the rhythmic unit remains constant while the beat changes:

Bartók: Concerto for Orchestra, 1st movement, bars 488-509 (see Appendix A, No. 9).

Copland, *El Salon Mexico.*

Dvořák: *Scherzo Capriccioso,* passage in 2/4 (bar 561).

Strauss, Richard: *Don Juan,* bar 30.

Strauss, Richard: *Don Quixote,* transition to Variation No. 8.

Stravinsky, *Le Sacre du Printemps,* 1st part—*Jeu du Rapt,* passage between Nos 43 and 48.

Stravinsky: *Les Noces,* Parts I and II.

Wagner: *Götterdämmerung,* Interlude between the Prelude and the 1st act (*Siegfried's Rhine Journey*), transition from *Schnell* 6/8 to *Rasch* 3/4.

If a string group is available, the 1st movement of Stravinsky's *Concerto for String Orchestra* is highly recommended for class study. The same composer's *Symphonies of Wind Instruments* also offers an excellent opportunity to apply the techniques which were here discussed.

Change of Tempo With Rhythmic
Relation Maintained

Sometimes the rhythm of the new tempo has a relationship with the previous rhythm, which may be indicated by the composer by means of such markings as *doppio movimento, mezzo tempo*, or ♩ = ♪, etc. Concerning this last indication, composers are not in agreement as to which note value represents the old tempo and which the new. In classic music the musical context gives the clue, while modern composers generally use the relation: ♩ (old) = ♪ (new).

Ex. 450: This exercise illustrates a number of typical changes of tempo and rhythm. Use 2-beat in the 6th measure, 1-beat in the 13th. Observe that the relation between bars 16 and 17 is based on the equality of the two bars.

Ex. 451: The marking "Tempo stretto come avanti" indicates that ♪♪♪ equals ♪♪♪; therefore, the quarter-beat equals the previous half-beat (note that, at this point, the tempo is taken more slowly than at the beginning of the movement).

FRANCK, *Symphony in D minor*

Ex. 452: In the Presto (1-beat), the whole measure equals the quarter-beat of the previous tempo.

BRAHMS, *Symphony No. 2*

Ex. 453: For an unmistakable indication of the tempo change (♪ = ♩), it may be helpful to subdivide the last quarter-beat in bar 2. In any case, "think" the eighth-note values in the old tempo just before starting the "Doppio mosso."

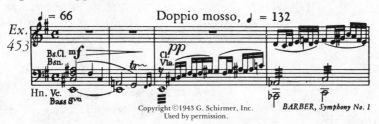

Copyright ©1943 G. Schirmer, Inc.
Used by permission.

BARBER, *Symphony No. 1*

Ex. 454: The quarter-beat of the Allegro is twice as fast as the quarter-value in the Lento.

Copyright 1943 by Aaron Copland, Renewed 1970.
Reprinted by permission of Aaron Copland and
Boosey & Hawkes, Inc., Sole Licensees and Publishers.

COPLAND, *A Lincoln Portrait*

Ex. 455: For bar 2 apply Diag. 59b; the eighth-beats are twice as fast as the quarter-beats in the preceding measure. The 2nd beat in each bar should be sufficiently sharp to bring out the syncopations.

HANSON, *Symphony No. 3*

Ex. 456: Subdivide the 3rd quarter-beat in bar 2; the second eighth of the subdivided beat serves as preparation for *Four* in the new tempo, which is twice as fast as the old tempo.

R. STRAUSS, *Tod und Verklärung*

Ex. 457: If the metronome markings are strictly observed, each of the slow beats in bar 5 equals *four* fast beats of the preceding tempo. Good control is needed to indicate the sudden change with calm, small gestures.

DUKAS, *L'Apprenti Sorcier*

Ex. 353: The tempo change is, in effect, ♪ = ♩.

Ex. 388: Change from slow to fast (♩ = ♩).

Additional examples for the study of tempo changes with rhythmic relation maintained:

Britten: *War Requiem, Dies Irae*—at No. 49 (five eighth-notes equal a quintuplet in the new tempo).

Carter: *The Minotaur, Suite*—passage beginning at No. 66.

Delius: *Brigg Fair*—passage between Nos. 38 and 39.

Kodály: *Psalmus Hungaricus*, transition at No. 9.

Mahler: Symphony No. 1, 1st movement—at No. 4.

Rimsky-Korsakov: *Scheherazade*, 2nd movement, *Moderato assai* 4/4 at F.

Schoenberg: Kammersymphonie—passage beginning with bar 249.

Sibelius: Symphony No. 3, 2nd movement, 13th bar after No. 6, *Tranquillo*.

Strauss, Richard: *Till Eulenspiegel, Gemächlich* 2/4, 19th bar, *doppelt so schnell*, 25th bar, *wieder noch einmal so langsam*.

Stravinsky: *L'Oiseau de Feu* (Suite), Finale—*Doppio Valore Maestoso* at No. 19.

Change of Tempo Without Rhythmic Relation

Some tempo changes occur without relationship between the last beat in the old tempo and the first beat in the new. If there is an opportunity in the music for a preparatory beat, the new tempo is established just as at the beginning of a piece. This is the case in Exx. 141, 275, and 295 (after a fermata), Ex. 298 (after an interruption), Exx. 308b and 330 (after a rest), Ex. 329 (after a sustained note), Ex. 293 (after the last beat in the bar, but feasible only because of the slow tempo which allows subdivision on the last count!), and Ex. 216 (at the end of a ritardando).

However, a sudden transition may leave no opportunity for a preparatory beat. This requires a clear and determined gesture, especially for the first few beats in the new tempo. The conductor must be absolutely sure of the tempo and the players must be convinced of his certainty. Still, some sudden changes are so difficult that they can be played satisfactorily only as a result of careful practice at rehearsal.

Ex. 458: The first 3 beats in the 2nd measure must be given without any hesitation or faltering, yet without rushing, and not too heavily. (The same is true for the 3rd bar of Ex. 267.)

Andantino moderato, (♩ = 76)   Un poco più animato, (♩ = 100)

NICOLAI, *The Merry Wives of Windsor—Overture*

Ex. 459: No interruption is intended in the 3rd bar; simply start the new tempo on *Three*.

ENESCO, *Roumanian Rhapsody No. 1*

Ex. 460: Use a simple and very clear wrist motion for the downbeat at Presto, addressing the 1st violins. (The first note in bar 6 has been changed to D by conductors who believe that the start of the violin run ought to be identical with that in the Leonore Overture No. 2. Beginning the run with C, they feel, anticipates the tonic chord and weakens the effect of the tutti entrance 21 measures later. The autograph is lost and no textual sources exist which deserve to be called authentic, unless the D found in one of Beethoven's sketches for Leonore No. 3 is considered sufficient evidence.)

BEETHOVEN, *Leonore Overture No. 3*

Ex. 461: Some conductors subdivide for the sudden poco meno, but it is better just to slow down the 1-beat. Allow the instruments time for the 2nd and 3rd quarter-notes in your calm and graceful upbeat.

J. STRAUSS, *Voices of Spring*

Ex. 462: The transition to a quicker tempo in bar 5 must be indicated with particular certainty because of the syncopation; use a precise staccato.

BEETHOVEN, *Symphony No. 4*

The following six examples show change of tempo in combination with change of the rhythmic pattern.

Ex. 463: The gesture on *Two* in bar 3 uses the accented upbeat and is timed as a preliminary beat in the slower tempo.

HARRIS, *When Johnny Comes Marching Home*

Ex. 464: In the 4th measure, an incisive *Two* is needed to establish the new tempo firmly.

WILLIAM SCHUMAN, *Symphony No. 3*

Ex. 437: Within no more than 4 bars, the quarter-beat changes abruptly from ♩ = 116 to ♩ = 80, and again to ♩ = 138.

Ex. 465: An energetic full-staccato beat is needed for the Vivo.

RÍMSKY-KORSAKOV, *Capriccio Espagnol*

Ex. 466: In bar 3, the composer indicates not only a change of pattern (1-beat) but also a suddenly faster tempo. Therefore lead the first 2 bars of the Più mosso with especially clear downbeats. The gradual increase of the tempo leads to a brief stop after bar 14 with a hurried ending of the pizzicato passage. After the interruption, direct the *meno* with 3-beat, poco espressivo. Bar 17 (*molto riten.*) is done non-espressivo, but in bar 18 beat *Two* and *Three* staccato to prepare for the detached notes, played hesitantly by the clarinets. For *a tempo primo* (♩. = 132), use staccato gestures, not too large but very determined.

Copyright ©1941 G. Schirmer, Inc.　BARBER, *Overture to The School for Scandal*
Used by permission.

Ex. 431 (bar 13): This illustrates a change to slower tempo and to the 3-beat pattern.

Additional examples for the study of sudden tempo changes without rhythmic relation:

Bartók: *Music for Strings, Percussion, and Celesta,* 3rd movement—bar 54 (5/4) ♩ = 80, bar 55 ♩ = 104.

Beethoven: Symphony No. 5, 2nd movement—bars 205 (*Più mosso*) and 218 (Tempo I).

Beethoven: Symphony No. 6, 3rd movement—bar 234 (*Presto*).

Berlioz: *Menuet des Feux-Follets* from *La Damnation de Faust*, several changes from *Moderato* to *Presto*.

Debussy: *La Mer*, 2nd movement—at No. 25.

Dvořák: Symphony No. 9. 3rd movement, *a tempo* at No. 2.

Janáček: *Sinfonietta*, 4th movement, at No. 7.

Mahler: Symphony No. 1, 4th movement, at No. 22.

Roussel: *Suite in F*, 3rd movement, 6 bars after No. 26 (*Allegro giocoso*).

Stravinsky: *Pulcinella Suite*—at Nos. 27 and 30.

Tchaikovsky: Symphony No. 5, 2nd movement—*Moderato con anima* (bar 66).

Verdi: *Aïda*, 2nd act, 2nd scene (Gran Finale)—start of the ballet music (*Più mosso*) at E.

Study and practice scores Numbers 7 to 9 discussed in the Appendix.

Chapter 29

FREE STYLE

Free Style of Conducting

IT OFTEN HAPPENS that a student attends a concert that is led by
an eminent conductor and finds that the leader's gestures do not
correspond with the patterns and methods studied so arduously.
He wonders if he has been wasting his time, and whether what he
has learned can be applied to actual conducting.

What this book has called good usage in conducting conforms to the traditional patterns, but it is not always easy to recognize the patterns, since there is room for considerable variation. Furthermore, the rapidity with which the gestures follow
each other makes it difficult to discern them. The student's
plight may be compared to that of a person with a good theoretical knowledge of a foreign language who, entering the country
where the language is spoken, has difficulty with the swiftness of
everyday speech. In both cases increasing experience and familiarity will clear up the confusion.

Nevertheless, the student is correct in concluding that the
conductor uses some gestures that do not conform to any of the
patterns. This is due to the fact that there are gestures that can
be described as "free style." Some of these gestures are discussed
below.

The direction of any beat may be changed to secure a particular result. For intense lyricism in 4-beat, it is effective to carry
② higher than usual and to reach ③ with a diagonal movement, especially when the 3rd beat is emphasized. In very strong
passages, downbeats may be used on each count to stress the attack. (This should not tempt the young conductor to adopt an
all-downbeat technique!)

Ex. 467: The chords in bars 5–7 are done by many conductors
with successive downbeats.

Allegro ma non troppo, ♩ = 88   *BEETHOVEN, Symphony No. 9*

Ex. 468: These bars conclude the entire movement. Since it would be awkward to end with an upward gesture, use a downbeat for *Two* in bar 4. This downbeat is a sharp motion to direct the accented off-beat.

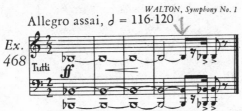

In fast 2-beat, the gesture easily becomes monotonous and does not lend itself to the directing of expressive passages. Therefore conductors sometimes use curved motions, carrying the baton to the right on *One* and to the left on *Two*. This method avoids the continual stress on the 1st beat, which in certain lyric passages (see Ex. 469) can become quite disturbing.

Also in 2-beat, it is possible to emphasize *Two* by using a not-too-large but energetic sideways stroke, preferably to the left, when an upward *Two* would be inconvenient; this means that the 1st beat is very small.

Ex. 470: The beginning of this movement (bars 1 and 3) can be done by beating *Two* to the left with a strong but short gesture.

It has already been pointed out that certain beats may be weakened in order to emphasize others by contrast. In free style the weakening may be carried to the point where such beats disappear altogether. In all cases, however, the 1st beat should be omitted only when there is no likelihood of a misunderstanding. Many players follow the music by counting bars, and need the downbeat. The same applies to skipping rests, which is done fairly often because the conductor does not want to make gestures that are not essential. For instance, in Ex. 179, the 4th and 5th eighth-beats may be omitted in bars 2 and 4, though the rhythm must be maintained strictly. Generally, a conductor with limited experience will do well to indicate all the rests if there is the slightest possibility of a misunderstanding.

In orchestral accompaniments, a careful handling of rests is required when the orchestra pauses for several successive measures. In each of these measures (*general pauses*) the first count should be indicated by a clear down-stroke, omitting the other counts. In many cases, this *free-style* procedure is more secure than the indication of all the counts. Not to beat at all during passages of this kind is advisable only if the players have been informed at which bar the conductor will resume the regular beat. This should generally be done in the measure that precedes the one in which the orchestra enters after the pause. (See the end of the violin cadenza in the first movement of Mendelssohn's Violin Concerto; from the beginning of the cadenza, do not beat for 35 bars, but resume the regular 2-beat one measure before the entrance of first violins, first flute, and first oboe.)

Whether to beat or omit rests is a particularly important problem in accompanying recitatives. Many Italian opera conductors traditionally use a downbeat for all chords regardless of the count on which they fall. This is practicable only when the orchestra parts include the words of the recitative; otherwise the beats must be very clear and the first counts must be unmistakable, even while the orchestra is waiting during several rests.

Not beating at all for a number of bars while the orchestra is playing must also be classified as a free-style characteristic. When not indulged in for the sake of showmanship, this can have a genuine musical purpose. Soft passages, similar in style to chamber music, may need little or no indication from the conductor. The fact that no beat is given may challenge the players' initiative and result in an especially well-balanced and delicate performance. Besides, it may be helpful for the young conductor to realize on such occasions that the musicians can to a certain extent play without him, and that he need not control every single count, nor every detail marked in the score. This realization may cure him of "overconducting" and holding the reins too tightly. It also will increase his poise and relaxation. But if the beat is stopped, it must be resumed smoothly at the proper moment, or the performance will become shaky.

It may sometimes be effective to beat with the left hand instead of the right. In Ex. 193 you may direct the tympani solo (bar 5) with the left hand, saving the right for the tutti in the next measure.

In certain syncopated passages in which the syncopation is in effect a change of time-signature, you may beat the accents instead of the rhythm. Do this only when all the instruments have the same rhythmic pattern and no misunderstanding is possible. The conductor must be sure that his clear-cut control allows him to return to the regular rhythm with absolute certainty.

Ex. 322: You may use 3 beats for the first two bars, beating on each *sf* and returning to 1-beat in bar 3, as though the music were written:

The use of free style for preparatory gestures has already been discussed on page 245. While free style adds variety to the beat and sometimes brings out effects which the regular pattern cannot achieve, it loses its meaning if used too frequently. It can be dangerous if it weakens the players' feeling of security, especially in unfamiliar music. Also, it may confuse an orchestra that is not highly experienced.

The Art of Accompaniment

In conducting an orchestral accompaniment, you face essentially the same problems as in accompanying a soloist at the piano, but the particular kind of alertness and flexibility that a good piano accompanist has are required to an even greater degree by the conductor: his gesture must both follow the soloist and lead the orchestra. For, even though the players adjust to the soloist to a certain extent, they must rely upon the leader for most of the coordination.

Perfect ensemble between the soloist and the orchestra is obtained more easily when the conductor and the soloist have worked out their interpretation beforehand. Even then the conductor must be ready for unexpected tempo modifications. However, considerable skill and attention are demanded of the leader in order to maintain a good ensemble when there has been limited rehearsal time.

Agreement on the starting tempo is essential when an introduction precedes the first solo entrance. The conductor must set the pace in a way that conforms to the soloist's playing. Lack of consistency in tempo could cause discomfort, if not embarrassment. Sometimes a brief orchestral introduction consists merely of broken chords, as at the beginning of Sibelius's Violin Concerto. To be sure of the tempo, the conductor might then hum to himself the solo theme before giving the upbeat.

A few technical hints follow. In slow tempo, resist the temptation to subdivide the beat unless subdivision is absolutely necessary. It is much better to use slightly larger and very calm gestures which, so to speak, contain the smaller values and make the musicians listen to the soloist. If they listen carefully, they will follow even rubato passages without the conductor's help. The desire to stay together with the soloist must not result in stiff gestures with overemphasized beats, or the accompaniment will drag. Do not hesitate unnecessarily on the counts, but keep the gesture moving with a light forearm. Be prepared to delay or hasten toward the next count. A special warning is given against waiting on the last count in the bar with uplifted arm; if a delay is necessary, move slowly upward, then come down quickly. Generally, such adjustments must not cause the rhythm to become uneven. Despite rhythmic nuances, the conductor cannot afford to lose sight of the basic rhythm. Both the soloist and the orchestra expect a certain firmness from the conductor.

This brings up the question of when the conductor should lead and when he should follow. To decide this, he must understand the nature of the instrument or voice that he is accompanying. There are cases in which it is evident that the soloist must follow the conductor's beat in order to achieve coordination.

Ex. 471: A new tempo begins, after the fermata, with a start after the count. The conductor must take the lead to assure coordination of the low strings with the piano part. The syncopated rhythm requires a very firm beat, based on complete understanding between soloist and conductor.

Ex. 471

Allegro moderato ($\bullet$= 128)   PROKOFIEV, *Piano Concerto No. 3*

Ex. 7: Most violin soloists prefer to follow the conductor's beat for the "exit" of the second trill.

On the other hand, the conductor should know where to wait for a singer to breathe, or for a difficult shift of position in the violin, or where to speed up with a quick run on the piano—to mention only a few such adjustments. It goes without saying that the conductor should listen carefully to the solo part. Above all, he must know it thoroughly. In rapid passages with many notes on each count, he must know the groupings of the notes within the bar so as to synchronize his beat with the soloist. It is sometimes easier to follow the left hand of a piano part when this is rhythmically simpler than the right. Also, it may help to watch the soloist when the ear alone is not adequate. For good dynamic balance, however, the conductor must rely on the ear alone. The dynamic marks, as printed in the parts, are more or less relative and must be corrected by the conductor's indications whenever necessary. If you cannot hear the soloist with reasonable ease, you may be sure that the audience cannot either.

The student should get some practical experience in accompanying instrumentalists and singers as soon as possible, even though he may only have at his disposal a piano or a small ensemble. Nos. 9–11 in the Appendix include typical examples of orchestral accompaniment. In this practice the soloist should occasionally avoid watching the conductor and may even make it hard for him by taking various liberties.

Aleatory Music

Aleatory music (*aleatorius*: "where the dice may fall") has gained new significance in contemporary music. Within a general trend towards improvisation in music, some composers do not restrict the performer to predetermined notes, rhythms, and dynamics. Instead, they welcome his participation in the creative process by letting him make choices within alternatives. This method of composing has brought about novel systems of notation in the form of charts, diagrams, and various geometrical figures. Although most of the time the traditional staves are used, the performer must learn how to read such scores and, in addition, observe the instructions which usually accompany aleatory works.

Characteristic of this style is the utilization of a great variety of sounds. Some effects are produced by handling traditional instruments in an unorthodox manner, others by including in the score unusual instruments and all sorts of mechanical devices. Consequently, the conductor, aside from studying the score, may have to undertake some investigation and experimentation as part of his advance planning. This includes assembling the needed properties and, in some cases, securing the services of expert players.

The conductor will not find it difficult to apply the beat patterns that have been discussed in this book to the direction of aleatory works. Improvisation may require a very flexible beat for timings that are done on the spur of the moment. Also, he will have to pay special attention to the giving of signals to individual performers, or groups of players, whose entries "happen by chance." As the timing is likely to differ from one performance to another, it is important to establish a clear understanding of the type and meaning of each signal. Usually, the players perform from full scores, or at least from cross-cued parts, which facilitates the rapport.

Chapter 30

APPLICATION OF
BATON TECHNIQUE

Applying Baton Technique to the Score

THE DISCUSSIONS in the Appendix show how to apply baton technique to a complete score. Some of these detailed suggestions may be considered too personal; in fact, certain passages can be directed in several different ways. The further the student advances, the more he will develop his own technique and will use the gestures that suit his artistic personality. Some musicians maintain that a detailed planning of gestures has little value, and that if the conductor knows the score thoroughly, his gestures will follow automatically. Since the gestures of even experienced conductors are not always adequate at first rehearsals, the inexperienced leader should certainly prepare himself as well as he can. As the foregoing study has shown, it is not always easy to coordinate the various motions. Especially in difficult passages, the student may have to conduct his imaginary orchestra again and again before the sequence of motions is smooth and fits the music.

In preparing to conduct a score the student should keep in mind two basic requirements: (1) A strong feeling for the rhythm of each individual part as well as for the whole, which combines different rhythms, is needed to direct the players with authority. (2) Only if all the dynamic gradations are firmly fixed in the leader's mind can his gestures be combined in a simple and natural way. Even highly talented young musicians, especially if their experience has been limited to the piano, often need great self-discipline to achieve certainty with regard to rhythm and dynamics.

Ex. 472: In order to direct this theme with conviction, the conductor must study its rhythmic structure, especially the frequent change from 6/4 to 12/8.

Molto agitato ed energico, ♩. = 76   WILLIAM SCHUMAN, *Symphony for Strings*

Ex. 472

Copyright © 1943 G. Schirmer, Inc.
Used by permission.

Ex. 473: A polyrhythmic passage of this type needs careful study. You must know the various rhythmic figures and the way they are combined or your gestures will lack firmness. The student will do well to direct each rhythmic pattern separately before he conducts the whole.

Molto allegro ♩ = 132   SCHOENBERG, *Five Pieces for Orchestra, No. 4*

Ex. 473

Furthermore, the importance of knowing the orchestration thoroughly cannot be overestimated, not only for cuing but for the conductor's planning as well. As the baton moves, the mind follows a succession of instrumental parts. *The conductor thinks in a line that contains all the important musical elements and interpretation marks in terms of the instruments.*

Which musical elements are important? The conductor must decide when he will direct the melody, how much attention he will give to the inner parts, and which details need special attention. The choice of "what to conduct" lends individuality to the interpretation. For example: when two groups play the melody, the larger one is usually led more directly, but if a particular orchestral color is desired (as strings with solo woodwinds, the woodwind color predominating), the smaller group is addressed. The effect of a passage may be greatly enhanced by directing counter-voices more strongly than the main melodic line. Generally speaking, however, it is unwise to pay too much attention to inner parts and to use elaborate gestures for a great number of small details, for this disturbs the logic of the overall musical picture and may easily become a mannerism.

Not every interpretation mark requires a gesture. The fact that all of the individual techniques have been discussed does not mean that they must *always* be applied. It is not necessary to indicate every accent or to lead every detail of the phrasing. This would result in an overloading of the gestures and would detract from the spontaneity of the performance. The mastery of baton technique is not an end in itself, and the student must develop a feeling for the proper use of this tool. He will then know how to use his gestures economically and will not miss the forest for the trees.

Another danger that the conductor must avoid is the tendency of his planned gestures to become so firmly fixed in his mind that during the performance he will not consider the players sufficiently. He must always remember that he is leading human beings and not the idealized orchestra of his private practicing. He must not let his imagination and temperament carry him away, causing him to lose sight of reality and to neglect the needs of the musicians. The solution is to have a clear conception of how the score should sound, and yet be able to adapt the gestures to the actual response of the players. The leader must be mentally and physically alert in order to sense the players' reactions and to control them even when things occur that he did not anticipate.

Factors such as the quality of the players are important, because with less-experienced musicians the conductor's concern is with elementary needs, while with well-trained players his indications are directed more toward interpretative ends. In experienced orchestras, the players themselves supply a good deal of precision and expression upon which the conductor can rely. Still, details of tempo, dynamics, and articulation that are *not* marked in the orchestral parts need stronger gestures than those that are. The results of rehearsal must also be considered: well-rehearsed details require less indication during the performance than those that have not been prepared.

Adjustments While in Action

No one can foresee at all times how the players will respond; hence, the conductor's ear must be keen enough to realize what the orchestra is doing and, if the results are not as desired, the gestures must be adjusted accordingly.

The importance of the ability to maintain a definite tempo has already been stressed. If the players hurry or drag the music, a firm beat must counteract this. It may even become necessary to use staccato or tenuto (especially the "dry" tenuto) although the music is legato. If the tempo threatens to become uneven in staccato, the sharpness of the beat should increase. Such corrective measures, however, must not take the form of jerky gestures. Caution must be exercised particularly in accelerating the tempo when the players are dragging, because the acceleration may become too great. On the other hand, the common error of using an enlarged, spasmodic beat sometimes causes the tempo to drag still more. The best way of maintaining control is with relatively small but firm beats. This is also important for cases when the conductor may have to correct his own tempo. In general, it is easier to speed up after having started somewhat slowly than to do the contrary. In slow tempo, a subdivided beat may effectively prevent hurrying.

But the beat is secondary; it is most important that the conductor's feeling for the tempo be so strong that it cannot be affected by any irregularities on the part of the orchestra. Even though the beat may have to yield to the players for one or two counts for the sake of ensemble, the conductor must be able to bring the orchestra back to the correct tempo with flexible but firm gestures. As an invaluable exercise, the student should practice with a pianist who can follow the beat as an orchestra would, but who deliberately slows down or hurries, forcing the student to find the proper gestures with which to lead him back to the original tempo. This exercise should be practiced with different rhythms, legato and staccato, and at different speeds.

Such flexibility is particularly useful in accompaniment because of unexpected delays, stops, and other emergencies. It is usually easier to wait than to catch up. If the latter is necessary, small beats are much more effective than large ones. Nervousness may lead to frantic motions that aggravate rather than help the situation. The conductor must train himself to remain calm in an emergency and should learn to anticipate difficulties before they arise. The same is true for adjusting entrances that are either missed or played prematurely. A useful technique to smooth out an early entrance is to hold the offender with a left-hand gesture while leading the rest of the group with the baton, being sure to bring the former into unity with the others. An angry wave of the hand only confuses the issue. The conductor's job is to help the performance and not to discipline the players.

The conductor's consideration for what the musicians need should include even such mechanical problems as putting on and taking off mutes, or turning pages between movements.

However well-rehearsed the ensemble and however well-marked the parts, only the actual sound of the music tells the conductor which gestures to use for dynamics. If the orchestra plays too loud in a *f* passage, the conductor may decrease the size of his gesture and even use the left hand to subdue the group. On the other hand, a *p* passage may not stand out sufficiently unless the conductor gives a large beat.

The degree of intensity in the gesture clearly depends upon the musicianship of the players. Occasionally the conductor will allow an individual player considerable freedom in the performance of a solo passage and will simply accompany him with the rest of the orchestra. For a well-balanced performance, the leader must sense how much emotional intensity the players have, so that his gestures will strengthen weak sections but not give unnecessary stimulation to groups that do not need it. However, it does not follow that the conductor should ever be lacking in intensity. He must never allow himself to adopt a passive attitude, for the orchestra expects that he will do his share of the work, and if he does not, it is inclined to lose interest.

To what extent the players watch the baton depends partly on the individual musician's technical ability and alertness. Yet, except for the rare occasions when his attention is completely absorbed by a very difficult passage, the average player gives a considerable part of his effort to watching the baton. If this were not so, it would be hard to explain the remarkable influence exercised by an able conductor at a first reading of unfamiliar music. Still, the conductor should cooperate with the players by assisting them with very clear and, if necessary, larger gestures, either in passages of great technical difficulty or when something goes wrong and decisive leadership is demanded.

The conductor's function, however, goes far beyond the mere exercise of control. His technique must be a means through which he vitalizes the orchestra. The music must always sing within him; then his gestures will not become mechanical. When technical mastery is combined with musical inspiration, the conductor makes his players feel that he is working *with* them. In the absence of these qualities, the players feel restricted and are affected *negatively*. A good conductor works as an artistic leader and not as a disciplinarian; he is stimulating and affects his players *positively*. Only a direct and positive approach inspires the players for a vital performance.

Chapter 31

SCORE STUDY

Purpose of Score Study

STUDYING A SCORE serves a double purpose: to learn the music in terms of notes and markings, and to establish a conception of the composition in the broadest sense. Except for the fact that reading an orchestral score is more demanding then the study of a solo part, the conductor's task as an interpreter is not unlike that of other musical performers. The working process, however, is different. The conductor's interpretative ideas must be developed before they can be applied to actual playing. In contrast, the solo performer, even if he started out by reading the music, enjoys the leisure of his studio for practical application. In other words, an instrumentalist's or vocalist's homework leads directly to a performance in public, while a conductor prior to rehearsing the orchestra must create in his inner ear an imaginary performance. This image must reflect all the aspects of music making, from minute details to the broad flow of the music from the first to the last measure.

Some of the conductor's ideas may change in the course of rehearsals. Still, beginning with the first rehearsal, he must face the orchestra with a clear conception of the score and be prepared to answer questions asked by musicians regarding the performance of their parts. His authority will suffer unless he can instruct the players quickly and efficiently.

Circumstances beyond the conductor's control can interfere with proper preparation, such as late arrival of music furnished by a soloist, or stepping in for an ill colleague. The ability to sight-read a score, sometimes used as a test in conductors competitions, may disclose presence of mind, technical skill, and a flair for quickly grasping the essentials of a certain musical style. It does not, however, tell about a conductor's potential as an interpreter. Interpreting music is a decision-making process that requires time to make choices concerning tempo, phrasing, articulation, sound balances, and other details in all their complexity.

Questions of this nature will be discussed in later chapters.

There we shall try to shed light on methods of how to "read be-hind the notes." Here we are concerned with the initial study of a score and ask, first of all, on what kind of score to base our study. This question is of considerable importance in regard to music written before 1900.

Selecting the Score

Strange as it may seem, interest in the reliability of orchestra materials is a rather recent trend among conductors. Speaking of the Viennese classics, for instance, it was long taken for granted that the *Gesamtausgaben*, published during the second-half of the nineteenth century, were beyond reproach. Although they were superior to earlier editions, the editors had often assumed a "father-knows-best" attitude and all too frequently had not ad-hered to the original text. One need only compare the old Mo-zart Edition's version of the "Haffner" Symphony K. 385 with the photocopy of the manuscript to discover alterations of notes, rhythms, phrasings, even of tempo signatures. It is not surpris-ing, therefore, that present recordings of the work, even when conducted by outstanding musicians, are not true to Mozart's text.

No matter how essential the reference to autographs, they are not always the most authentic sources. Beethoven, for exam-ple, used to enter corrections, not only in fair copies written by copyists for the publisher, but also in printed proofs. Moreover, composers have made significant changes long after publication but failed to inform the publisher. The far-reaching corrections Mahler made in his symphonies are now included in revised edi-tions, as are important alterations made by Debussy in his *Noc-turnes*. Nevertheless, these works are still sometimes performed without the composers' corrections by conductors who remain unaware of authentic sources.

One more word about the selection of editions within the classic repertory: Although, as a rule, a conductor must rely on the research done by musicologists, he should learn about editor-ial methods and keep informed about available publications. Since the Second World War, great strides have been made in re-publishing the orchestral works of many of the great masters. The new volumes are relatively expensive but available at music libraries where they can be consulted by conducting students. It is to be hoped that before long these editions will be completed and less costly study scores will be printed. Regrettably, not all study scores now on the market live up to the claim of being *Urtexts*.

Methods of Score Study

The study of unfamiliar scores proceeds in steps, although the order of steps may vary. Agreement exists regarding the first step: perusing the score on a getting-acquainted basis. Many conductors then undertake a form analysis in terms of phrase groups and larger segments. This may go hand in hand with, or be followed by, an investigation of the harmonic and contrapuntal structure. In the case of serial compositions, the tone row, or smaller units, must be determined and pursued throughout all permutations.

When studying the orchestration, the conductor must make it a habit to clarify in his mind what each player is doing at any given moment, not merely which notes he is playing but, equally important, how he is to perform them in regard to rhythm, dynamics, and other markings. Painstaking attention to these elements during score study will bear fruit when orchestra rehearsals begin, and the conductor, thanks to solid preparation, is able to "be with the players," a feeling equally satisfying for the leader as for the orchestra (see the comments on pp. 76 and 307).

The caution recommended against using recordings for the practice of baton technique (see p. 76) also applies to score study. Aside from the risk of imprinting in one's mind the interpretative ideas of another person or getting confused by listening to different versions, a young conductor, in order to become a master of his craft, must learn to study a score without leaning on outside help. Symphonic recordings appeared on the market no more than 50 years ago, and the outstanding conductors of the recent past, who had to do without them, were none the worse for it.

Not all schools of music offer special courses in score reading and score playing. A conducting student, whose education has been deficient in this respect, must fill the gap by self-training. First, he should play, on the keyboard, Bach chorales printed with the original clefs on four staves, then string quartets, chamber music with transposing wind instruments, and finally orchestral music. In class work, several students should get together, taking turns in playing and checking on each other's performance. Some musicians, thanks to talent or hard work or both, excel in playing from full scores, but more modest efforts are no less valuable. Those who do not play the piano at all and must forgo this self-testing exercise use methods which they have found most useful, relying on their inner ear and making sure that no detail in the score has slipped their attention.

This brings up the question whether playing the piano is indispensable for a conductor. The answer is: not indispensable, but highly desirable. Very few orchestra leaders of prominence have been totally devoid of keyboard facility. If Arturo Toscanini, whose instrument was the cello, went to the trouble of practicing the piano to the point that he could coach singers without the help of an accompanist, a young musician ought to make a similar effort.

Marking a Score

A widespread, though not commendable, habit among conductors is to start entering pencil marks the moment they open a score for study, including signs which merely duplicate printed ones. It is not uncommon, for instance, for a change to alla breve to result in a page being disfigured by three large ¢ signs marked in red or blue on the top, center, and bottom of the page. There is no taboo against an occasional mark to facilitate score reading, but a conductor must not proceed indiscriminately and make marking a compulsive routine. People who defend the messing up of scores should be very sure that they are not deficient in score reading — not to mention the nuisance they cause others who have to use the same copy and will suffer from the idiosyncrasies of colleagues.

Unless the legibility of a score is poor, it should not be necessary to pencil in signs for cuing. A conductor should at least wait to enter signs that duplicate printed notation until, in the course of rehearsals, he finds that he needs warning signals to feel secure.

Marking phrase groups can be useful when the metrical structure of a composition changes frequently. Being reminded of irregular bar grouping, a conductor concentrates with greater ease on the many other details which require his attention.

The primary function of score marking is to enter all the information that the conductor wishes to be added to the printed orchestra parts for the sake of clarification and of reducing the need for verbal comments in rehearsal (see Ch. 35).

Memorizing a Score

Some musicians absorb music so quickly that they know it from memory after thorough score study. Those who find memorizing more difficult should not force themselves to an effort which can be nerve-racking in performance without being appreciated by the orchestra. Players dislike to sense a strain in their leader's mind if it can be attributed to his insistence to conduct without score. Although, in the eyes of the public, dispensing with the conductor's stand has become a status symbol, a young conductor must not forget that, unless he can do without score in rehearsal, he may not know the music as well as he pretends. He should also remember that the quality of the orchestra's performance does not improve by the absence of the conductor's stand, but has at times been jeopardized by a sudden loss of memory on the leader's part.

Some prominent conductors prefer to have the score available in performance, no matter how sporadically they make use of it. Knowing the music from memory is not an end in itself but a means to maintain eye communication with the players. In fact, certain passages can be directed effectively only if the conductor's eyes "are not in the score." Here are a few examples: (1) the beginning of a piece (giving the first beat while looking down to the music would not be conducive to an inspired start!), (2) a sudden tempo change (looking at the players calls for better attention), (3) incisive short chords (lack of precision is quickly remedied by eye communication), (4) chorus attacks (chorus singers do not react well to the beat unless addressed directly by the conductor).

Generally speaking, the conductor's attitude toward memorizing the music should be dictated by common sense. In performance, he should use the score as little as possible, but spending many hours on memorizing for the purpose of public display could be a waste of time which he might put to better use by probing more deeply into the background of a composition.

Interpretation of a Score

There is no shortcut to arrive at a valid conception of a work, nor is there a proven and generally accepted method to guide a conducting student in his efforts as an interpreter of music. Musicianship, performing experience, acquired knowledge, and intuition—all these elements work together in a growing process that leads to bringing technical mastery of a score in line with the performer's emotional involvement. Differences in personality and artistic leanings account for the considerable variety in readings of the same work. Although the ability to express and project personal feelings is essential in the performance of music, young conductors should not take refuge in the categorical statement "this is the way I feel the music" in order to avoid argument. The same music can be "felt" in several different ways, as proven by eminent conductors who changed their interpretation of a work in the course of continued study and increasing knowledge.

The initial approach to the study of a score may depend on circumstance. Recalling a very impressive performance, live or recorded, a conductor may be inclined to adopt a similar interpretation. Even negative memories of readings by other conductors can condition his mind. Facing an unfamiliar score written in a style totally outside his experience, a conductor, although free of preconceived notions, may still have a problem in approaching new musical territory. In this case, a recording led by a conductor who specializes in this type of music can be helpful, as can recordings of contemporary works directed by the composers.

No matter how much conductors differ in their methods of score study, they share a fundamental motive: they want to do justice to the music and its composer. Here the consensus ends. Non-musicians often believe that within the framework of a musical score and performance traditions the preservation of the composer's intentions is assured. Professionals know better. Traditions are tenuous, the score does not tell everything, and each conductor claims the right to serve the composer according to his artistic views and musical taste. The following comments, being directed to young conductors with flexible minds, are intended to present an open view of choices on the way from initial score study to final preparation for the orchestra rehearsals.

Different Attitudes to Interpretation

Attitudes toward musical interpretation oscillate between two extremes. One extreme would be marked by taking unrestricted liberties with the score, the other by literal adherence to it. In the first instance, a performer "re-creates" the music by molding the score according to his personal judgment. This can include changing notes, markings, tempo instructions, and orchestration. Examples of recent date include romanticized and re-orchestrated versions of Handel's *Messiah*, which could still be heard in the nineteen-fifties. Conductors who preferred an arrangement to the *Urtext* obviously believed that vesting *Messiah* with modern devices was a legitimate means of conveying its spirit to our audiences.

Due to the now-prevailing approach to baroque music, arrangements of this type have almost become a relic from the past. In the field of post-baroque music, however, it would not be difficult to pinpoint liberties taken by conductors who place their individual tastes before stylistic considerations. They believe in the philosophy that masterworks, in order to stay alive, must be reshaped in line with the artistic climate of each generation. Rather than attempting to perform the classics according to original concepts, they try to bring out the overall effect that the composers, supposedly, had intended. It has even been suggested that composers would have given their approval, had they lived in our time.

Musicians who advocate adherence to the composer's ideas challenge this theory. If the public's receptivity, they ask, is indeed conditioned by shifting psychological trends, how can it be explained that historically oriented performances are enjoyed by present audiences no less than modernized versions. If it is true that in our "fast-moving" society some music of the past cannot be appreciated unless played at a quicker pace, how can it be justified that some other, equally old, music is now often performed more slowly than marked by the composer? If conductors are praised as masters of the "Mozart style," how does one account for a surprising lack of unanimity in their readings of Mozart's works? How do we then define style? Perhaps we should, in this context, speak rather of shifting performance fashions and limit the use of the word "style" to demonstrable musical realities based on historical sources.

The Quest for Authenticity

A young conductor, reluctant to accept questionable concepts of style and distrustful of traditions that cannot be traced to the composer, will have to learn how to make his choices.

While a truly authentic performance is out of our reach, the quest for authenticity, despite its utopian nature, remains a worthwhile challenge. Admitting that ultimate truth is unobtainable is one thing; another is trying to eliminate avoidable stylistic errors. Besides, utilizing information about a composer's intentions need not lead to impersonal music making, as little as identifying with another person need deprive us of human warmth and understanding.

The quest for authenticity must not be mistaken for a puritan approach in the sense of the everything-is-in-the-score maxim which, earlier in our century, led some musicians to apply modern usage to eighteenth-century works. They went so far as to object to rhythmic alterations in baroque music, to any added appogiaturas and other embellishments in Mozart operas, and to any unwritten tempo modifications. They failed to recognize that literal rendition can distort a composer's ideas as much as the taking of unwarranted liberties.

Aside from using a reliable score and learning about performance practices, a conductor should look into a work's general background. Seeing a single work in the perspective of the composer's entire output will widen and intensify his understanding. Mozart's instrumental works, for instance, cannot be appreciated without knowledge of his operas. Insight into Schubert's and Schumann's symphonies requires familiarity with their songs and piano compositions. Extended to other composers, these examples open up a wide field of study. If remaining a "student for life" has been called the mark of a true artist, this certainly applies to conductors who are expected to master a repertory larger and more varied than the one of any other musical performer.

Chapter 32

CHOICE OF TEMPO

General Considerations

ORCHESTRA PLAYERS, when asked about the conductor's primary function, are likely to single out the setting of the pace. Similarly, a composer's first concern, when entrusting his score to a conductor, is the grasp of the proper tempo. Conductors themselves, when studying an unfamiliar score, try right from the start to feel the music's pulse, knowing that a well-chosen tempo will make a variety of musical details fall into place, which otherwise might turn out awkward and unconvincing. They also know that the choice of tempo can be marked by pitfalls. Tempo markings are vague, be they worded in Italian or the vernacular. Metronome indications do not always hit the mark, as admitted by composers when their markings are put to a test in performance. No wonder that Mozart called the choice of tempo not only the most essential, but the trickiest thing in music.

Any attempt to determine, once and for all, the "right" tempo for a piece of music would be simplistic and mechanical. There is consensus, however, that a performance would suffer without the benefit of a "basic" tempo, which in spite of occasional modifications can be generally maintained. How to determine a basic tempo cannot be put into rules, but it has long been recognized that only by viewing a movement in its entirety can we hope to capture its pulse. Thus, Leopold Mozart suggested in his *Violinschule* (1756) that before deciding on the tempo of a movement one should look for a characteristic passage, often occurring later in the piece, which might be more enlightening than its beginning.

In general terms, the choice of tempo is based on tempo markings, the rhythmical and formal structure of a composition, its style and orchestration. Moreover, the pacing should be reasonable in the sense of being playable (or singable) and effective by allowing the unfolding of phrases and, at the same time, should make an orchestra sound its best. With musical performance not being a science but an individualistic craft, all these elements pass through the medium of the performer's personality.

To make the pulse of the music his own is of particular significance for the conductor whose effectiveness depends on a secure
feeling for the beat, something that does not develop overnight.
A conductor must have "lived with the music" in order to project
its pulse with conviction and spontaneity.

Application of a Chosen Tempo

The conductor's preparatory study does not always lead to a
valid concept of the tempo, mainly because working in the studio
lacks certain features that mark orchestral teamwork in the concert hall. Acoustics could be the reason, but aside from this a
conductor may discover in rehearsal that a chosen tempo does
not "work" with the orchestra. Misjudgment of this kind need
not be explained by lack of experience. Conductors of proven
ability have sometimes made tempo adjustments during rehearsals or in the course of performances. A notable instance occurred
at a Bayreuth Festival in the 1930s when a famous conductor
modified his pacing of a Wagner opera to such an extent that,
from the first to the fourth performance, the total playing time
decreased by twenty minutes. It is of interest that witnessing musicians were inclined to attribute the maestro's change of mind to
psychological factors.

That the conductor's beat, set in motion by a mental impulse, can be conditioned by his state of mind is not astonishing.
Nervousness, fatigue, over-enthusiasm, and other psychological
causes can lead to directions that are at variance with the original scheme, whereby the conductor is not always aware of the
shift of tempo.

Special precaution against straying from the basic pace is
needed in rehearsal. Playing a passage many times over can
cause the beat to slow down, particularly when the repeats serve
to clarify the musical texture. Having completed his corrections,
the conductor should let the orchestra repeat a longer section for
the sake of continuity and make sure that the correct speed is resumed. Some conductors (Toscanini is said to have been among
them) have found it useful occasionally to consult a pocket metronome in rehearsal to check tempo fluctuations.

A psychological influence on the choice of tempo of a different sort has been noticed in recording sessions. Listening to a
playback between "takes" can make a conductor alter a tempo

that does not seem to produce the desired effect. The impression on a listener who hears mechanically reproduced music in a room can be different from that in a concert hall or in an opera house. One could argue against such a double standard in tempo choice, but it is undeniable that a conductor's pacing of a live performance is not always identical with the one applied to his recording of the same work—perhaps one of the reasons why conductors are rarely satisfied with their recordings and dislike listening to them; it is also a warning to students not to rely on recordings in matters of tempo!

Tempo Modifications

The nature of certain compositions suggests a strictly maintained pulse. Many dances, perpetual-motion-like pieces, or movements built primarily on rhythmic propulsion require a persistent beat from the first to the final measure. Beethoven's *Allegretto scherzando* in his Eighth Symphony would suffer unless performed in this fashion (Ex. 369). These instances, however, are rare when seen in the perspective of all the music written by classic and romantic composers. In the light of most of their works, relentless adherence to a fixed tempo would put a straitjacket on the performer. It would prevent him from letting the music breathe and from giving meaning to the rise and fall of a melodic line. The need for subtle flexibility in the pacing of music has led some composers to use metronome markings that suggest a tempo span rather than a fixed speed. In place of $\quarternote = 80$, for example, they might prefer to write $\quarternote = 76$–84.

Thinking in terms of a tempo span, which implies minor modifications without losing sight of the basic pulse, is a useful means to preserve the essential character of the music as reflected in its rhythm. As an example, we select Wagner's *Meistersinger* Prelude and assume as its basic tempo $\quarternote = 108$ (see Ex. 336). Increasing the speed to $\quarternote = 120$, or slowing it down to $\quarternote = 96$, would change the music's character noticeably, while it is maintained by keeping the tempo within a span of $\quarternote = 104$–112.

When, or when not, to deviate from the regular beat is closely linked to a conductor's sensitivity and empathy for the music, but also to his learning and insight. Subtle tempo modifications, often hardly noticed by the listener, serve different purposes. Relaxing the pulse may assure clarity in intricate passages, render significance to a phrase, or underline an unexpected modulation. Picking up the speed may put a lively theme into sharper relief or allow freer rein to the musical momentum. Still, a conductor should test the validity of such modifications by letting the music, at least once, pass through his mind in strict tempo. He will then be his own judge as to where the music fares better by being played at straight speed, or where sticking to a regular beat would be pedantic and hinder the music from conveying its meaning to the listener.

Tempo Relations

The examples for tempo relations quoted in Chapter 28 referred to cases where composers had entered specific indications in the scores. Such relations, however, had existed long before composers began to express them by mathematical formulas. They can be divided into two categories: manifest and latent relations.

We speak of a manifest tempo relation when a musical episode returns, or is anticipated, in the form of a quotation, be it in identical or altered notation.

Ex. 474: The theme of the slow introduction returns, in shortened form, in the fast section to precede the recapitulation. The tempo relation is ♪ = ♩.

Adagio maestoso (♩= 80)   MOZART, Serenade No. 9 (K. 320)

Allegro con spirito ($\mathatwo = 80$)

Ex. 475: The Overture to *Der Fliegende Holländer* contains a quotation of *Senta's Ballad*, heard in the 2nd act of the opera. Note that Wagner indicated the metronome for the *Ballad*; the overture has no metronome markings (see p. 111).

Più lento. ♩ = 100

WAGNER, *Der fliegende Hollander*

Quotations of this kind are frequently found in operatic overtures. Since the musical ideas were conceived to serve a dramatic function, familiarity with the opera provides a better insight into the expression and tempo of the quoted passage than the study of the overture alone. The same is true for orchestral excerpts from operas, such as selections from Wagner's *Ring* cycle. Knowledge of the entire work is needed to grasp the style of the music and its dramatic connotation.

An interesting manifest tempo relation, shown in Exx. 476a and 476b, occurs in the Ball Scene in the first Finale of *Don Giovanni*. Although Mozart's intentions are unmistakable, they are not always observed in performance.

Ex. 476a: Prior to the Ball Scene, an invisible stage band plays this Contredanse, marked *Allegretto*. Consistent with the usage of the time, a tempo of ♩ = 100–104 can be assumed. This is to continue, after the entrance of the pit orchestra, for the remaining section in 2/4, including the passage in D minor quoted after the double bar.

Ex. 476b: Like the Contredanse, a Minuet was played backstage right after the conclusion of the section in 2/4. Now, in the Ball Scene, it is not only repeated, but put in conjunction with the Contredanse and a previously not-heard German Dance. To make the combination possible, Mozart chose a fast German Dance in 3/8 and a moderately fast Minuet (the "slow Italian type," see p. 341). Thus, within a tempo span of ♩ = 96–104, Mozart made it possible for the three dances to be played to the same beat.

A latent tempo relation, although not always provable, exists when, at a tempo change, the musical context suggests a continuation of the music's pulse. Three examples, taken from overtures of Mozart and Beethoven, serve as illustrations.

Ex. 477: The transition from the introduction, *Andante* ₵, to the *Allegro* ₵ is marked by rapidly repeated notes, 32nd-notes in the *Andante* (second violins and violas) and eighth-notes in the *Allegro* (violas and cellos), calling for an uninterrupted flow with the relation ♪ = o. (For a smooth transition, it is useful to apply 1-beat to the first few *Allegro* bars before changing to 2-beat.)

Ex. 269: In the Overture to *Die Entführung aus dem Serail*, a tempo relation can be established between the fast and slow sections by the formula o = ♪ (one measure of the Presto equals the eighth-beat

of the *Andante*). The *Andante* is quoted from the opera's opening aria and offers a manifest tempo relation. The example shows the return to the *Presto*.

Ex. 478: Here again, latent and manifest tempo relations are combined. A rhythmic figure, first heard in the horns, then in timpani, establishes the relation $\textbf{\textit{d}} = \textbf{\textit{♪}}$ for the transition from *Un poco sostenuto* $\textbf{C}$ to *Adagio* 3/4. The theme of the *Adagio* is taken from the tenor aria in the opera, previously quoted in the introduction of the overture.

Ex. 478

Manifest tempo relations are rarely subject to controversy, but there can be disagreement in regard to latent relations. Some conductors, for example, maintain that, in symphonies of the classic Viennese school, introductions are invariably linked to the main sections by a precise rhythmic relation. Even though in many instances a good case can be made for assuming such a relation, it would seem wrong to exclude the element of surprise as created by contrasting tempi. In the case of the four Beethoven symphonies that begin with an introduction, the composer's metronome markings leave no doubt that the fast sections are to start with a new rhythmic impulse.

Metronome

Mälzel's metronome, now mostly replaced by electric or watch-like devices, was first hailed as the salvation from forcing music into "tempi ordinari," to quote Beethoven. Unhappy with the traditional Italian tempo markings, he praised the invention as a means to give full expression to the "free genius." The enthusiasm did not last. Still, in spite of being maligned for being unreliable and misleading, the metronome has survived. Beginning with Berlioz, metronome markings are found in most French scores, and many nineteenth-century composers in other countries followed suit. Today, virtually all composers make use of metronome indications.

Beethoven's use of the metronome is of special interest, not merely because he was the first outstanding musician to experiment with it, but in view of considerable controversy regarding his metronome markings. The fact is that he continued using it, even after he had come to recognize its limitations. Shortly before his death, he urged his publisher to wait with printing the score of the *Missa solemnis* until the metronome list would be ready—a plan that he did not live to carry out. Not only from letters to his publishers, but from conversation books, we know how Beethoven labored before deciding on metronome figures. He seems to have experienced the frustration that is all too familiar to every musician who has tried his hand at fixing tempi metronomically. A certain speed may now appear convincing but is objectionable when tested the next morning, or a metronome figure that fits the beginning of a piece may become questionable when applied to other sections of the same movement.

In short, the pulse of living music cannot be captured by a mechanical device, which explains why composer-conductors have not always observed their own markings. Stravinsky, for one, who had long insisted on strict adherence to his metronome figures, came to admit that, with increasing experience in conducting his works, he sometimes revised his original ideas about tempo (without, unfortunately, having these changes entered into the printed scores).

In spite of these odds, even the most skeptical conductor would welcome metronome markings by Bach, Mozart, and other masters, had they been able to avail themselves of the device. In Beethoven's case, the critics of his metronome figures have failed to explain why, sometimes within the same work or movement, some of his markings are readily accepted, others flatly rejected. Perhaps they forget that the metronome was never intended to pinpoint the speed of music. It was meant to provide information regarding the character of the music and to prevent the performer from straying too far from the composer's intention. For the conductor, metronome indications are invaluable as a guide to define a tempo span that preserves the character of the music.

The third movement of Beethoven's Seventh Symphony (see Appendix A, No. 4) may serve as an example. It bears two markings: *Presto* 3/4, $\downarrow$. = 132, for the main section, *Assai meno presto*, $\downarrow$. = 84 for the Trio. The *Presto* is usually performed at a speed identical with, or at least close to, Beethoven's metronome. It is not uncommon, however, for the Trio to be played as slowly as $\downarrow$. = 60, to the effect that it assumes a character quite different from the one reflected in the composer's marking. A less excessive slowing down, say a speed of $\downarrow$. = 72, would still conform to *assai meno presto* and remain within a reasonable tempo span of $\downarrow$. = 72–84.

Further discussion of Beethoven's metronome markings will be found in Chapter 34.

Chapter 33

PERFORMANCE PRACTICE (I)

> "Very few men investigate. Hence, most men are led by authority; and the errors of learned men are received as truth and incorporated into public opinion."
>
> *Noah Webster (1816)*

The Study of Performance Practice

PERFORMANCE PRACTICE REFERS to rules and habits of former times, which served to bridge the gap between the notation and execution of music. Throughout the eighteenth century students were guided by textbooks filled with musical examples "this way it is written" and "this way it is played." Some suggestions differed from one text to another, as could be expected in a time when taking liberties with notes and rhythms was based partly on rules, partly on the taste of each performer.

No clear line can be drawn to mark the end of ambiguity in music notation. Liberties continued, especially in opera, far into the nineteenth century. Even Schubert was obliged to accept changes in his songs made by a famous baritone friend. Generally speaking, however, and particularly in orchestral and other ensemble music, the written text has ceased to be subject to the performer's discretion since the days of Beethoven.

In 1832 Ludwig Spohr published his *Violinschule*. There he expressed the view of the time by distinguishing between *richtiger Vortrag* and *schöner Vortrag*. "Correct" execution included true pitch, exact rhythm, steady tempo, and observation of the composer's markings. "Beautiful" execution required a refined treatment of dynamics, accents, and phrasing. Moreover, it called for tempo modifications. Passion was to be expressed by increasing the speed; tenderness and sadness by slowing it down. Students were advised to develop taste and feeling and to emulate the outstanding performers of the time. A footnote informed the reader, merely as a matter of historical interest, that former customs could be looked up in Leopold Mozart's book.

Spohr's belief that current habits superseded former performance styles was in line with a firmly rooted tradition. Mozart had not hesitated to rewrite the scores of Handel oratorios according to the ideas of his generation. Likewise, when Wagner edited Palestrina's "Stabat Mater," he transformed renaissance music into a romantic piece charged with explosive passion. From Wagner's essay *Über das Dirigieren* we learn much about his thoughts on interpretation. He had no qualms about making changes in classic scores but chided conductors who took liberties with his own works.

Ours is the first century which has seen an increasing interest in former performance practices. Thanks to the efforts of music scholars, a reorientation toward baroque music had been initiated early in the century. At present, courses in baroque style are included in the programs of many music schools, often in conjunction with performing groups. However, more recent studies, which are devoted to the performance of post-baroque and nineteenth-century music, have made little inroad into practical music making. Relatively few musicians seem to take interest in these questions. Besides, sources of information are not easily accessible and have still to be summarized. Time will tell whether, in the wake of scholarly investigations, a reorientation toward post-baroque music will enter the mainstream of musical performance.

Not all conducting students participate in musicological studies. Within existing curricula, questions of interpretation are discussed in classes that primarily serve the training of performing skills. Some instructors take interest in the history of musical performance; others are content with handing down to their pupils the more-or-less valid traditions inherited from their teachers.

A conductor, while working out his interpretative ideas, must be prepared to make his own choices. His education, therefore, should provide information on the broadest possible basis and encourage curiosity in every field of music, including historical studies. Awareness of style, far from being a hindrance to a conductor's personal involvement, enables him to decide with better understanding how to apply former customs to present realities, such as the instruments now in use, the training of the players, the size of concert halls, and other facts which are part of our musical daily life.

Old vs. Modern Instruments

Just as it seems unlikely that the classic masters would have listened to our orchestras with undiluted pleasure, we would probably not have been satisfied with the orchestral sound of their time. Improved intonation, evenness of tone, technical precision, increase in the number of string players—all this speaks in favor of modern orchestras. Yet our forefathers would hardly have appreciated the overly brilliant sound, the raise of pitch, and the sheer loudness often accompanied by muddiness in the lower ranges—all part of the overall sound produced by our wind and string instruments. Thinking in terms of sound levels, the present *mezzoforte* would, at Mozart's time, have equaled a *forte*, if not a *fortissimo*. It has become customary, therefore, to adjust present playing habits in line with stylistic considerations when we perform pre-romantic music.

Reducing the number of string players for better balance is only part of the adjustments. The conductor must attempt to achieve the mellowness combined with crispness of sound that marked eighteenth-century music making.

Chamber music groups that perform on eighteenth-century instruments have found that application of the required techniques often furnishes the answer to questions of interpretation. The nature of the old instruments helps to determine speed, phrasing, and other details of performance. For the conductor, these findings are of more than theoretical interest, because he can draw conclusions for the performance on modern instruments.

An invaluable source for the study of string playing during the second half of the eighteenth century is Leopold Mozart's *Violinschule*. It is available in an English translation and should be required reading for conductors. Aside from violin playing, the book comments on many aspects of music performance in general. No less than 75 out of a total of 268 pages are devoted to bowing and phrasing. The great variety of bowing will surprise those who believe that, in Mozart's time, bowing was handled in a rather square and unsophisticated fashion.

Ex. 479: Successive up-bow passages are suggested as a "successful" technique. For each up-bow, more strength is to be applied to the first note, or the first two notes, than is used for the subsequent notes, which are to be slurred "quietly and gently." As an alternative, one may "also try" to play the exercise with up-bow for the first half of the bar, down-bow for the second.

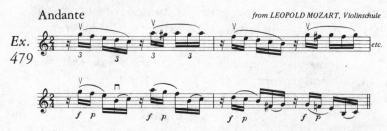

Ex. 480: Here, successive up-bows are recommended for detached playing. Putting a "short stress" on each note makes the music "bolder and gives it more spirit."

It must not be forgotten that, in Mozart's time, the bow, shorter than a *Tourte* bow and of different shape, produced a lighter tone. Moreover, string sonority has since been affected by a number of mechanical alterations (bridge, sound post, bass-bar, neck, chin rest) and by replacing catgut by other materials for the strings. Although we now use modernized instruments and a different bow, Leopold Mozart's teachings remain significant, if for no other reason than that they played an important role in the education of his famous son.

Baroque Music

The following comments refer to the late baroque of the eighteenth century and are limited to an outline of basic questions. To gain deeper insight into the baroque style and its application in performance, a conductor must consult reference books and acquire knowledge of baroque instruments. Texts do not always furnish ready answers, because the intermixture of rules and liberties, which is peculiar to this style, often calls for the performer's judgment, no less now than in the old days.

Depending on their national background, the authors of the time differed in matters of tempo. Within each school, however, the speed of music was defined according to tempo categories, often with reference to mathematical formulas. This included the pacing of the dances that have come down to us in the form of suites. Some authors even utilized mechanical devices which preceded Mälzel's metronome. All this information has been compiled by scholars, such as Dolmetsch, Donington, Neumann, and Sachs (see the bibliography at the end of Ch. 34).

Quantz, in his text on flute playing, measured tempi by tracing them to the human pulse. His figures were later translated into metronome speeds. For example, a *Siciliano* 12/8 required 4 beats per measure at about ♩. = 52. The same pulse should be generally applied to movements in 12/8, as to the *Largo ma non tanto* in Bach's Concerto for Two Violins (see Ex. 385).

A question related to tempo concerns the slowing down of cadences that conclude a section. If not exaggerated, such ritards are stylistically justified. They must, however, not be applied as a matter of routine. C.P.E. Bach pointed out that a "concluding trill" should be slowed down only at the end of a piece, and that music of "fiery or sad" nature was to be played in strict tempo to its conclusion — in the first instance in order not to stop the momentum, in the second not to carry the sad expression too far.

Turning to dynamics, the so-called terrace dynamics, an alternation of soft and loud sections without intermediate shadings, relate only to music written for organ or harpsichord. Its general application would not conform to baroque practice, as little as would romanticized performances with excessive dynamic markings. The dynamic range was by far not as extensive as ours. Dramatic crescendos and diminuendos were still a thing of the future. Yet performers knew of subtle dynamic gradations within a melodic line. Music created in the "era of sensitivity" did not lack expressiveness. It was for good reason that C.P.E. Bach praised the clavichord, which had been his father's favored *clavier*, as an instrument that permitted dynamic shadings.

In the eighteenth century, the art of phrasing was an important part of music education. It was often left to the performer's taste, which explains the scarcity of phrasing marks in many baroque scores. In the case of Bach, the vacuum is filled by fairly frequent indications as, for instance, in the carefully phrased violin part of the "Christe eleison" in the B-minor Mass. Other sections of the Mass offer further examples, as do the scores of the *St. Matthew Passion*, a number of cantatas, the Brandenburg Concertos, and sonatas for various solo instruments. These phrasings, which are distinguished by much variety, are a guideline for marking those Bach scores that lack phrasing. It should be noted that baroque phrasing cannot be separated from articulation, ornamentation, and the "inequality of notes." Obviously, this presents problems in ensemble playing, which existed already in the old days. Quantz instructed "good leaders" to practice unmarked passages with the tutti players because, as he put it, the "greatest beauty in performing required that all play the same way."

Three of Bach's Brandenburg Concertos call for doubling of the string parts. For performances in large concert halls, the number of strings may also have to be augmented for the other three concertos, but it should be kept in line with the character of a chamber orchestra. In regard to both wind and string instruments, the practice of letting the number of players depend on a given situation can be traced back to Handel. Throughout the *Messiah* score he marked *con ripieno* (all strings) or *senza ripieno* (small string group) but altered the signs when he produced the work at different places and with different orchestras. Sometimes Handel's orchestral introductions, though marked *forte* bear the sign *senza ripieno*, but, when the same passage is repeated, we find the sign *con ripieno*. This would not make sense, unless we assume that Handel, seated at the keyboard while attacking a new tempo, felt more secure by having the beginning played only by the musicians placed near him. Once the pace was established, everyone could join in. This precaution now being superfluous, we may confidently start those numbers with full orchestra.

Conductors should examine the printed keyboard parts needed for the baroque continuo. Some modern arrangements are too elaborate, others too monotonous. A continuo setting in Bach's hand can be studied in the Harpsichord Concerto No. 6 in F-major (BWV 1057), a transcription of the fourth Brandenburg Concerto. When rewriting the solo violin for the harpsichord, the composer combined the solo playing with continuo accompaniment.

For secco recitatives in oratorio and opera, the keyboard was joined by cello and doublebass (earlier by viola da gamba and violone). Chords, even when written in long notes in the score, could be shortened in performance. When Bach wrote out the

low string parts for the *St. Matthew Passion*, he used quarter-notes for those chords, with rests in between. It is difficult to understand, therefore, why some conductors insist on a persistently sustained bass line, even for the secco recitatives in Mozart operas.

About one-half of the twenty-seven instruments (not counting keyboard instruments) that Bach utilized have no equivalent in a modern orchestra. The tone color of those that still exist has changed due to differences in construction. To what degree the baroque style is approximated in a performance by a modern orchestra depends on the conductor's ideas and the musicians' ability to adjust their playing habits.

The conductor must decide how obsolete instruments are best replaced. The *flute à bec* can no longer be called obsolete thanks to the revival of recorders. Still, whether recorders, limited in sound volume, can be used for the fourth Brandenburg Concerto and other works of Bach, has to be determined in view of a hall's acoustics. The *cornetto* (no relation to the cornet!), a woodwind instrument of the once widely used family of *Zinken*, is found in scores of Bach, Handel, and Gluck. A trumpet usually serves as replacement, although the two instruments have little in common. Within the oboe family, an English horn must substitute for the *oboe da caccia* and the *oboe d'amore*, unless players trained to perform on the old instruments are available.

The piano has no place in the baroque orchestra. A harpsichord must be chosen, even if the acoustics make amplification necessary. When an organ is needed, a good electric organ may be preferable to a larger instrument with pipes whose construction does not lend itself to the baroque style.

Haydn

After the completion of the new edition of Haydn's symphonies, the formerly used, often greatly distorted, printed parts are now being replaced in orchestra libraries. A set of study scores includes textual notes, relating to source materials and allowing one to study alternate versions. Conductors should also consult H.C. Robbin Landon's book *Joseph Haydn and his Symphonies*, an important source of information in regard to all aspects of performance practice.

Haydn's habit of marking phrasing only partially did not pre-

sent a problem to his musicians who were familiar with their director's preferences. When supplementing unmarked passages with slurs, we cannot do better than emulate the composer's phrasing patterns. In the case of triplets, it is sometimes difficult to determine from an autograph whether a small slur calls for legato or is merely a triplet sign on top of detached notes. It might happen, therefore, that a conductor disagrees with an editor's choice.

Early Haydn and Mozart symphonies, scored for strings and a small wind group, were performed with harpsichord. The direction was divided between the concertmaster and the *maestro* at the keyboard who supported the orchestra by improvising his part in thoroughbass fashion. When the orchestral setting became more compact, the need for complementing it on the keyboard decreased. Yet, when Haydn directed his symphonies in London during the early 1790s, he was seated at the keyboard (during his first visit, a harpsichord, later a pianoforte) and would occasionally play a passage not indicated in the score. Generally speaking, a harpsichord should be added, at least to Haydn's first 40 symphonies.

Although the continuo keyboard in Haydn's late oratorios is scored for *cembalo*, a *hammerklavier* modeled after the early pianofortes seems to be more appropriate (see p. 344). Into the nineteenth century, the terms *cembalo* and *clavicembalo* remained in use but also applied to instruments with hammers.

Haydn's use of the trombones in "The Creation" and "The Seasons" can serve as a lesson in performance practice. The altos, tenors, and basses of a choir were at that time often supported by trombones (formerly, so were the sopranos, but the use of soprano trombones or *cornettos* had been discontinued). The participation of trombones was marked in the scores by *colla parte*, though details were usually worked out in rehearsal. Haydn, by writing out the trombone parts, left no doubt which choral passages needed brass support.

Mozart

Orchestra materials for a number of Mozart symphonies and concertos are available in the new Mozart edition (the abbreviation NMA stands for *Neue Mozart-Ausgabe*). Inaccurate parts must be corrected to conform to the authentic full scores.

A frequently occurring error, which can obscure Mozart's intentions regarding the tempo, is the incorrect printing of the signs C and ₵. We have the composer's written statement that an alla breve sign served to indicate a considerably quicker pace, although we cannot be certain that Mozart always used this sign to mark double tempo as taught by contemporary theorists. Equally important as relating to speed, an alla breve determines the metrical structure within the measure. In an Adagio C , for instance, the eighth-notes are the counting units, but in an Adagio ₵ the quarter-notes are so used.

Ex. 481: Marked ₵ by Mozart, the willful change to C has been perpetuated in all editions prior to the NMA. The music is felt in 4 calm pulses per measure, but the conductor may subdivide certain counts for clearer definition, as for the 32nd-notes in the timpani. Study the entire introduction to the symphony, keeping the subdivided beats very small and maintaining the flow of the music. (This introduction has been performed as slowly as ♪ = 63. Aside from ignoring the signature ₵ , such an interpretation disregards the relationship between the descending scales in bar 2 and their recurrence in bar 72ff. of the *Allegro*. See p. 343).

Adagio, (♩ = 50–54)   MOZART, *Symphony No. 39, K. 543*

As a general rule, our conducting patterns (which did not even exist in Mozart's days) must never interfere with the music's pulse. Primary concern is the feeling for the meter, while the number of beats is merely a practical consideration. The Andante ₵ in *Eine kleine Nachtmusik* (Ex. 37) is to be felt in two quiet units regardless of the conducting pattern. The same applies to movements in 2/4 or 6/8 time, when the tempo marking is Andante or faster.

Ex. 482: The angular pattern of a regular 4-beat would not allow a tender flow of the melodic line in this *Andante con moto*. A gracefully subdivided 2-beat is recommended (see p. 116). Richard Strauss suggested that this movement, as well as the movements quoted in Exx. 179 and 483, must be felt and "possibly conducted" without subdivision.

Ex. 483: A regular 6-beat would put undue emphasis on each eighth-count and fail to give life to the swaying repeated notes. Subdivision with a feeling of 2 pulses should be applied to the beginning and similar sections of the movement, but a different treatment is required for bars such as those quoted in Ex. 313.

Mozart was meticulous in the choice of tempo and could be critical of performers whom he believed to be guilty of rushing or dragging. He favored fluency but objected to pushing the speed to a point where the notes could no longer be heard distinctly. His tempo indications were carefully chosen within an established order of tempo categories, as demonstrated by corrections he made in his manuscripts. As a typical example, the first movement of the G-minor Symphony, K.550, was originally marked *Allegro assai*. This was crossed out by Mozart and replaced by the slower *Molto Allegro*, while *Allegro assai* remained for the much livelier finale of the symphony. For the slow movement in the String Quartet, K. 465, he changed *Adagio* to *Andante cantabile* to indicate a more fluent pace. Conductors should, therefore, not fall for the temptation to perform the Andante cantabile in the "Jupiter" Symphony (Ex. 179) as an Adagio!

The following list of tempo categories conforms to the order found in textbooks that were in use in Mozart's days. They were divided into four groups: slow, moderately slow, moderately fast, and fast.

Grave	Moderato
Largo	Allegretto
Adagio	
	Allegro
Larghetto	Allegro molto
Andantino	Allegro assai
Andante	Presto
	Prestissimo

It should be noted that Larghetto was included in the Andante group, that Andantino was slightly slower than Andante, and that Allegro assai indicated a speed almost as fast as Presto.

Numerous modifying words filled the need for differentiation. Using Andante as an example, Mozart added words such as *cantabile, sostenuto, moderato, or maestoso* to ask for a somewhat slower pace, while a more flowing Andante was marked by *con moto* or *molto. Più andante* ("more going") was an equivalent to *più mosso.*

The minuet tempo deserves a special word. Mozart distinguished between the regular minuet, mostly marked Allegretto, and the slow minuet which he called "Italian" (see p. 326). The regular minuet had one pulse to the measure, at a speed of ♩. = 56–66. The slower type, often marked "Tempo di Menuetto" as in the *Rondeau* of the Violin Concerto in A-major (K. 219), called for a more deliberate pace, ♩ = ca. 96. When the 14-year-old Mozart first encountered the slow minuet in Bologna, he was surprised that it had "so many notes" and, therefore, required a slower tempo.

Like Mozart's tempo indications, his markings for dynamics show care and musical logic. They must, of course, be understood within the practice of his time.

Ex. 484: The woodwinds end softly, although the last note of their phrase coincides with a *forte* in the other instruments. Musical logic prevailed over considerations of balance, whereby it must be remembered that the relatively moderate *forte* sound of Mozart's orchestra made the contrast less noticeable (see Ex. 481 for the beat pattern).

The two different uses to which Mozart put the *fp* sign are explained in his father's *Violinschule*: it could indicate a strong and sudden accent or a moderately emphatic attack followed immediately by a decrescendo. The first type, creating a dramatic effect, appears frequently in Mozart's operas, as in the second finale of *Don Giovanni* during the Commendatore scene. Examples for the second type are found in the overture to *Le Nozze di Figaro*.

Ex. 485: Musical and technical reasons speak against a literal *fp*. As to the low strings, the bow action makes it virtually impossible to play four equally strong notes in quick succession before a sudden *p*, nor can the violins sustain a *forte* until lifting the bow for the retake needed to begin the subsequent passage in *p*. Accordingly, the first half in bars 1 and 3 must be played *f* $>$ *p* by the entire orchestra.

Ex. 486: The playful nature of this theme calls for a quick diminuendo after the downbeats in bars 1–6, rather than for drastic accents (see p. 368).

Ex. 481: In bar 2, literal observance of the notation would make the strings sustain the *forte* for the entire half-note in contradiction to the *piano* in the winds. It can be assumed that Mozart expected the winds to make a decrescendo leading to *piano*.

Mozart indicated staccato by dots or wedges. Wedges, in the shape of small vertical lines, had long been in use before the appearance of dots. Now, wedges served a double purpose: to shorten a note or to give emphasis to a note, short or long. Mozart's inconsistent use of the two signs can be confusing, as in the passage quoted in Ex. 16. In the autograph, some of the 16th-notes are marked with dots, others with wedges. Here, as in many other cases, editors and performers have no choice but to rely on their judgment.

Ex. 487: The first three notes of the melody have wedges, but only the first two are short. The third wedge calls for an accent (like "leaning on a note") on the sustained A, which is tied to the next note. The *fp* signs in the accompaniment must be understood as $f > p$. In the last measure, the autograph again shows Mozart's inconsistency: dots are mixed with wedges.

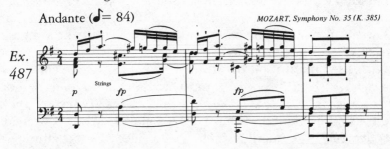

The proper application of "strength" and "weakness" within a melodic phrase was discussed in all textbooks of the time. Mannerisms resulting in faulty accents were criticized, often with reference to the reciting of poetry. Just as a spoken line could be spoiled by undue stress to a word, music would suffer from wrong accentuation. A valuable source of information is D.G. Türk's *Klavierschule* (1789), which contains a detailed discussion of accentuation, embellishments, and other questions of interpretation.

A comprehensive study of Mozart's use of embellishments is still missing. Three chapters in his father's *Violinschule* deal with ornamentation but do not furnish answers to all questions. Edward Dannreuther's *Musical Ornamentation* contains a compilation of other contemporary sources that explain the meaning of ornamental symbols. In order to instruct their players properly, conductors should take advantage of this information.

Taking textual liberties with solo parts in the form of improvised embellishments and variations was not only legitimate practice in Mozart's days, but an essential part of instrumental and vocal training. At present, attempts are being made to revive what for a long time had been a lost art. It should be remembered, however, that only those musicians who mastered the craft of composition were considered competent to change the written text. The problem does not come up in orchestral music, because in ensemble playing performers were not supposed to go beyond the written ornamentation.

As a performer on the keyboard, Mozart excelled in the art of improvising variations, which played a special role in the *da capo* sections of slow movements. He was also among the first composers to discard the harpsichord. Since about 1777 he gave preference to the *hammerclavier*, then called fortepiano. The instrument that he purchased around 1782 is still in existence. When in Vienna, he used it for all solo appearances and also for accompanying in the opera pit. Its sound, different from a harpsichord and a modern piano, fits perfectly into the orchestral texture of Mozart's orchestra.

An instrument used by Mozart for its distinctive color is the basset horn. It must not be replaced by a bass clarinet. Conductors should see to it that a pair of basset horns are part of the orchestra's equipment and that clarinet players are encouraged to practice the instrument, which is also needed for a number of Richard Strauss's works.

Chapter 34

PERFORMANCE PRACTICE (II)

Beethoven

LITTLE IS KNOWN about Beethoven as conductor of his works, but reports tell about the way he performed his piano music. He insisted on a perfect legato to produce a singing tone. Calling himself a "tone poet," he regarded music a means to project his most personal emotions and visions. Thus, his playing was highly expressive, even rhetorical, and marked by tempo modifications that could be combined with drastic dynamic effects, such as broadening the pace for a big crescendo. Still, he was intent on rhythmic precision and on setting the right basic tempo. Much can be learned about Beethoven's performance style from Carl Czerny's comments on the composer's piano works, including his chamber music and concertos (they are available in English translation). Czerny had first-hand knowledge of Beethoven's intentions, probably more so than any other pupil, which makes his detailed notes and metronome suggestions a valuable source of information.

Beethoven's symphonies include a total of 60 metronome indications. More than twenty seem to fit the music perfectly. Some of the remaining markings appear to be "on the fast side"; a few even suggest misjudgment, as can be expected whenever a composer determines the metronome without testing the speed repeatedly in performance.

If we keep in mind that the metronome's function does not go beyond determining the tempo character of a composition, accepting Beethoven's markings at face value would be as wrong as dismissing them altogether. The metronome $\eighthnote = 92$ for the Larghetto in the Second Symphony (Ex. 89) is among those markings that have met with disbelief. Yet, this indication may have made sense to the composer. First, the time signature 3/8 calls for a light flow of the melody; secondly, in his arrangement for piano trio Beethoven amended the marking to "Larghetto quasi Andante" (in line with 18th-century tradition, see p. 341). Most important, there is reason to assume that $\eighthnote = 92$ was meant to indicate the upper speed limit for the entire movement which, according to testimony, was to be played with tempo modifications. Aside from speeding, or slowing, a number of passages, the secondary theme (beginning at measures 75 and 239) was to have the character of an Allegretto. Starting the movement at $\flat = 84$, which appears to be appropriate for the main theme, would remain within a reasonable tempo span.

Significant conclusions can be drawn from the way Beethoven used metronome indications within the same work, no matter how inconclusive his tempo markings may have been. The first movement of the *Pastoral* Symphony is marked Allegro ma non tanto 2/4, $\downarrow = 66$. The metronome for the Allegro 2/4 in the third movement is $\downarrow = 132$, which clearly indicates that, in the composer's mind, the two tempi were to be identical. The soundness of his judgment, however, has been questioned. Although most conductors accept Beethoven's metronome in the third movement, they contend that the speed for the beginning of the symphony is excessive and that the music calls for a 2-beat. Perhaps they forget that Beethoven, not concerned with beating patterns, wished to make sure that the first movement was felt in one leisurely pulse per measure. In fact, the "ma non tanto" would not have made sense if combined with the marking $\downarrow = 132$. In practical terms, if we again assume that Beethoven's metronome refers to the upper speed limit for the entire movement within a span of $\downarrow = 56$–66, a 2-beat at $\downarrow = 112$ would not rush the beginning and would allow for a flexible pacing of the movement, which contains numerous passages that lend themselves convincingly to a 1-beat without jeopardizing the conductor's control. In the third movement, however, the impetuous rustic dance was conceived in two forceful beats; hence the metronome $\downarrow = 132$.

Beethoven carefully checked and rechecked the metronome chart for the Ninth Symphony at various times. Even if his metronome may not have been entirely accurate, he would certainly have noticed any significant deviation from one beat per second once he had put the movable weight of the pendulum on 60. It seems unlikely, therefore, that he was far off the mark when he indicated $\downarrow = 60$ for the Adagio molto e cantabile 4/4. It has been said, with some justification, that Beethoven, when determining the metronome speeds for his first six symphonies, saw these works, composed much earlier, in a different light from when they were conceived. This argument, however, would not be valid in the case of the Ninth. Interestingly, its autograph shows that "e cantabile" was added in large letters as a modifying afterthought to the original, much smaller, "Adagio molto." "Cantabile" held a special meaning for Beethoven, who once said, "Good singing was my guide; I strove to write as flowingly as possible. . . ." When played at ♩ = 40, as the Adagio has often been performed, the melody is no longer singable in terms of human song. Moreover, the second subject of the movement, Andante moderato 3/4, is marked ♩ = 63, leaving no doubt that Beethoven felt little difference in the pacing of the two themes.

Another disputed metronome marking in the Ninth Symphony concerns the Trio of the second movement, Presto ₵, ♩ = 116 (o = 116, found in some editions, was a printer's error). The preceding Molto vivace 3/4, ♩. = 116, leads directly into the Trio with a stringendo of 8 bars. What the composer's intentions were can only be guessed. The implicit tempo relation is as puzzling as the sudden throwback to a measured and seemingly slow 2-beat after an exciting increase in speed. Erasures and instructions to the copyist in the autograph show that the Trio had been planned as a Presto 2/4, but was changed by turning two 2/4 bars into one alla breve bar throughout the Trio (note that the marking Presto, ♩ = 116, makes good sense when applied to a 2/4 meter!). As one of several solutions, none of which can claim authenticity, one might reduce the tempo somewhat after the fermata in bar 395. This allows for an acceleration, but still permits the tempo relation ♩. = ♩ from the last 3/4 measure to the first alla breve bar. Conductors' preferences vary widely in regard to the speed of the Presto. Some stay close to Beethoven's metronome by playing the Trio at ♩ = 126, others take it as fast as ♩ = 152. The "poco ritard." at the end of the Trio speaks against exaggerated speed, because slowing down just for the concluding bar would be meaningless if the tempo is rushed.

The meaning of traditional signs is often subject to a composer's habits. In Beethoven's scores, a simple *f* frequently replaces a *sf*, both in *forte* and *fortissimo* passages. In soft passages, the word *dolce* is used, not to ask for still softer playing, but to indicate a gentle espressivo.

In a letter written in 1825, Beethoven complained about a copyist who had failed to pay attention to details in copying the score of the string quartet, Op. 132. Everything, he wrote, was to be copied exactly according to the manuscript, in particular, slurs and dynamics. For staccato, he pointed out that "it is not indifferent" whether to put wedges or dots. Early prints of Beethoven's symphonies still made this distinction, which is entirely neglected in present editions.

Ex. 488: A set of handwritten parts for the Seventh Symphony, still extant, had been corrected by the composer for its first performance. From these corrections we can conclude that, after a fully sustained quarter-note (*ten.*), the 2 eighth-notes, played up-bow and down-bow, are to be detached sharply before the on-the-string portato in the 2nd bar (see Ex. 352).

Eighteenth-century practice did not require sustaining each note to its full value. Consequently, the *tenuto* sign served to preclude, in the absence of a slur, a break before the following note. *Ten.* appears in Mozart scores, as in the first movement of the Symphony in E-flat major (K. 543). Beethoven, continuing the tradition, applied it importantly to the main themes in the finale of his violin concerto and of the *Coriolanus* Overture (see Ex. 384).

It is often assumed that all trills in Beethoven's music are to begin on the main note. Actually, he never abandoned entirely the eighteenth-century custom of starting trills on the auxiliary, as can be seen from measured trills, such as in the Sixth Symphony (second movement, solo flute, bar 131) or in the Ninth (third movement, 1st violins, bar 129). Moreover, Beethoven's fingerings in his piano music show alternate use of the two styles.

Ex. 489: In the 2nd violins, the melodic line calls for a trill starting on the main note, while in violas and bassoons it must begin on the auxiliary. Repeating the E in the lower voice would weaken the impact.

The absence of grace notes at the end of a trill does not always mean that the composer would have objected to an "after-beat."

Ex. 89: For the Larghetto theme in the Second Symphony, the after-beat is not marked in the score but is found in Beethoven's arrangement of the work for piano trio. The trill itself should begin on the upper note. Repeating the C♯ would interfere with *cantabile* playing.

Ex. 490: Here, the trill has a written exit. Opinions differ on whether to start it on the main or the upper note. Repeating the C♯ gives stronger impact to the *sf*; also, it brings out more effectively the broken chord of the dominant-seventh.

The treatment of grace notes, especially when appearing in groups of two or three notes, varied in Beethoven's days. No rule determined whether such ornaments were to be played on the beat or to be anticipated. Sometimes, grace notes slurred to a downbeat note demand anticipation, although they are written after the bar line.

Ex. 491: It is inconceivable that Beethoven would have expected the winds to play the *gruppetti* on the downbeat.

Exx. 492a and b: Although tied to the following notes, these grace notes must be anticipated.

Ex. 493: Two grace notes in the form of an ascending third were usually played on the beat.

Ex. 494: These grace notes have been interpreted in three different ways. The first and second styles conform to optional practice in Beethoven's time. The third, now adopted by many conductors, came into use around 1920. The first style deserves preference, because repeating the same note on three successive downbeats seems alien to the composer's manner of shaping a melody. Moreover, for a later-occurring variation, Beethoven let the note D, not the B, fall on the downbeat.

The interpretation of the grace notes in the *Marcia funebre* of the Third Symphony remains controversial. Some conductors insist on playing the grace notes in the double basses on the beat. Others, who believe that they should be anticipated, refer to the repeat in the *Minore*. There the notation is changed, in one instance, from grace notes to a triplet before the bar line. The autograph has long disappeared and the sources are not always conclusive, which explains why some details in the present editions of the *Eroica* are based on editors' guesswork. The following example speaks in favor of anticipated triplet figures.

Ex. 495: A comparison between an entry in one of Beethoven's sketchbooks and the final version is of interest. Originally, the composer had the strings play the triplet in the 9th measure on the downbeat. For the final version, he changed his mind, putting the triplets before the bar line.

Uncertainty also exists in regard to a passage preceding the repeat in the *Eroica's* first movement.

Ex. 496: In early prints, bars 150 and 151 are repeated, thus extending the end of the exposition by two bars. The *Revisionsbericht* in the Eulenburg study score leaves it to conductors to decide between the alternate versions. Especially when the repeat is observed, the longer version, allowing four bars for the decrescendo, seems more appropriate than the shorter one. It must be remembered that repeating the exposition had been an afterthought on the part of the composer after a first hearing of the work at a private concert. Only then did he write the first ending and have his brother mail it to the publisher, which perhaps accounts for the textual confusion.

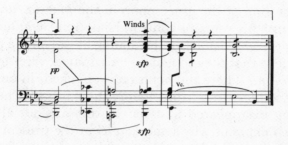

Beethoven's firm decision to have the exposition in the *Eroica* repeated is the more noteworthy, as the work was then criticized for being too long. The change must have been motivated by the composer's regard for structural balance. Although structural weight in music is to be measured by substance as well as by duration, an exposition of merely 155 bars, followed by a development section of 246 bars, and a recapitulation (including the coda) of 294 bars would have been no more than an introduction of ideas without carrying the weight that Beethoven wished to impart to the exposition within the movement's total form.

Arguments about the merits of observing repeat signs are of long standing. F. A. Habeneck (1781–1849), whom Wagner respected as an outstanding interpreter of Beethoven's symphonies, used to skip all repeats. Felix Weingartner, regarded to be no less of an expert a century later, recommended not repeating the expositions in the first movements of Beethoven's third, fourth, sixth, and seventh symphonies. In our time, many conductors take a different stand, with the Seventh remaining the only one whose first movement is generally believed to be more effective when the repeat sign is disregarded.

Music in the Romantic Era

The heading is taken from the title chosen by Alfred Einstein for his informative and highly readable book on romanticism in music. In regard to performance practice, it must be kept in mind that early romantic composers, including Schubert, Mendelssohn, Schumann, and Berlioz, did not expect their music to be treated in a willful manner. Schubert, for one, insisted that his markings were to be observed meticulously, that nothing was to be added, and a steady tempo maintained at all times. It was Liszt and Wagner who turned to individualism in music interpretation. Liszt's numerous pupils, and conductors under Wagner's influence, included some of the most prominent performers of their time. They promoted the new trend, which was to cast its shadow well into our century.

This raises the question of whether the liberties taken by the proponents of the Liszt-Wagner school were essentially different from those suggested, for instance, in Spohr's teachings (see p. 331). One need only read the instructions that Hans von Bülow gave his students regarding the interpretation of Beethoven's fifth piano concerto to recognize that what had formerly been minor modifications had now become drastic alterations. What had been a desire to bring music to life through subtle shadings and inflections had now turned into demonstrative manipulation. As a typical and fairly recent example, a conductor grown up in this tradition would start the Allegro vivace in Schubert's Overture to *Die Zauberharfe* (D. 644) at a speed of $\d = 92$, but make an abrupt accelerando in the 24th bar, leading to $\d = 126$ for the tutti entrance.

Letters, memoirs, and other contemporary writings tell about nineteenth-century performance practice and provide a wide field of study for curious conductors. Some of the source material has been presented by scholars in musical periodicals and other publications. The following brief comments, limited to a small number of composers, bring up points of particular interest to conducting students and are meant to encourage further investigation.

Schubert

Of Schubert's orchestral works the first three symphonies are available in the new Schubert Edition. Symphony No. 8 can be studied in its authentic form thanks to the facsimile print of the autograph and two study score editions, both with textual notes. Current orchestra materials contain numerous errors. (According to the new Deutsch Catalog [1978], Schubert wrote only eight symphonies; the spurious No. 7 is no longer counted. Consequently, in the new numbering, the Unfinished is No. 7, and the "Great" C major is No. 8. It will no doubt take several years for the new numbering to become generally accepted. These two symphonies are therefore listed in this book according to the old numbering.)

The correct time-signature for the introduction of Symphony No. 9 is alla breve. The marking C, which appears in all editions, is misleading. If "felt in four," the opening theme loses the character of a merry *Wanderlied* and deprives the downbeat accents of their natural impact (see Ex. 306). Consequently, they are often "underplayed" in performance. Moreover, the repeat of the theme at the end of the movement (bars 672ff.) must relate to the introduction.

Schubert's habit of writing overly large accent signs can be confusing. Editors have sometimes mistaken them for diminuendo, as in the final measure of Symphony No. 9. Here, the huge accent sign is combined with a *sf*, a combination not unusual in Schubert's manuscripts. Also, he frequently used this sign to accentuate a phrase. (Diminuendo signs that indicate a phrase accent appear occasionally in Beethoven's scores, as in the Leonore Overture No. 1, bar 112; Brahms used it frequently, as in his Second Symphony, third movement, bar 4.)

Ex. 497: The diminuendo sign is a phrase accent. It does not lead from *pp* to a still softer sound, but calls for a slight increase in volume in bar 4, leading back to *pp*.

Ex. 90: The autograph leaves no doubt about Schubert's intention. The signs in bars 25 and 27 are accents. Therefore, the *p* in bar 29 is to be understood as a piano subito.

Of Schubert's 87 metronome indications, 65 belong to the opera *Alfonso und Estrella*, the others to songs. Although limited in number, they tell a story: all the songs, and most of the vocal pieces in the opera, are marked to perfection, but for several orchestral sections the metronome seems to exceed a reasonable speed. In other words, when guided by the sung word, the composer was on safe grounds, but disregard for orchestral limitations made him misjudge some of the quick tempi. There is more to learn: "Andante molto," for Mozart still a lively Andante, now signified a slow Andante. Andantino was now considered to be faster than Andante. Larghetto, however, still in the tradition of Mozart and Beethoven, was only slightly slower than Andante.

Furthermore, Schubert's metronome markings prove the significance of the alla breve sign. Even for a song as slow as *Der Wanderer (Sehr langsam* ¢, ♩ = 63) he did not choose 4/4 as time-signature, but marked it alla breve — too slow for the metronome's calibration (♩ = 31). In contrast, *Der Tod und das Mädchen*, with the indication *Mässig* (= Andante) ¢, ♩ = 54, was to be felt in 2 sustained, but not overly slow, beats.

Mendelssohn

Mendelssohn's and Schumann's rather frequent use of the metronome is more revealing than their Italian or German tempo markings. In general, overly fast or slow speeds were avoided. Larghetto, Andante, Andantino, and alla breve were applied as in Schubert's scores. Mendelssohn, for many years a busy conductor, was known for elegance, precision, and a gentle expressiveness. It is no wonder that he was attacked by Wagner, who criticized his readings of the classic masters for being superficial. As a teacher, Mendelssohn categorically forbade any unmarked ritardando and wanted written tempo modifications to be kept to a minimum. He disliked sentimentality, recommended a flowing pace, but objected to nervous rushing. A pupil of the composer stated, in 1880, that conductors performed Mendelssohn's works "much too slowly."

Mendelssohn's letters make for interesting reading. From his correspondence with Ferdinand David, who premiered the Violin Concerto, Op. 64, we learn details about the performance of this work. We also read that, in spite of admiration for Liszt's genius, Mendelssohn was critical of his exaggerations in the performance of classic composers and of his lack of respect for the printed text.

Schumann

To quote from Schumann's writings: "It is equally bad to drag as to rush. — Don't strive for bravura; try to produce the impression the composer had in mind, anything else would be distortion. — If you want to grow, associate with scores, not with virtuosos."

Unfortunately, Schumann's choice of German words for tempo markings does not always help to read his mind. "Ziemlich langsam," for instance, for the introduction of his Fourth Symphony, was meant to be the equivalent of "Andante con moto," as can be seen from the first version of the work. Conductors can be misled by the German words, unless they trust the composer's metronome.

It has been said that Schumann's metronome was faulty, a statement that is neither provable nor likely. The thirteen piano pieces in his cycle *Kinderscenen* lack tempo indications, but are marked with metronome. Some of these markings are readily accepted by pianists; others are firmly rejected. The pace for the famous *Träumerei*, ♩ = 100, seems overly fast and was adjusted to ♩ = 80 by the composer's foremost interpreter, his wife Clara. Pianists who choose a slower tempo forget that the music was meant to reflect the dream of a child, not of a sentimental teenager. Generally speaking, early romantic composers did not want their slow movements performed with excessive languor.

Berlioz

Unhappy experiences with conductors who failed to grasp the spirit of his music made Berlioz take up conducting. From his writings we know about his ideas regarding interpretation. Present music writers would classify him as a "literal" conductor. He expected from the performers strict observance of every marking, insisted on firm rhythm, and expressed displeasure with what he called the "sempre tempo rubato" style of the Wagnerites. Speaking of the conductor's individual feeling, Berlioz remarked: "The question here does not concern the conductor's but the composer's feeling. Therefore, composers must not neglect marking their works with metronome indications and it is the conductor's duty to study them well. For conductors to neglect this study is committing an act of improbity."

Ideas about performance are part of Berlioz's *Traité d'instrumentation* and are also reflected in his very personal way of scoring. The doubling of bassoons, the combination of two trumpets with two cornets, divided strings, and other new devices—all this shows an intense involvement both in the potential of each instrument and the exploration of the total orchestral sound. Berlioz was essentially a dramatic composer and his orchestral writing must be seen in the light of his operas and choral works.

Orchestra parts of Berlioz's compositions are heavily edited. An authentic edition of the scores is under way. Some standard works, including the *Symphonie fantastique,* are already available. The Largo ($\downarrow = 56$) at the beginning represents another case where the metronome is more enlightening than the Italian term, which might suggest a slower pace than intended for the melody, which recalls a love song written when the composer was in his teens (in his memoirs, Berlioz quotes the words underlying the music).

Wagner

No other composer has given instructions to conductors as specific as those published by Wagner for the performance of the Overture to *Tannhäuser* and the 1st act Prelude to *Die Meistersinger*. Not included in the scores, his comments must be looked up in the composer's collected writings—which may explain why they are rarely observed. True, Wagner's turgid prose can be confusing, and available English translations are unsatisfactory, but the wishes of a great composer-conductor ought not to be neglected. In Appendix B, the instructions are presented in a wording which, it is hoped, will be helpful.

Confusion has also been caused by Wagner's unrealistic metronome markings. If performed according to metronome, the playing time of the *Tannhäuser* Overture would be at least fifteen minutes. However, Wagner stated that, under his direction, it lasted only twelve minutes. In contrast to the metronome for the beginning, $\downarrow = 50$, he wanted this music to be played "not dragging, in walking motion," so a speed of about $\downarrow = 60$ would be more in line with his intention. It is no wonder that Wagner despaired about using the metronome and discarded it after *Tannhäuser*.

Authentic modifications of the printed text in Wagner's operas were preserved by Felix Mottl. Included in the full scores, and vocal scores, published by C. F. Peters, they are an indispensable source of information for conductors.

Wagner believed that music can be brought to life only by a freely shaped melodic line, for which he used the Greek word *melos*. Within this line, however, he insisted on strict rhythm, such as dotted notes and unhurried triplets. In the interest of the music's broad flow, he wanted Allegro passages in 4/4 time to be directed with a 2-beat whenever possible (see Ex. 388). He liked a full orchestral sound with a minimum of 32 violins, 12 violas, 12 celli, and 8 basses. The brass had to have power and brilliance; the solo woodwind players had to perform with intensity and expression. Yet, for his operas, the composer expected every word to be projected clearly from the stage and established the rule that, for all sung passages, the dynamic signs in the orchestra were to be lowered by one degree: a *p* became a *pp, mf* was changed to *p,* and so on.

In the Overture to *Rienzi,* and occasionally in other scores, Wagner used turns to begin on the lower note. Most of the time, however, turns in his operas start on the upper note, always in accordance to notation.

Wagner's sometimes overly long slurs in string passages leave the bowing up to the players. Like Richard Strauss, Wagner was in favor of "free bowing." He was not an expert at writing for the harp. The harp part in *Tannhäuser* must be arranged to be playable. In *Isoldes Liebestod*, rewriting the part from B-major to Cb-major is welcomed by harpists.

Brahms

Some textual changes made by Brahms after the publication of his scores are missing in the edition of his collected works. A copy of *Ein Deutsches Requiem*, used by the composer for conducting, contains black and red marks to modify tempo, phrasing, dynamics, and orchestration. Particularly with regard to the music's pacing, Brahms avoided being too specific in printed editions. Metronome indications were included in the original score of the *Requiem*, but later omitted. Among Brahms's orchestral works, only the second Piano Concerto has printed metronome markings, all of which seem well-chosen.

Regarding the performance of his Fourth Symphony the composer remarked:

I have entered some tempo modifications in the score with pencil. For a first performance they may be useful, even necessary. Unfortunately, they often appear then in print (in my works and those of others)—where in most cases they do not belong. Such exaggerations are needed only as long as orchestras (or soloists) are not familiar with a work. Then I often find myself that I cannot do enough pushing or holding back to come near the desired expression, passionate or quiet. Once a work has been completely absorbed, such markings should, in my opinion, be discarded. The more one deviates from this rule, the less artistic, I believe, the performance becomes. I experience frequently with my older compositions how everything just falls into place and how superfluous some of those markings are! However, nowadays people like to make a big impression with what they call a free artistic interpretation. . . .

Two signs for dynamics, then no longer in use, were revived by Brahms: the ambiguous *pf* and $>$ for accenting a phrase (see p. 354); *pf*, originally standing for *piano* followed by *forte*, later turned into an abbreviation of *poco forte*. In Brahms's scores, *poco forte* is often written out and calls for a sound level between *mf* and *f*.

When Brahms started composing for orchestra, most double bass players had abandoned the old system of tuning the four strings in fifths, with C as the lowest pitch. Except for the *Requiem* where, for the concluding section of No. 3, some players must lower the E-string to D, Brahms refrained from writing notes below E. The same is true for Wagner beginning with *Tannhäuser* (in *Tristan und Isolde* he required lowering the E-string to C#, but not until *Parsifal* did he expect to find players with five-string instruments). Opinions differ as to what extent double bass players should take advantage of the C-string when performing Brahms. Similar changes have never been suggested for Wagner's works, perhaps because he skillfully avoided awkward shifting of octaves. In the case of Brahms, one might point to piano arrangements of orchestral works in which he sometimes utilized the lower range on the keyboard. Nevertheless, conductors must not sanction alterations without careful study of the musical context.

If we are to believe reports by musicians who performed Brahms's symphonies under his direction, the composer would not have approved of the rushed tempi we now sometimes hear. His music making was relaxed. The kind of excitement that is kindled by a hard-driven pace was not germane to Brahms's nature. Nor would he have been happy with the changes that have been inflicted on the timpani part in the Coda that concludes his First Symphony. He might have wondered whether adding a roll, or altering the rhythm, would give a deeper meaning to his music and its message.

Bruckner

Bruckner's symphonies have been published in several different versions. In some cases it is questionable whether an "original" version presents the composer's final thought. Reliable information is found in Deryk Cooke's résumé *The Bruckner Problem Simplified*.

The tempo markings in the first editions, heavily edited by the composer's assistants, do not always conform to the original ones. Partial metronome indications were added by the editors who, we can assume, knew about their master's intentions.

Three of Bruckner's symphonies require a quartet of Wagner tubas. These instruments, rarely used in the repertory, must be kept in good shape to produce a satisfactory sound. To allow ample time for practice, instruments and parts must be available to the players several weeks prior to rehearsals. Even then, intonation problems must be worked out in sectional rehearsals, preferably in combination with the other brass players.

In interpreting Bruckner's music, the conductor's foremost task is to present a reading that puts all the segments of a broadly conceived symphonic form into proper proportion. The very genesis of Bruckner's music points to structural problems. With the composer's consent, segments of his symphonies were cut, then restored, then altered again. Even Wilhelm Furtwängler, a prominent interpreter of this music, omitted certain passages in the printed score during the early years of his conducting career (at that time he also shortened the second movement of Schubert's Ninth). In our days, Bruckner enthusiasts frown on any tampering with the text, although a look into the background of the Third Symphony reveals the impossibility of determining what the correct text is. These comments do not imply a critique of Bruckner's music but want to impress on young conductors that the interpretation of these monumental works is a challenging undertaking that goes far beyond learning the score.

Late Romantic Music

Almost one-half of this chapter has been devoted to questions related to the performance of Beethoven's works, questions more numerous than those to be solved in the interpretation of the masters who followed him. In particular, when performing music written during the past 100 years, conductors can rely on a method of scoring that includes instructions more complete and more precise than those in older music. Looking at Mahler's scores, for instance, the new method is evident from the first to the last page. The composer's subsequent revisions have been mentioned. As compared to the first editions, the final versions of Mahler's symphonies contain significant changes in regard to orchestration and dynamics, which goes to show that, although an experienced conductor, Mahler was not immune to misjudgment.

Strauss's ability as an orchestrator is as remarkable in his early scores as in later works. His indications of dynamics, carefully calculated for each instrument, are a built-in protection against imbalances, planned to let every leading voice, both in the orchestra and from the opera stage, stand out distinctly. Strauss was unhappy when his signs were not observed. Why was it, he asked, that balance was achieved when he conducted but all too often neglected under other conductors' direction? (It must not be forgotten that Strauss led with small gestures and a minimum of physical effort.) "Tempi! Metronome!" was another of his demands. On the other hand, his mind was open to practical considerations: for his orchestration of a song (*Wiegenlied*, Op. 41, 1), he provided two sets of violin figurations to be used, depending on the tempo that best suited the singer's breath technique.

Most French scores, from Bizet and Saint-Saëns to Debussy and Ravel, leave few doubts about the composers' intentions. The French leaning toward practical reasoning, together with expertise in orchestration, produced a technique of scoring that rarely brings up questions other than those whose solution requires familiarity with the music's style, based on broad knowledge of French music in general. Pierre Monteux's and Charles Münch's interpretations proved that variances in detail are compatible with preserving an idiomatic reading. As to the adherence to the composer's text, French musicians of that period, following in the steps of Berlioz, rejected unjustified liberties. We recall Debussy making mockery of the "universal nightmare" caused by the "transcendental interpretation" of masterworks, and Ravel chiding a famous conductor for the "ridiculous" treatment of one of his compositions.

Russian composers of the late nineteenth-century felt no differently regarding the interpretation of their works. Rimsky-Korsakov's memoirs tell about conductors taking unwarranted liberties and misjudging tempi. Craftsmanship in orchestral scoring was of a high order among Russian composers of that generation, including explicit marking and well-chosen metronome indications. Nicolai Malko, a conductor whose musical education was rooted in the best tradition of his country, remarked that Tchaikovsky wanted his symphonies played "like Beethoven." This would speak against a present trend to exploit Tchaikovsky's music for a conductor's ego-trip, much in contrast to the admirable self-discipline that distinguished this composer's lifework.

Comments on performance practices in nineteenth-century opera will be part of a later chapter.

Bibliography

This list of publications in the field of performance practice is limited to works published in English. The selection has been made in view of a young conductor's needs. Most of the books include reference to sources for further study. (Pb) indicates paperback edition.

Babitz, Sol. *Early Music Laboratory* (Series of Bulletins)

Bach, C. Ph. Em. *Treatise on Keyboard Playing*

Badura-Skoda, Eva and Paul. *Interpreting Mozart* (Pb)

Beethoven, Symphony No. 5, revised score with textual notes in German by Peter Gülke, published by C. F. Peters as part of a complete new set. (A volume containing symphonies Nos. 6–8 is expected to be published in 1980 as part of the Bonn Edition of Beethoven's works.)

Czerny, Carl. *On the Performance of Beethoven's Piano Works* (Pb)

Dannreuther, Edward. *Musical Ornamentation* (Pb)

Dart, Thurston. *The Interpretation of Music* (Pb)

Dolmetsch, Arnold. *The Interpretation of the Music of the 17th and 18th Centuries*

Donnington, Robert. *The Interpretation of Early Music*

Dorian, Frederick. *The History of Music in Performance* (Pb)

Emery, Walter. *Bach's Ornaments*

Keller, Hermann. *Phrasing and Articulation* (Pb)

Landon, H. C. Robbins. *Joseph Haydn and His Symphonies*

Mozart, Leopold. *Treatise on the Fundamental Principles of Violin Playing*

Neumann, Frederick. *Ornamentation in Baroque and Post-Baroque Music*

Norton Critical Scores. (Symphonies: Beethoven No. 5, Berlioz Fantastique, Mozart K. 550, Schubert No. 8) (Pb)

Quantz, Johann Joachim. *On Playing the Flute* (Pb)

Sachs, Curt. *Rhythm and Tempo*

Terry, Charles Sanford. *Bach's Ornamentation*

Tosi, Pier Francesco. *Observations on the Florid Song*

Türk, Daniel Gottlob. *School of Clavichord Playing* (a translation of Türk's *Klavierschule* by Raymond H. Haggh)

Vinquist, Mary, and Zaslaw, Neal. *Performance Practice: A Bibliography* (Pb)

Weingartner, Felix. *On the Performance of Beethoven's Symphonies* (Pb)

Chapter 35

PREPARATION OF ORCHESTRA MATERIALS

CAREFUL PREPARATION of orchestra parts requires many hours of work, but time and effort are well spent. Rehearsal hours, often restricted and costly, must be put to the best possible use. Verbal explanations to clear up textual questions not only waste the orchestra's time, but disrupt the momentum that is essential for effective rehearsing. The conductor must, therefore, see to it that parts, in good condition and properly marked, be ready for distribution to the players prior to the first rehearsal.

Examination of Materials

A distinction must be made between merely transferring into the orchestra parts those marks that the conductor had entered into the full score (see p. 316) and the more time-consuming collating of score and parts in regard to every textual detail. Only thorough examination of each part makes the parts conform to the correct text and assures the discovery of misprints.

Musicians cannot do their best when playing from poorly printed, torn, or messy parts. To be told "the material is so bad that we can hardly read the notes" is frustrating for a conductor who is about to bring out fine points of interpretation. Awkward page turns can also be annoying. They can upset coordination in the strings or ruin the effect of a forceful tutti attack. To arrange for page turning during a pause, a portion of a page may have to be rewritten and used as an insert. Other deficiencies to be watched include missing *arco* signs after a *pizzicato*, discrepancies regarding *con sordino* and *senza sordino* (strings and brass), and errors in the notation of clefs or key signatures.

Quick identification of any place in the score is of vital importance in rehearsal. The old system of rehearsal letters or numbers is less practical than the successive bar numbering found in newer editions. If bar numbers are missing, they should be added to the parts.

Marking Parts

Although conductors' views on the need and nature of supplementary markings vary, their usefulness is beyond question. Orchestra musicians prefer playing from well-marked parts to using erasers and pencils continually during rehearsal. They remember conductors who, while rehearsing a relatively simple and short work, had bowings and dynamics changed in every measure, with the result that the rest of the program remained under-rehearsed.

Whenever needed, partial indication of articulation must be completed. Frequently, the context leaves no doubt, as at the start of the 3rd movement of Beethoven's Sixth Symphony, where only the first four notes bear staccato dots. Similarly, in Ex. 452 it is clear that staccato playing goes on when the marking stops after four bars. Still, each case is to be judged on its merits, and analogy must not be made a rule in the absence of articulation signs.

Ex. 498: This example is typical of "streamlining," an editor's impulse to substitute analogy for the variety intended by the composer. After having played tongued notes for 4 bars, the clarinets change to slurring with the *pp*. To prevent a misunderstanding, Dvořák, in addition to the slurs, marked the 5th measure *legato*. Nevertheless, the older editions printed slurs for each of the six bars. (The new Dvořák edition, published in Prague, must be consulted for all the works of the composer.)

Ex. 498: Allegro con fuoco ♩ = 152 — DVORAK. Symphony No. 9 — legato

Ex. 356: The 16th-notes in bar 2 are not marked staccato. Beethoven wanted the *pp* in the 3rd measure to coincide with a change of bowing style. The staccato must not be "given away" while the winds still play legato.

Ex. 165: In older editions, several legato signs were added to Haydn's text, another instance of analogy replacing the intended variety.

Aside from articulation and phrasing (along with breathing signs for the winds), useful information to be entered into orchestra parts includes: the number of beats per measure that the conductor intends to use; skipping of repeats, holds and breaks; and ritards that exceed minor tempo modifications.

Signs for dynamics are entered to replace the printed ones or to provide additional information. Usually, they serve to improve orchestral balance, be it to prevent one group of instruments from overpowering another or to help a solo player to be heard without forcing his tone. Sometimes signs are added for a special effect the conductor wishes to achieve, such as the expressive molding of a phrase or a cogent dramatic contrast.

Ex. 499: Note that Mozart's marking for this entire passage is simply *piano*! For the sake of "animation," Felix Weingartner recommended playing the first bar with crescendo, followed by a *piano subito* (six measures earlier, the same phrase was to be done "in simple piano"). For the rest of the example he suggested the following "phrasing."

Ex. 500: A sudden piano followed by a big crescendo is sometimes inserted for a strong buildup towards the end of a piece. Italian conductors follow an old tradition by inserting dynamics in bars 3–7. In the case of the Overture to *Don Pasquale*, this effect had the sanction of Arturo Toscanini.

Whatever the merits of added or changed dynamics, it must be kept in mind that the effect exercised on the players by written signs is quite different from the directions they receive by means of gestures. Unless planned with caution, written signs can lead to unwanted exaggerations that do not conform to the music's style. In general, a conductor should avoid overloading orchestra parts with pencil marks and trust his ability to communicate expression without the help of written signs. In Ex.

499, for instance, only the signs added to bars 10 and 11 and 14 and 15 can claim justification. Even here, espressivo playing in the low strings can be obtained just as effectively, and with more delicacy, by the conductor's gesture alone.

Still, there are cases when practical reasons demand a change of printed signs. Two examples follow, the first from Brahms's Symphony No. 1, the other from Mozart's Overture to *Le Nozze di Figaro*.

Ex. 355: It is advisable to replace the *f* in bar 5 by *meno forte*. String players rarely react properly to a simple *f* that immediately follows a *ff*. Any gesture to subdue the players for the sudden change of dynamics would have to be overly dramatic.

Ex. 486: Unless the strings are marked *pp* in bars 7 and 8, the staccato notes of oboes and flutes (edited orchestra parts erroneously print legato) are not heard sufficiently. Indicating the *pp* to the strings by a gesture would be too fussy. Counting on a pit orchestra with no more than 14 string players, Mozart could not have foreseen this problem. (For similar reasons, strings and brass must be marked *fp* in bars 262–263, 276–277, and 280–281 of the same overture.)

Bow Marking

Printed bowing signs began to appear sporadically in orchestral scores about 100 years ago. Russian and French composers made the start, while German musicians were slow in adopting the habit. In fact, Richard Strauss advocated individual bowing to allow each player to find the solution best suited to his technique. Yet, when acting as a conductor, Strauss would ask for a special bowing style, as for the beginning of Mozart's Symphony in G minor, K. 550. Here he preferred to have the violins start with down-bow.

Most present-day composers include bowing signs in their scores. By now unified bowing is taken for granted to such an extent that string players feel uncomfortable when asked to proceed on their own instead of emulating the concertmaster's bowing. Nevertheless, some string passages in the works of Wagner, Brahms, Bruckner, and Strauss profit from individual bowing.

Bowing signs have been added, anonymously, to string parts within the classic repertory. They are often pedantic, unimaginative, and distort the original phrasing. Whenever necessary, they must be corrected. Sound, expression, and rhythmic incisiveness depend to a considerable extent on bow action. A young conductor who has never played a string instrument can learn about bowing technique by playing chamber music with fine string players and by discussing all pertinent questions with the section leaders of the orchestra. In time, and with the help of some experimentation, he will develop sufficient know-how to mark string parts in line with his interpretative ideas. It would be unwise, however, not to change bowing signs, if during rehearsals other solutions turn out to be more effective. Also, preferences may differ from one string group to another.

As an example for marking a string part, Appendix C reproduces the first violin part of Mozart's Symphony No. 35.

Changing the Composer's Text

Some alterations of the printed text were discussed on the preceding pages. For a long time, conductors have taken it upon themselves to change notes, rhythms, orchestration, and the order of movements. If we add cuts, dynamics, and phrasing, a list of all the tamperings with scores might easily fill as many volumes as the music itself. Although arguments about the rationality of those more-or-less arbitrary changes are likely to continue as long as music is performed by human beings, it can be stated that, in the course of the last few decades, musicians have turned to respect the composer's text to a much higher degree than former generations. Many musical performers now believe that the aim of score study is not merely to learn *what* is written, but *why* the music was written in a certain way. Before questioning the validity of a composer's scoring, conductors are now inclined to give him, as it were, the benefit of the doubt!

Ex. 501a: For the return of the triplet motive (second time), the composer added violas and horns for fuller chords and a different tone color. In this new context, he lengthened the concluding notes to quarter-notes.

Ex. 501b: The trills (second violins) are longer the first time than in the repeat. This could be explained by the switch to the E string, which produces a sound different from that on the A string, or simply

by a composer's wish for variety. (Why shouldn't there be variety in music as in nature, which inspired the music!)

Ex. 501b

In neither case would it make good sense to establish an analogy that Beethoven had not intended.

In Haydn's and Mozart's scores it happens not infrequently that the concluding note at the end of phrase groups is of different length for one or several instruments as compared to the notation for the rest of the orchestra. Discrepancies of this kind do not always favor a unified ensemble. Still, the notation should not be altered without a study of the musical context.

Ex. 502: For 4 bars, the winds play dotted quarter-notes, the violins and violas eighth-notes, while the low strings are coordinated with the quarter-notes of the singers. The two last measures present a problem: to have the low strings continue with quarter-notes would not serve any apparent purpose, but would upset the ensemble. A change to eighth-notes is therefore suggested.

Ex. 502

Ex. 503a and b: In bar 3 of the first example, the beginning of the flute solo would be covered by the violins, unless their quarter-note is shortened to conform to the release of the winds. No such change would be in order in the 3rd measure of b, where the appogiatura on the downbeat justifies a slightly longer chord in the string accompaniment.

Ex. 504: In bars 2 and 4, the half-notes in low strings and bassoons must not be shortened, although they are sustained beyond the tutti chords. The three ponderous half-notes are an important musical statement, quoted from the opera's second finale where they echo the ghostly knocking at the door.

Changing the Orchestration

Conductors alter the composer's orchestration to clarify the thematic structure for the benefit of the listener or to obtain an orchestral sound that is more to their liking. These changes include shifting notes from one instrument to another, adding instruments for a fuller orchestral texture, or lightening it by letting some instruments pause. Furthermore, in view of technical imperfections that curtailed the composers' choices in former times, orchestra parts are adjusted to take advantage of our superior instruments.

Ex. 505: The horn passage that introduces the second theme of the movement (see Ex. 351) is given here to the bassoons, obviously because the notes A and B could not be produced on horns in E♭ in Beethoven's time. Most conductors find the bassoon sound inadequate in this context and have horns play the first 3 measures, either alone or in combination with the bassoons (sometimes the bassoons are supported by one horn only).

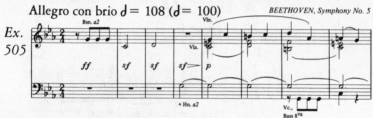

Ex. 506: To expect a bassoonist to play these low notes *pppppp*, as suggested by the overly anxious composer, would be unrealistic. A bass clarinet usually substitutes. (Thanks to electronic sound control, the substitution is not needed in recorded performances.)

Ex. 507: Even with doubled woodwinds, the inner voices do not stand out sufficiently unless horn and trumpet parts are changed. Three trumpets are needed for this arrangement. The violas, scored in unison with the celli, are more helpful when they participate in the melodic line (Schubert could not count on more than two or three celli as part of a small string group!). Arrangements of this type are suggested only for orchestras with large string groups performing in big halls.

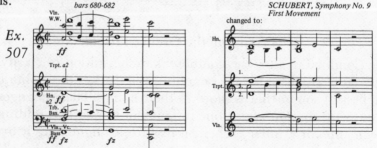

The change in Ex. 502 follows a recommendation of Felix Weingartner. Best known among his writings are the comments on the interpretation of Beethoven's symphonies (see the bibliography on p. 362). In spite of its controversial nature, Weingartner's study is a valuable introduction into the problems of orchestral balance in Beethoven's scores. Warned of these problems, a conductor is better prepared to find his own solutions.

Wagner was the first to revise the orchestration of Beethoven's symphonies and to publish his recommendations. In the second movement of the Seventh, for instance, he had the trumpets double the clarinets in bars 75-90, which meant leading the first trumpet to a high B in bar 84.

Ex. 508: The coordination of trumpets and timpani, typical of the classic style, was disregarded by Wagner (see p. 332). Having performed the work in this manner, he proudly reported: "The effect was so excellent that no one among the listeners felt to lose, but rather to gain, which on the other hand did not impress anyone as a novelty or a change." (Wagner's German prose is as confusing as this literal translation!)

BEETHOVEN, Symphony No. 7

Weingartner, who does not subscribe to Wagner's arrangement, suggests letting the second trumpet play the E an octave lower in the interest of better balance, a reasonable change in this particular case. Not all the alterations, however, that Weingartner recommends for second horn and second trumpet, should be accepted without examining the musical context.

Ex. 509a presents the original text, while Weingartner's changes have been added in Ex. 509b. The changes concern mostly dynamics. Also, in bars 5-7, the second horn is lowered by one octave. At first sight, analogy seems to speak in favor of this alteration. Yet, if the lower F would have been essential in the composer's mind, he could have given it to the second bassoon, just as he scored this instrument independently in the symphony's second movement. In this case, there is no compelling reason to alter Beethoven's text. Should the "a due" for the horns disturb the balance, the second horn pauses. Doubling the flute for the crescendo, as Weingartner suggests, can be useful, but his arbitrary additional markings for dynamics are questionable.

Ex.
509a

BEETHOVEN, *Symphony No. 1*
First Movement, bars 124-137

Ex.
509b

The authenticity of the *p* in the 13th bar of Ex. 509b is un-
certain, except for the first violins. The autograph, as for Beethoven's Symphonies Nos. 2 and 3, has disappeared. Still, it is to
be hoped that conductors will be less dependent on guessing once

the nine symphonies can be studied from a thoroughly re-searched edition.

Problems such as the orchestration of the second theme in the Scherzo of the Ninth (bars 93ff.) will remain. Doubling the woodwinds by four horns, as it has become customary since Wagner's time, introduces an orchestral color quite alien to the Beethoven sound. Yet playing the theme as scored is even more unsatisfactory, with or without doubling, while marking the strings p (as it has been tried) quenches the rhythmic impact. Weingartner, who devotes no fewer than 70 pages to the inter-pretation of the Ninth, used to add a pair of trumpets to carry the melody at the repeat. One wonders whether he would not have changed his mind, had he lived longer, just as he aban-doned some other all too radical changes in later years.

In his revision of Schumann's symphonies, Weingartner re-orchestrated entire passages. Other conductors limit changes to dynamics and avoid some of the doubling but add woodwind doubling to f passages. Even purists admit that Schumann's sym-phonies, when played exactly as scored, suffer from lack of the-matic clarity and from want of contrast which obscures the struc-tural build-up.

In the first and last movements of Schumann's Fourth Sym-phony, some timpani notes clash with the harmonic setting. "Wrong notes" in the timpani also occur in works of other com-posers of the same period. Unlike the classic masters, they ac-cepted dissonances for the sake of an important timpani effect. Taking advantage of the modern device that permits a quick change of pitch, conductors now substitute notes that fit the har-mony. Filling in timpani notes, however, where a composer wrote a pause is quite another matter. The intermittent use of kettledrums was a characteristic feature of the classic orchestra. Tempting as it may be to add timpani notes to the *Tempest* sec-tion in Beethoven's Sixth Symphony (beginning with bar 78), it would introduce an element foreign to the composer's style. In fact, the "delayed" timpani entrance in bar 106, after a pause of 22 measures, heightens its effect.

Similar caution should be observed in regard to shifting dou-ble bass passages to the lower octave, a procedure that was dis-cussed in reference to Brahms's scoring. Players and conductors should view questions of orchestral setting within the broad as-pect of an entire work and not from the narrow angle of a single passage in an individual part. The double bass line in the 4th and 5th movements of Beethoven's Sixth Symphony proves this point. After having made repeated use of the C string for the *Tempest* music, the composer refrained from using it for the first section of the finale, yet returned to taking advantage of the low bass notes for the movement's climax (bar 175ff.). The alterations of the bass part sometimes made in the first section are therefore not justifiable.

Doubling

"To double woodwinds is indispensable in forte, and whenever they are playing an important theme" is a quote from the notes added by Richard Strauss to Berlioz's text on orchestration. Strauss was then thinking of older works, because, in his own scores, based on a string group of 16-16-12-10-8, he balanced winds against strings without the need of doubling.

Wind doubling dates from the eighteenth century. When Haydn made use of it during his last visit to London, his string players probably numbered 12-12-6-4-5, a far cry from his resources in Esterháza, (5-5-2-2-2). Mozart, at least on one occasion, enjoyed the luxury of a large string group and doubled winds. Rules for doubling did not exist. Similar to modern custom, arrangements were made according to changing conditions and available forces, always with the purpose to achieve a better sound balance. (When Beethoven negotiated the terms for the first performance of his Ninth Symphony, he requested a string group of 12-12-10-6-6 and double woodwinds.)

Within our standard repertory, wind doubling is used in the performance of Bach and Handel oratorios (when presented in large halls), rarely in a Haydn or Mozart symphony, but frequently for works of Beethoven (Symphonies Nos. 3, 5, 6, 7, and 9), Schubert (Symphonies Nos. 8 and 9), Schumann, Brahms, Bruckner, and Tchaikovsky. This list is not complete. It remains within the discretion of the conductor to augment any section, including the brass, or to double a single instrument in filling the needs of a given situation.

Doubling must be marked clearly in individual parts to indicate which measures are to be performed by the assistant players. In the case of orchestras with only one extra player in a section, the conductor determines whether doubling applies to the first or second voice. Sometimes it will be necessary to have a special part written for the assistant musician. Yet doubling remains subject to change. Only while rehearsing in the concert hall can a conductor judge with certainty where doubling is required, keeping in mind that acoustical and stylistic considerations are of equal significance.

On the other hand, doubling indicated in the score by the composer may upset the equilibrium. Particularly in works of classic composers, notes that are scored for two wind players in unison may sound too heavy. In these cases, most of which concern horns and trumpets in the higher ranges, it might be helpful to let one of the players pause (see p. 374).

Lightening the string sound by a temporary reduction of the number of players is common practice, either for passages that require the refined sound of a chamber orchestra or to assure discrete accompaniment. It is believed that in Mozart's concertos *tutti* and *solo* were not simply meant to indicate entrances for soloists (they usually played with the orchestra tutti), but in the sense of the former *con ripieno* and *senza ripieno* (see p. 336). In all these cases, conductors would do best to wait for the rehearsal to determine how many string stands are to participate or whether they prefer to have the inside players pause. The same method applies when a score calls for only half a string section. Once the decision is made, the number of stands or players must be marked in the string parts with clear indication where the reduction begins and where the tutti is resumed.

Retouching vs. Arranging

Borrowing a term from painting and photography, the technique of making minor changes in an orchestral score to clarify the musical texture has been called retouching. It leaves the music's structure and expression intact, and it does not interfere with the composer's conception. Conductors who subject a score to more drastic alterations are overstepping the boundary of interpretation by entering the field of musical arrangements. The line between retouching and arranging may not always be easily definable, but little doubt exists that the rewriting of entire passages, as it was mentioned in connection with Schumann's symphonies, exceeds retouching.

Composers have frequently made use of these techniques when revising their works. Mahler's revised scores have been mentioned. Wagner rewrote the score of *Der fliegende Holländer*. The changes made by Mozart in the second version of the first movement of the *Paris* Symphony (K. 297) did not go beyond retouching. The second version of Schumann's Symphony No. 4, however, is for the most part an arrangement of the original one.

A conductor's function is to interpret music. As the survey in the preceding chapter showed, the masters of the past wished their works to be interpreted the way they were conceived. There are no guidelines for conductors to determine which textual changes are compatible with the "quest for authenticity." Unqualified answers cannot be expected in a field where many questions are argumentative. Several questions have been discussed in connection with previous examples. The following ones offer additional material to appraise the pros and cons in regard to textual changes.

Ex. 510: Some conductors have made the strings continue their pizzicato through the end of the movement, although the parts used in 1813 under the composer's supervision contain the *arco* signs. Another change, heard not long ago, lengthened the last note of the 1st violins, for no other reason than that a conductor liked it better this way.

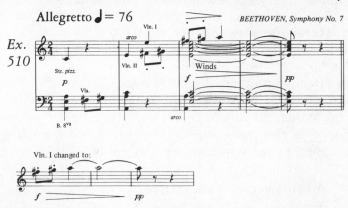

Ex. 511: According to Weingartner's report, Hans von Bülow made the strings play pizzicato in bar 3, presumably to soften the contrast between the *dolce* of the flute and the string chord marked *f*. Yet Beethoven could have prescribed pizzicato had he wished to create this

effect. For a large orchestra, as compared to Beethoven's smaller group, the *f* might be reduced to *mf.*

Ex. 126: In bar 13, shortening the first note of the violins to a 16th-note, followed by a 16th-rest, assures incisive and coordinated playing. Such a change in notation may not be necessary for a well-trained orchestra, but it often helps to make the violins lift the bow before attacking the next note; in other words, it is a practical device that in no way interferes with the musical context.

Ex. 345: A similar, and equally legitimate, change in notation is useful in the 3rd measure. Crossing out the first of the four 16th-notes on the 4th count (flutes and violins) makes for better ensemble playing. Besides, it may serve rehearsal time.

Ex. 256b: The conductor must decide whether the first violins should make a short break after the fermata in bar 4, or to go, without interruption, into the repeated note C, now played softly. The notation in the symphony's original version shows that Schumann did not intend a break, because he connected the two notes by a tie. When performed this way, the up-bow in the fifth bar must be unnoticeable in order not to interrupt the line.

An effective method to give a legato line in the strings the definition derived from detached playing is a divisi in unison, as used by Mahler in Ex. 512. To apply this device without the sanction of a composer would clearly fall into the category of "arranging." Ex. 513 presents what might be called a borderline case.

Ex. 513a and b: Only the melodic lines are quoted. In the original version, which utilizes only strings, the playing is legato throughout. In the final version, Schumann added a flute and an oboe to the 3rd bar for legato, while violins and violas play detached double notes to achieve a more energetic crescendo. This may work with a small string ensemble. When the symphony is performed by a large orchestra, the two wind instruments are outweighed by violins and violas which obscure the legato line. A better result is achieved by a divisi, with half of the violins and violas continuing the legato pattern.

Chapter 36

REHEARSAL TECHNIQUES

A FREQUENTLY HEARD question is whether the conductor fulfills his most important function in rehearsal or in performance. No simple answer is possible. A wide scope of musical and psychological aspects exists in evaluating the work accomplished by a conductor and his team of players. People familiar with the inside workings smile at fanciful exaggerations such as the observation that a famous maestro "plays on his orchestra like on an instrument" and, by contrast, are amused when told that, with all the essential work completed in rehearsal, "the performance runs by itself." They are aware of numerous details whose proper rendition requires verbal clarification, or of passages where, without adequate rehearsals, the conductor will be wise to conform to the orchestra's established ways, lest he invite disaster. Also, they have seen a conductor harm a performance, no matter how well rehearsed, by an awkward gesture or, worse, when his spiritual forces fail him, lead a routine performance instead of an inspired one.

Similar to the conductor's baton technique, which may be defined as a highly individualized craft to evoke specific responses on the part of the players with the most effective gestures, his verbal communication in rehearsal must be equally specific, easily understandable, and congruous with his musical intentions. While rehearsal techniques vary according to each conductor's individuality, habits, and preferences, valid generalizations can be arrived at, and pertinent advice be given, supported by musical and psychological experience. The application of these techniques must fit changing rehearsal conditions and depends on the type of orchestra the conductor is to direct.

Rehearsal Planning

The following comments are offered with professional orchestras in mind, although not all communities in the United States can afford an orchestra that need not be augmented by students or amateur players. The conductor's handling of rehearsals would then have to take into account the different levels of musical skill and the divergencies in the players' general attitude, which cannot possibly be the same for those pursuing their training or avocation and professionals who come to earn their livelihood. Even when working with fully trained and experienced players, the conductor varies his rehearsal techniques according to the quality of the group and the kind of program that is to be prepared within a certain number of rehearsal hours. In some orchestras, the strings may be superior to the winds, or vice versa, so that more rehearsal time must be allotted to some sections.

The question arises as to how many players are familiar with the music from previous experience, how long ago a work was performed, and whether it was under the direction of the present conductor. The fact that a composition was last played under a different director can be a disadvantage or may be beneficial, the latter being the case if the preparation had been thorough and precise. Even a reading quite dissimilar in tempo and expression will then be adopted by the orchestra quickly and with reasonable ease. Aside from familiarity with the program, the technical capacity of an orchestra and acoustical contingencies all affect the planning of rehearsals. Unfortunately, not all orchestras enjoy the use of their concert halls for preliminary work.

It has been said that the music director, if nothing else, is a "time-saver." Orchestras performing without a leader must rehearse more hours and, incidentally, they usually rely for advice on the concertmaster or another knowledgeable musician who attends rehearsals with critical ears.

In planning his schedule, the conductor makes certain that, within the total number of rehearsal hours, each composition receives its fair share of preparation. Technically intricate works and difficult contemporary music, whose reading is sometimes aggravated by poorly printed parts, require extra rehearsal time. Therefore, in devising his programs, the conductor will do well not to overload them with such scores. Also, he will attempt to commence readings of unfamiliar works several weeks prior to performance, possibly in sectional sessions which allow string and wind players to rehearse at different times.

When the conductor decides exactly what to practice at each meeting, he is led by considerations too diversified to be enumerated, but, knowing the capacity of his players, he can frequently foretell to the minute how much work will be accomplished. Obviously, a guest director finds himself in a situation unlike that of the permanent leader and may have to arrange his schedule from day to day. But even the regular head of an orchestra must be flexible to meet situations such as a musician's sudden illness or the late arrival of solo artists. The threat of emergencies has caused some organizations to insist that all musicians be present for the duration of every rehearsal. However, keeping musicians sitting around in idleness for long periods is hardly desirable. A well-planned schedule permits excusing those players who are not needed during the initial or concluding portions of a session.

It would be unwise for a guest conductor to change the orchestra's seating arrangement, unless he finds, after an hour's rehearsing, that the present seating is detrimental to the performance. To make a change merely for his personal convenience would defeat its purpose. Musicians need time to adjust to a different placement because their sense of ensemble depends largely on the way they hear themselves and their colleagues on stage. The merits of seating systems are not discussed here because their evaluation is linked to conditions of enormous variety. A conductor must "know" his orchestra and his hall before he can hope to arrive at the most satisfactory solution. Leopold Stokowski, an expert in these matters, never stopped experimenting with seating arrangements during a long career. One requirement, however, never changes: the conductor must be seen by all the players.

Efficient Rehearsing

Before starting a rehearsal the conductor greets the orchestra briefly, assures himself that all the musicians for whom the score calls are present, and makes certain that the tuning of the instruments has been completed. Generally, conductors should be cautioned against making speeches, giving detailed instructions prior to actual playing, or attempting to enlighten the orchestra by musical analyses. Professional musicians tend to be critical and suspicious of words until convinced in terms of music. The suggestion that the conductor quickly ascertain whether everybody is ready to rehearse is justified and also useful at concert time. It would be embarrassing for the director (and this has actually happened) to be forced to stop a performance because a musician, mistaken about the order of the program, remained in the musician's lounge instead of being on stage.

Careful tuning must not only precede a rehearsal but be repeated during its progress whenever the intonation is out of line. Problems of intonation, partly due to the nature of the instruments and different for strings, winds, and percussion, arise from various sources and cannot all be solved by tuning. Instruments must be in perfect shape, each player's technical ability must be matched by a keen ear and, last but not least, all musicians must make a constant effort to maintain a unified pitch by listening to their colleagues' playing. Keyboard instruments and harps add special complications, because in spite of the best efforts, the orchestra's pitch is apt to rise in the course of several hours' playing. Still, initial tuning is the first step toward achieving true pitch. The concertmaster usually supervises tuning, which should be completed before the rehearsal begins and must never be permitted to degenerate to a perfunctory routine.

Whether to use an electrical device to sound the A or adhere to the time-honored custom of letting the solo oboe give the pitch remains a matter of opinion. The manner in which the tuning is handled is most important. Sounding the A for two or three seconds and letting the entire orchestra plunge immediately into the all-too-familiar chaos of "tuning up" cannot produce good results. Stringed instruments, woodwinds, and brasses must check the A separately while the others maintain silence. String players are to spend sufficient time on careful tuning of all their strings so that there would not be an unpleasant surprise should all violins and violas be asked to sound, let us say, their open G strings in unison. Another useful test is to spend a few rehearsal minutes on letting the orchestra play a C-major scale. The resulting increased awareness of pitch may prove to be rewarding.

With the rehearsal under way, it is for the conductor to decide when to interrupt for corrections or discussions. Experience alone teaches him up to what point his gestures and facial expressions will suffice to communicate his intentions to the players, and which details make verbal clarification imperative. In the first instance, he will rely on his skill with the baton and will refrain from repeating a passage if he is sure that he can straighten out imperfections without explanation when the same music is played later on. However, he will not waste time repeating a page over and over if problems at this particular place call for discussion. Some conductors first go through an extended portion of a piece without interrupting. There may be a virtue in this procedure if a composition is new to both conductor and orchestra; some kind of perspective can then be gained as a guide for further rehearsal work. Otherwise its value is doubtful, and letting errors pass just for the purpose of "playing through" is usually a waste of time. This is not to advocate stopping the music for every mishap. A musician frequently notices his error at least as quickly as the conductor and would rightly resent it if a fuss were made over every wrong note, an oversight of change of key or clef, or a misunderstanding perhaps caused by blurred print. In such cases an exchange of glances settles the matter. But the conductor must not hesitate to act when technical or stylistic details render explication necessary or when the general quality of playing is not satisfactory. It is the conductor's responsibility to establish the highest possible level of performance from the very beginning of a rehearsal. Indeed, the first five minutes are often decisive for the results of a working session.

Facing an orchestra for the very first time, a guest conductor may prefer a slightly different approach, just as beginning a conversation with a new acquaintance has its psychological implications. The conductor's primary objective is to evaluate the orchestra quickly, to feel the musicians' reaction to the beat, and to give them a chance to adjust to a conducting style that might differ from the ways of the permanent leader. Therefore, rather than to start out with music unfamiliar to the orchestra, he should first rehearse a standard work on the program and continue for at least five minutes without interrupting. To do this effectively, he must not look at the score. Only this way can he communicate with all the players and find out to what extent he succeeds to convey his ideas to them by gestures and facial expression.

Four principal objectives must be kept in mind in preparing an orchestra for performance: familiarity with the music for flawless reading; apprehension of the tempi and their modifications; coordination of dynamics, rhythm, articulation, and phrasing; and a conception of style and spirit germane to the composition. It should be added that the success of a rehearsal depends to a large extent on the orchestra's general training in ensemble playing and the conductor's discernment in applying rehearsal techniques without losing sight of his final target: a performance that combines precision with expressiveness, balanced sound with animation. He will gain time for essential practice if the players are accustomed to watching him to the best of their ability.

A well-trained, attentive orchestra need not be instructed about tempo, about slowing down or speeding up, about holds, breaks, and other elementary details, because skilled musicians are able and willing to follow a clear beat and to be guided by telling gestures. They also expect authority and efficiency from their leader when he finds it necessary to discuss passages whose rendition needs verbal explanation. The ability to express himself plainly and concisely is an important part of the conductor's craft. It is his responsibility to keep up the momentum of the rehearsal while the music is interrupted. Here are some practical suggestions.

1. Before interrupting, be sure of what you are going to say.

2. Educate your orchestra so that everyone stops right at your signal and then observes silence.

3. Speak loud enough to be heard by the entire orchestra. Begin your comments without hesitation and whenever possible formulate them in terms of clearly defined technical advice. If you ask for a certain kind of expression, sing the phrase no matter how unattractive your voice, rather than indulge in poetical language. (Paul Hindemith, when a young concertmaster, once reported in exasperation: "Now we have rehearsed Brahms's *First* under three conductors within a few weeks and each time we arrived at the horn solo in the finale, the conductor started talking about the sunrise.")

4. Never say, "Once more" after interrupting without giving a good reason, unless things have gone wrong to such an extent that the necessity for repeating is obvious.

5. Frequently remarks are addressed not to all musicians but to sections or individual players. In this case, first identify the instruments concerned, then the passage in question, then explain why you are not satisfied. Discussions of extended solo passages ought to take place in private, which is preferable to lengthy explanations in the presence of the orchestra.

6. Do not discuss musical details without being sure that the players have turned to the right page and know exactly what you are talking about.

7. Once you have begun working on a passage you must persist until improvement is noticeable, unless a player is not capable of coping with a particular problem because of technical limitations. (Even a taskmaster such as Toscanini, in rehearsing Debussy's *Fêtes* with a renowned European orchestra, went on without fussing when he noticed that some bars were beyond the capacity of a certain player.)

8. Announce distinctly and unmistakably the place where the music is to be resumed. When playing from parts without bar numbers, some musicians, in order to find the place, may have to count many measures of rest. Allow then sufficient time and perhaps repeat the announcement. When singers participate, do not forget to give them word cue and pitch.

9. After proper announcement, resume the music as soon as practicable and without lingering.

10. Spoken comments while the musicians are playing should be used sparingly by the conductor.

11. Do not spend so much time on the first movement of a work, or the first act of an opera, that the remaining portions will be under-rehearsed.

12. Do not rehearse every piece each time in its entirety. To play in rehearsal, other than the final one, long stretches of music without problems is a waste of time. Use rehearsals for passages that need work.

This list of suggestions, by no means complete, can be augmented by helpful advice of various kinds found in the writings of practiced and resourceful musicians, including the amusing set of rules which Richard Strauss once proposed to young conductors.

Technical Advice and Its Application in Rehearsal

Some supplementary words seem to be in order to affirm the superiority of technical advice as compared to more or less general criticism. With regard to dynamics, we know that disapproval indicated by saying "too loud" or "too soft" rarely remedies the fault if the material is not marked properly. Composers are sometimes loath to admit that their printed markings are misleading but usually change their minds quickly when attending a rehearsal of their work. As previously suggested, parts should be marked beforehand by the conductor. However, no matter how experienced, he may have to revise markings in rehearsal. Acoustics is a frequent cause for modification; peculiarities of the performing musicians another. After all, and fortunately so, music is not made by machines but by human beings, notwithstanding the present trend of electronic music.

Methods other than markings can improve dynamics. String players may have to be instructed to include more notes in one bow for greater softness or to change the bow frequently to develop more strength. Pressing the bow on the strings, or moving it slightly, obviously affects the dynamics, as well as the bow's traveling speed. Again, the best sonority may be achieved by playing a passage in another position, that is, on a different string. Conductors knowing the nature of each instrument are familiar with these and many other tricks of the trade and obtain quick results with some experimentation in rehearsal. *"Probieren ist selbstverständlich, aufs Ausprobieren kommt es an,"* is a phrase of Otto Klemperer—rehearsing is taken for granted; what matters is experimenting.

To appraise the sound balance, the conductor may have to listen from the rear of the hall, letting his assistant lead the orchestra. As a rule, though, familiarity with stage and auditorium enables him to judge the overall effect from the podium in spite of the greatly distorted sound picture which, unavoidably, the conductor must endure. In most halls the sound level of trumpets and trombones is just right if the conductor barely hears them. The same is true for horns in *piano* passages, while they often must be encouraged to bring out a *forte marcato*. Woodwind solo lines should hit the conductor's ears quite strongly to make sure that their sound carries into the auditorium. This, of course, must not be accomplished by forcing the tone, which would hurt the solo instrument's sound quality and intonation. The solution lies in having the accompanying instruments play more softly, but no amount of entreaty will help unless the musicians listen to the solo passage, so that they themselves can hear it clearly. In general, whenever essential details of the orchestral texture are covered by heavy accompaniment, it is useful to let players demonstrate an obscured passage to the rest of the orchestra by performing it alone. In this and similar situations, the seating arrangement is of considerable importance. Music written for chamber orchestra and other unusual combinations may make special seating desirable to achieve a better blending of sound or to bring out solo lines with more distinction.

For articulation in wind instruments, the conductor may have to discuss different ways of tonguing. Unified articulation in strings requires a clear understanding of the various bowing styles, both for "off-string" and "on-string" playing, while for molding of phrases the players must know when to lift the bow for a moment or which portion of the bow to use for a group of notes. Nor must one forget the rule that every note is to be held for its correct value, not longer and not shorter; and furthermore, that one is not to drop the end of a phrase by making an uncalled-for *diminuendo*. The discussion of such basic elements of good music making points vividly to the twofold function of rehearsing. Rehearsals, while serving to prepare a program, must also be aimed toward the long-range purpose of training a team of musicians by creating understanding between the orchestra and its leader, as well as cooperation between the players themselves.

Good playing habits must become second nature. The rendition of works from the wide scope of music literature benefits from accumulated knowledge shared by all members of the group. This includes numerous questions of style such as embellishments, whose execution often calls for comment. Once aware of such problems, players will not begin every trill (to mention only one of the most frequently occurring ornaments) on the main note as a matter of routine but be anxious to have the question discussed in rehearsal.

In many ways the success of a rehearsal is contingent on the cooperation of the orchestra members. This includes studying the music prior to the first rehearsal. As a general observation, percussionists are likely to outdo their colleagues in this regard. Especially when a score requires quick alternation of numerous instruments, percussion players often memorize their parts. Most wind players and string section leaders prepare themselves thoroughly for the first reading. It is indicative of an orchestra's team spirit to what extent all its members make a similar effort. Special attention must be given to contemporary compositions that utilize instruments and sound devices outside an orchestra's standard equipment. In the discussion of aleatory music (see p. 306), it was pointed out that preparations are to begin long before rehearsing. Often the conductor will have to consult with musicians individually, be it to clarify an unusual method of music notation or to make sure that all needed paraphernalia will be in readiness.

Versatility is indicative of a professional orchestra. To do justice to music from many periods and of diverse national backgrounds, the conductor must establish a conception of musical styles so that his musicians are ready to change their approach from one composition to another. After having rehearsed a Tchaikovsky symphony for an hour, the orchestra may sound heavy in a Mozart work that follows next, but when asked to recall the orchestral texture required for Mozart, skilled players will adjust their performance without hesitation. In establishing high standards in the performance of a large repertoire, the members of an orchestra acquire both technical virtuosity and musical insight. Versatility and skill are linked together. After a subtle reading of a Haydn symphony, a Debussy work will receive a more delicate treatment; painstaking delivery of intricate rhythms in contemporary pieces can sharpen rhythmic awareness in classical music. This is not meant to imply that rehearsal techniques are the same in all these instances.

The conductor's methods vary according to the character and technical aspects of music. Selecting a sequence of measures typical of a composition's style and using it for extended practicing sets a valuable pattern for the entire rehearsal. Tricky passages often call for special attention. For a correct reading of certain rapid runs or for securing good intonation in spite of troublesome intervals, each string section or small wind group may have to play alone to "clean up" their lines before the *tutti* is "put together." Another useful device is to single out instruments from various sections that happen to play a difficult passage in unison or are faced with the same intricate rhythm, for the purpose of repeating those bars for perfect coordination. This method of "dissecting" is very helpful in rehearsing polyrhythmic patterns in contemporary music, because it serves to throw light on episodes whose musical context might otherwise remain obscured. In so-called pointilistic music, there is an added problem for the players who, unlike the conductor, are not aided by the full score and find themselves in need of orientation. To learn in rehearsal how their entries relate to other instruments can be a tedious and time-consuming process; it could be facilitated by including in each player's part a condensed score of complementary voices, showing how brief cues, frequently only one or two notes falling on an off-beat, fit into the whole.

The Psychology of the Conductor-Orchestra Relation

So far, the technical aspect of rehearsing has received preference, although, directly or by innuendo, questions connected with psychology have come into view. It has been pointed out that the conductor must try to formulate his ideas so that whatever he intends to communicate to his players finds attentive and willing ears. In rehearsing a professional orchestra, the director's position cannot be explained simply in conventional terms referring to leader-group relationship but, for a number of reasons, deserves special consideration in terms of group psychology.

First of all, the director deals with a heterogeneous group of individualists, a circumstance that is not only unavoidable but desirable. It is not skill alone that makes a first-rate orchestra player; he must be an artist in his own right, with the temperament and qualities characteristic of a performer. Secondly, by virtue of their talent, ability, and experience, musicians are likely to be critical, sometimes even resentful, of their leader. Many of them consider themselves, not always without reason, at least his equal when it comes to interpreting and rehearsing music. Thirdly, excellence in performance cannot be expected from musicians merely obeying orders, but only if they are motivated by an impulse derived directly from the music to which they devote their skills, hearts, and minds. If education is the art of opening people's minds, then the conductor's function in rehearsal must be called educational, not in the sense of formal teaching but of bringing to the fore all the best qualities latent in his musicians. To accomplish this he must be regarded by his group as *primus inter pares*.

Exercising authority in rehearsal is a challenge not easily met by a young conductor who has to give directions to musicians older and more experienced than he. He is not supported by a set of incontestable regulations like a young lieutenant commanding his platoon. In fact, he may feel that he must almost "fake" an authority, which is made difficult by the many critical eyes focused on him. However, a conductor's thorough knowledge of the score, clear beat, and enthusiasm for the music help to overcome an orchestra's mental resistance to his limited experience.

Psychologists have noted that adults as members of a group develop juvenile traits—unfairness or even rudeness—which they would never permit themselves when acting as individuals. Thus the conduct of usually well-controlled and reasonable people can turn into mischievous classroom behavior if the leader of the group lacks authority. This problem does not exist for a conductor who knows how to maintain discipline without forgetting his sense of humor, who combines firmness with diplomacy, and, still more important, who keeps interest alive throughout the rehearsal by impressing on each player that his cooperation is essential. When the conductor notices lack of attention, he should first ask himself if perhaps his leadership has been deficient.

It must be added, though, that it is difficult for a young conductor to judge who is to blame for unsatisfactory results, he or the orchestra. Nowadays it seems almost superfluous to warn against falling victim to what could be called an occupational disease among conductors a generation ago, namely, the loss of a sense of proportion caused by an egocentric "power complex" which made them act unfairly and rudely toward the orchestra. Conductors are liable to err as much as players, and it would be unwise to try to hide an error. As Pierre Monteux once told his students: "When you make a mistake you must admit it, but of course"—he added with a twinkle—"you must not make mistakes too often."

Much has been written to unveil for the general public the secret world of orchestra rehearsals. The stories and anecdotes found in books and other publications are legion. They tell, not always accurately, about the legendary abilities or eccentricities of famous musicians. Tales of this sort are a boon to hero worshipers but of limited interest to professionals. They rarely hit a musically significant point and sometimes even support mediocrity, as in the often-repeated story of the orchestra player who, after having listened impatiently to the famous maestro's explanations, retorted brusquely: "Just tell us whether you want this passage played *forte* or *piano*." If the story is true, this man was either a disagreeable person or a semi-educated musician unable to realize that the sweat and toil the creators of great music put into their work obliges us to make every possible effort in bringing their compositions to life. It cannot be done in terms of mechanical measurements alone. There are many gradations of *piano* and *forte*, numerous ways of playing *staccato*, and many other means of musical expression which evade definition. Likewise there are limits to the conductor's efforts to translate his intentions into technical language. The intrinsic meaning of music, the subtleness of a phrase, or the dramatic impact of an emotional outburst may not be felt by all the players unless the conductor possesses the suggestive power of revealing what is "behind the notes." How to do this cannot be taught. Each conductor must find his own way to project his feelings, by virtue of his personality, by singing a phrase with the appropriate expression, or by hitting on the illuminating word.

A flair for what to say, and what not to say, is part of a conductor's psychological perception and calls for presence of mind. To know how to word criticisms, to feel when to give encouragement, to sense when a tense moment is best relieved by a joking remark, all this affects the relationship between the leader and his group. Still, the reason why one conductor wins the cooperation of an orchestra while another fails is difficult to explain. It would be wrong to assume that there is a certain type of personality or a particular trend in musicianship which appeals to players, but it is safe to state that there is one attitude which they resent, the "chummy" approach of pseudo-camaraderie. Basically, it is not a question of liking or disliking their leader but of feeling respect for him. Unless musicians respect the conductor, they will not "play for him," as the saying goes. This feeling, of course, must be mutual and evident in the way the conductor comports himself in working with his orchestra.

The Conductor-Soloist Relation

Rehearsals with guest soloists can be irksome due to limited time and differences in musical taste. The first circumstance usually proves to be less serious, because with the help of an expeditious rehearsal an attentive orchestra led by a conductor who has mastered the art of accompaniment has little, if any, trouble as far as coordination is concerned. It is the general style and details of interpretation that can cause embarrassment. It is therefore essential that conductor and soloist meet prior to the rehearsal to discuss important points and try to establish a general understanding. It is comforting to know, though, that most artists of real stature are eager to cooperate with the orchestra. In any event, the conductor need not fear loss of prestige by trying to adjust the accompaniment to suit the soloist, as long as this can be done without jeopardizing the orchestra's playing. His main concern is to achieve the best possible performance, and it would be unreasonable to expect the soloist to alter substantially, within the span of a brief rehearsal, a rendition which has become part of himself.

Once the conductor has consented to the choice of solo artist, it is his duty to show courtesy to a guest in spite of disagreement and disappointment; he would be ill-advised to demonstrate his feelings to the orchestra or, worse, to the public. Unfortunately, a few soloists believe that they have discovered the one and only way to do justice to a composer and his work. Even in these extreme cases, a conductor who is not equally foolish should remain master of the situation. Again, some diplomacy and the right word said at the proper moment will help.

Concluding Remarks

This survey of psychological factors that make their influence felt in the conductor's work would be incomplete without giving some thought to a problem he shares with performers in general. It stems from the dualistic nature of artistic activities and must be solved by balancing emotional impulses with rational control, a complicated process and not necessarily the same in rehearsal and actual performance. Bruno Walter once remarked that, in rehearsal, while working with full mental intensity, he was careful not to be carried away emotionally, not just for the sake of saving physical strength but in the interest of undivided concentration on the orchestra's delivery of the music. Other performers have spoken about the "control mechanism" whose functioning they consider to be of fundamental importance, and they have warned against being "a hundred per cent absorbed." Without listening with an alert mind and adjusting gestures to whatever the moment demands, the conductor would cease functioning as a leader. Conducting students, due to nervousness and involvement in their preconceived ideas, often do not hear what is actually going on in the orchestra and must first learn the art of unbiased listening. The simplest and most effective method for self-education is to stop beating and let the orchestra play by itself. As a rule, the student is surprised to find how much momentum is provided by the players without his efforts and that he had been wasting gestures on details which needed no directions. He also notices that he perceives the sound of the orchestra with greater clarity and objectivity, to the benefit of his overall judgment (see p. 302).

Another point which sometimes escapes attention is closely related, namely, the invaluable opportunity for the conductor to utilize rehearsals for testing his rendition of a work, particularly a composition he leads for the first time. Musicians called to go over a familiar piece have been heard to remark that they could have played as well without rehearsal, which was needed only by the conductor. While such a statement should be taken with a grain of salt, it is certainly true that the conductor "needs" rehearsals; they are no less essential for him than for his players. The primary consideration is not *who needs* a rehearsal but *what use* is being made of it. Indeed, the fact that the conductor, while working with the orchestra, still has to decide on details of interpretation that are of vital importance to the performance should contribute to making a rehearsal an exciting experience. It is the happy combination of objectivity and initiative, rationalization and feeling, discernment and intuition that, in addition to technical ability, is the decisive factor in leading a successful rehearsal.

Chapter 37

CONDUCTING OPERA

THE OPERA PIT has been called a training ground for young conductors because of the special skill that is needed to control stage and orchestra within a musical style that is marked by frequent changes of tempo and meter. Clear, yet flexible, gestures are essential for the coordination of rubato passages, fermatas, and other peculiarities of operatic singing. All this, together with problems caused by last-minute emergencies as they are bound to occur in a theater, requires musical leadership that combines authority with presence of mind.

In terms of baton technique, conducting an opera is not different from leading symphonic music. Special attention must be given to the visibility of the beat. The choice of gesture may depend on the orchestra's seating in the pit and on the distance from the performers on stage. Also, problems of lighting are quite common. The conductor must make sure that his beat is always visible to all performers.

Dissimilarities between symphonic and operatic conducting can be traced partly to the difference in art form, partly to the working conditions that prevail in opera companies. A discussion of the opera conductor's work must therefore be divided between questions of interpretation and those that deal with practical matters.

Studying an Opera Score

Inspired by the story and its leading characters, an opera composer attempts to integrate music, words, and stage action. Therefore, an opera conductor's first concern should be to review the libretto and its background. When studying the score his attention must be equally divided between orchestra and voices. Singing the vocal lines to himself will help to fix them firmly in his mind. Their meaning and expression are inseparable from the musical interpretation of an opera.

This leads to the question of language. In the case of an opera written in a language the conductor does not speak, he still must know the meaning and inflection of every word. Neither dictionaries nor printed translations provide the information needed to appreciate the subtle relationship between words and music. A conductor will, therefore, benefit from being advised by a musical assistant who masters the language and can clear up questions of diction.

Performing opera in translation brings about problems of a different kind. Whatever the merits of an English version, the conductor may find that it interferes with his interpretation of the music. This can be caused by words that hinder good singing, unwarranted changes of notes and rhythms, or the choice of a phrase that implies a meaning so different from the original that it no longer corresponds to the musical expression. Operatic translators, by substituting words and meanings, often become arbiters of style, both musically and dramatically. It is interesting to note that opera composers usually do not mind omitting or adding notes within a musical phrase, as long as its inflection and essential character are preserved and its delivery made more effective by the change.

Performance Practice in Opera

Authentic editions of operas are still in short supply. Most dramatic works of Gluck, Mozart, and other German composers exist in reliable publications, but of the Italian standard operas, only Rossini's *Il Barbiere di Siviglia* is available in a researched edition. Among French operas, the score of Bizet's *Carmen* has been published in its original version, including numerous passages that the composer, presumably under pressure, had eliminated during rehearsals.

Carmen is not the only opera whose final version is in doubt. We shall never know Mozart's preference regarding the *Prague* and *Vienna* versions of *Don Giovanni*. Italian composers of the nineteenth century have, in the course of various productions, made changes in their scores without disclosing which alterations were meant to be permanent. When Verdi rewrote sections of *Il Trovatore* for the Paris Opera, he omitted some passages, adjusted cadenzas to suit the local cast, but he also introduced new ideas of considerable interest. Yet, the printed vocal score of this version has found little attention.

Making cuts in operas, a time-honored procedure, has been

subject to much controversy. Some omissions have the sanction of the composers, but most cuts must be ascribed to conductors who, for various reasons, considered it desirable to shorten the music, sometimes only by a few measures, then again by leaving out entire sections. Cuts, no matter how obscure their origin, tend to become habit-forming. A typical example is the omission of ten bars in the *Duettino* No. 14 in *Le Nozze di Figaro*. Although their authenticity is assured, and restoring them would lengthen the duet merely by a few seconds, the truncated version remains common practice.

To decide on deletions in an opera is not an easy matter. Even if not handicapped by financial limitations or casting problems, a conductor must not make up his mind about accepting a traditional cut, or restoring a previously omitted section, until he has taken time for careful study. Not every printed score deserves to be called authentic. Few composers acted like Puccini who, having made drastic cuts in *Madama Butterfly* after an unsuccessful premiere, demanded that the original vocal score be withdrawn. In fact, to insist on uncut performances indiscriminately might lead to being holier than the pope! Leonora's *Cabaletta* in the 4th act of *Il Trovatore* is an example. This section has recently been restored (although with a cut!) by musicians who believe it to possess musical and dramatic significance. Their opinion was not shared by Verdi who, four years after the work's premiere, cut the *Cabaletta* when he produced the opera in Paris.

Cuts are merely one aspect of "traditions" in opera that a conductor must neither accept without investigation nor reject summarily. Gustav Mahler saw in tradition nothing but "the most recent bad performance," although he did not tell by what yardstick the quality of a performance was to be judged. Seen in proper perspective, tradition has its place in opera. Pierre Monteux's reading of *Pelléas et Mélisande*, for instance, followed instructions received from Debussy. Similarly, thanks to lifelong collaboration with the composer, Arturo Toscanini's interpretation of Puccini's operas could claim a high degree of authenticity. Seen in this light, contemporary interpretations that are now being preserved by recordings will provide documentary evidence beyond the merely written information on past performance practices.

An operatic tradition that has rightly been challenged is the unrestrained addition of high notes for no other purpose than to show off a vocalist's top range. It developed in the nineteenth century among singers of the Italian school and must not be confused with the eighteenth-century practice of displaying vocal virtuosity through improvised ornaments and variations. In fact, in Mozart's time it would have been considered bad taste to interrupt the flow of the music by inserting, or even sustaining, a high note.

Generally speaking, a line must be drawn between operas in which taking liberties with the vocal writing is stylistically justified and those that were meant to be sung strictly according to notation. The first opera composer to reject changes was Gluck who, in the preface to one of his works, stated:

> *The more one strives for perfection and truth, the more important become correctness and accuracy. One example is the aria 'Che farò senza Euridice' from the opera 'Orfeo.' The slightest change, be it its pace or expression, would turn it into a comic song for a marionette theater. In an opera of this kind, any note sustained too long or too briefly, any change of tempo, any grace note, trill, or figuration, would completely ruin the effect of a scene.*

Mozart did not subscribe to Gluck's austere principles. Relying on singers with solid musical training, he expected them to adorn solo parts with grace notes and variations. If necessary, he assisted them. One of Mozart's embellished versions of an aria has been preserved. He wrote it for the slow section in the concert aria *Non so, d'onde viene* (K. 294), which shows that variations were not limited to the repeat of a melody but could be applied right from the beginning (see NMA II/7/2).

According to Tosi's treatise on ornamental song, an eighteenth-century classic, improvised embellishments were "the most laudable part" of a singer's ability and "the greatest delight for connoisseurs." His enthusiastic statement was tempered by a warning: perfection in this art required "understanding, imagination, adherence to strict tempo, profound knowledge of harmony, and exquisite taste." Mozart's contemporary, Johann A. Hiller, expressing similar thoughts in a book on vocal ornamentation, suggested that performers without thorough schooling in composition should leave the composer's text unchanged, words to be taken to heart by conductors and singers who attempt to restore former performance practices.

It is not surprising that Mozart wanted secco recitatives to be treated with complete freedom, almost like spoken dialogue, using the singing voice only occasionally. For the supper scene in the 2nd act of *Don Giovanni*, he encouraged the artists to improvise their lines even while the orchestra was playing, and he did not mind that every performance turned out to be different.

Mozart's operatic scores reveal his intense involvement with the stage, but they cannot be set apart from his orchestral works. Whether designed for the theater or the concert hall, music created in the same workshop possesses common traits within the totality of a composer's style. Questions of Mozart interpretation, as discussed in previous chapters, therefore apply as well to his operas. One might go one step further by stating that his dramatic works, like those of other German composers, do not conceal a close link to instrumental conception.

Verdi seems to have had this in mind when he claimed that, beginning with Rossini, Italian composers were "melodists," in contrast to the German school which remained focused on "harmonization and orchestration." (He named Haydn, Mozart, Beethoven, Mendelssohn, Schumann, and Wagner as non-melodists.) Although Verdi's judgment is to be taken with a grain of salt, it helps to understand the nature of Italian opera during the first half of the nineteenth century. The fact that many of these works were scored with accompaniments as stereotypical as their metric structure, harmonic setting, and orchestration had at one time led to a condescending attitude towards Rossini, Bellini, Donizetti, and the early Verdi. Now brought back to the repertory, many of these works retain their effectiveness thanks to the emotional impact of *bel canto* lyricism.

For the conductor, operas of this period carry problems caused, first of all, by the lack of authentic editions. The present materials are full of spurious notes, rhythms, and markings, not to mention the question of discrepant versions. All this leaves room for argument and highly individual interpretation, making it difficult, if not impossible, to outline performance practices. That a tradition was lost is borne out by the lack of unanimity among Italian conductors. It seems symptomatic that, even in the case of Verdi's operas, the authority of a Toscanini, who still performed under the composer's direction and on several occasions discussed with him the interpretation of his works, did not find general recognition among his younger colleagues.

Deviation from written notes was taken for granted in the

days of Rossini and Donizetti, but how and to what extent notes were changed can no longer be ascertained. Source material is limited to variations and cadenzas compiled by song masters of the time, whose musical competence was disputable. Mathilde Marchesi's collection, still used by coloratura sopranos, includes nine different cadenzas to *Ah! fors'è lui* in *La Traviata*, all written in Rossini fashion, which would hardly have pleased Verdi who had his own way of writing cadenzas. Tracing the gradual change in Verdi's use of cadenzas is of considerable interest. Before abandoning them altogether for his last three operas, he had, beginning with *Un ballo in maschera*, developed a technique to integrate cadenzas with the concluding bars in an aria in order to preclude any change.

This was in line with Verdi's increasing reluctance to make concessions to singers and conductors. His letters testify to his displeasure when he learned about infringements on his sovereignty as composer. When a conductor had changed a *mf* to *ff* in the Overture to *La forza del destino* (bar 168), Verdi exploded: "The principle that conductors create music leads to the abyss . . . a path to bad taste and falsification."

Verdi prepared metronome indications with care but did not find merit in determining the duration of an entire piece. Signs such as *col canto, a piacere,* and fermatas allowed for rhythmic flexibility. The custom of increasing the speed during the concluding sections of pieces with strong dramatic momentum can be called idiomatic, but, aside from such occasional liberties, Verdi's music was meant to be performed with a firm feeling for the rhythm and a steady pace.

No information exists as to how Verdi reacted to the insertion of high notes. It can be assumed that he permitted some changes, at least through the middle period of his career. It would be difficult to imagine, for instance, that he expected a tenor to adhere to the written G at the end of *Di quella pira* in *Il Trovatore*.

Top notes have always been an obsession with opera singers as a stimulant for applause and an expedient on the road to fame. Conductors objecting to abuses have been defamed as purists. Sixty years ago, the general manager of the Metropolitan Opera, overruling the conductor, requested a soprano to end Micaëla's aria in *Carmen* with a high Bb—the conductor, a prominent French musician, left the company.

It is not unusual for composers to write optional top notes, letting a singer choose between the higher and lower version. Even then, vocalists sometimes prefer to perform an aria in a lower key rather than to forgo the effect of a high note. Under the right circumstances, transposing the music has a legitimate place in opera, namely, as a means to adjust the vocal range to individual needs. When Mozart transposed the aria *Mi tradì* in *Don Giovanni* from E♭ to D-major, he was not concerned about single notes but was thinking of the soprano's *tessitura*. In contrast, the two transpositions frequently heard in the 1st act of Puccini's *La Bohème* (Rodolfo's aria and the final duet) serve no other purpose than to allow the tenor to reach out for more comfortable top notes (although the higher versions are optional!). In this instance, the printed orchestra parts provide alternate versions. Most of the time, orchestra parts must be written in the desired key, because string players are not accustomed to transpose music at sight.

Puccini's scores are notable for meticulous marking. He indicated minute tempo changes, dynamics, expression, articulation, even some bowings. Yet his operas are usually performed with additional modifications, some of them authorized by the composer, if we are to believe the comments published by one of his co-workers (Luigi Ricci, *Puccini—Interprete di se stesso*). Puccini, like many opera composers, did not always consider questions of orchestral balance. A large band in the pit, playing accompaniments marked *f* or *ff*, drowns out even the biggest voices. Aside from changing the printed dynamics, conductors will do well to keep the beat small and resist the temptation to indulge in demonstrative gestures for an emotional outpour.

Performance practices with relation to Wagner, Strauss, and their contemporaries in France were discussed in Chapter 34.

Rehearsing Opera

A symphonic program, consisting of about eighty minutes of music, is usually prepared in four rehearsals. One might expect that full-length operas of 120 to 200 minutes (not counting intermissions) would require a proportionate number of rehearsal hours, divided into reading sessions and stage rehearsals. An opera such as Strauss' *Der Rosenkavalier*, no less exacting than, say, his *Till Eulenspiegel*, would then call for at least eight rehearsals, not taking into account time-consuming scenery changes and other problems on stage. Yet the facts of operatic life tell otherwise: rehearsal conditions that are taken for granted in the concert hall would in opera be regarded a luxury that financially hard-pressed managers can ill afford.

To make the best use of rehearsal time, more than musical competence is demanded from an opera conductor. With the ever-present specter of overtime for orchestra, chorus, and stagehands, he is often forced to pinch minutes. Under these circumstances, even the most accomplished musician would be at a disadvantage without knowledge of the theater and meticulous advance planning. Advice on how to prevent trouble is offered here in the form of suggestions which supplement an earlier list (see p. 387).

1. As a first step, meet with the stage director to establish an understanding in regard to the general conception of the work and its realization in performance. Discuss cuts and, if an opera is sung in translation, clear up textual questions.

2. Arrange that all vocal artists receive early information pertinent to the performance. If there could be doubt about the correct version, well-marked vocal scores must be sent to them. This includes the person in charge of training the chorus.

3. Operatic orchestra materials are often messy and of poor legibility. Advance checking and marking of orchestra parts is therefore of the essence.

4. Participate as extensively as possible in the coaching of the singers. If an assistant is in charge, instruct him about tempi and other points of interpretation.

5. Once the entire company is assembled for rehearsals, intelligent day-to-day planning is needed to obtain the best results. During ensemble sessions with piano avoid having singers sit around idly for long periods. Their time is put to better use by working individually with the stage director.

6. Once the soloists have memorized their roles and sung the entire opera in ensemble, room rehearsals for staging should start. To believe that musical preparation ends when staging begins would be unrealistic.

7. Be present at all staging sessions. This way you are involved in working out details of acting to be integrated with the music. Also, you retain musical control. Tempi get easily out of hand when singers concentrate on stage business.

8. Make sure that the pacing during piano rehearsals conforms to performance tempi. It is disconcerting to singers to hear a conductor change tempi when orchestra rehearsals commence.

9. Attend several chorus room rehearsals to secure a good understanding. Once the pacing is set for a choral group, noticeable tempo changes are risky and often result in shaky performances. Similarly, if an opera involves dancing, tempi must be discussed with the choreographer. It is helpful to tape record a piano version of the ballet music to be used for rehearsals.

10. The coordination of backstage music is facilitated by the use of video monitors. Still, music played or sung behind the scene is often a source of trouble. In order not to waste rehearsal time, discuss with the assistant not only tempi, but questions of location.

Rehearsal planning is linked to the availability of solo artists. Late arrivals restrict ensemble study. Competence and experience on the part of individual performers are no substitute for the team work which results from daily rehearsals by the entire cast for several weeks.

Much also depends on the conductor's ability to work with singers. Rehearsing vocalists is quite different from directing instrumentalists. Extensive experience in vocal coaching is needed to identify with the performers on stage. Their job is not always appreciated by musicians who have never tried to step into an opera singer's shoes. Aside from being concerned with music, words, acting, and vocal technique, singers must maintain communication with the leader in the pit and fellow performers on stage. (An occasional attempt to take a singer's place is a valuable lesson for opera conductors!)

It would be unreasonable to expect artists to sing with full voice in all rehearsals. In fact, a conductor should insist that the members of his cast save their vocal strength for those occasions when balancing the ensemble, with or without orchestra, makes it imperative for all to sing the way they would in performance.

It is customary to arrange for at least one orchestra session together with the singing cast prior to the first stage rehearsal with orchestra. In fact, singers should attend most orchestra readings. Especially in the case of *bel canto* operas, having the players perform lengthy simple accompaniments without hearing the singing voice would be almost meaningless. Orchestra readings should, therefore, not coincide with staging sessions.

Except for the final dress rehearsal, scenes need not be taken in order but should be scheduled to allow for a maximum of working time. An aria can sometimes be done in front of the curtain during a long scenery change. Spoken dialogue or secco recitatives can be omitted for the first stage session with orchestra. Immediately preceding the final rehearsal, a complete run-through with the piano in the pit provides ample time for corrections.

Conducting in the Pit

An opera conductor assumes the dual role of leader and accompanist. When to lead and when to "go with the stage" cannot be formulated. Such decisions, often made on the spur of the moment, depend on unpredictable circumstances. Still, it is the conductor's responsibility never to lose sight of the musical and dramatic conception throughout the performance, as it is his duty to coordinate the ensemble and to guide the singers with the sympathetic understanding they need to do their vocal best. A tug-of-war would be out of place in the presence of an audience. Disagreements are to be straightened out in rehearsal prior to the next performance.

Eye communication, whose importance has come up repeatedly, is of special significance in opera conducting. In order to "be with the performers," a conductor must keep sight of the stage most of the time. True, if a work has been thoroughly prepared, singers should not look down to the pit except in crucial moments, but the conductor ought to be ready to meet their eyes whenever need be. This does not imply that the orchestra takes second place. Conductorial skill requires constant awareness of all happenings on stage and in the pit. Quick glances directed to the musicians, together with efficient stick technique, assure orchestral control.

How to seat orchestra players in an opera pit has never been determined to everyone's satisfaction. Placing an orchestra in a lengthy rectangle creates problems of coordination and sound balance that must be solved according to existing conditions. Aside from visual inconvenience, the distance in seating makes it difficult, if not impossible, for musicians to hear the other players. As one example, a timpanist playing in unison with a double bass pizzicato (usually at the opposite end of the pit) must rely on the conductor's beat for a unified attack.

The conductor himself faces the dilemma of receiving a grossly distorted sound, both from stage and pit. Unless he examines the acoustics by listening to a performance from different locations in the hall, he is bound to misjudge balances. Often it is the brass or percussion that overwhelms the ensemble, but sometimes the blame must go to the high overtones of a piccolo or a triangle. Then again it happens that violin passages played on the E string upset the balance, whereas a switch to the A or D strings can make these instruments almost inaudible.

In many houses the orchestral sound is not sufficiently projected to the stage, so that singers may not hear a soft accompaniment, such as at the beginning of the *Habanera* in *Carmen*. Here, conductors have on occasion asked the orchestra to perform the first measures *forte*, but the problem is better solved by the use of amplification with backstage speakers that are heard by the singers, though not by the audience.

Chapter 38

CONDUCTING CHORAL WORKS
WITH ORCHESTRA

INSTRUCTION ON HOW to train and direct choruses is found in textbooks dealing exclusively with the art of ensemble singing. The following comments concentrate on the question of whether directing choral works in combination with instruments requires an approach that differs from leading an a cappella group.

The direction of any musical performance is based on the relation between gesture and response, a relation that is subject to the individuality of the leader and the reaction of the performers. Thus, vocalists may react differently to a gesture than string or wind players. Within the framework of generally accepted beating patterns, a conductor must therefore develop techniques that are effective in relation to a chorus and are also easily understood by instrumentalists.

It would be unrealistic to claim that the baton technique usually applied to directing a professional symphony orchestra is identical with practices commonly employed in conducting an unaccompanied group of voices. First of all, a choral director can dispense with the use of a baton. The singers, placed close to his stand and, as a rule, performing from memory, are in a position to follow his most subtle hand motions. Moreover, thanks to ample rehearsal time, which allows frequent repeats of the same passages, his group is familiar with all the details of his interpretation. Consequently, he will be understood by his singers even when using "free-style" gestures to a greater extent than customary in orchestral conducting. Such gestures, if used skillfully for the sake of spontaneous expression, are sometimes more effective than conservative leadership.

Choral directors with limited orchestral experience may find that the players' reaction to their beat does not correspond to their expectation. The lack of understanding is usually more noticeable during purely instrumental sections. Once the voices join in, professional musicians are likely to adjust to the rhythm of the chorus. Such problems, relatively minor in the performance of classic music, increase in connection with intricate twentieth-century scores.

To what extent a choral expert succeeds in acquiring the skill needed to control orchestral playing is a matter of ambition and opportunity. He cannot hope to achieve the desired results in the course of a few rehearsals without having learned to anticipate how an orchestra reacts to his gestures and verbal instructions. Such knowledge is also useful in preparing a chorus for singing with the orchestra. Technically speaking, a last-minute switch from a more or less improvised manner of directing to "professional" conducting should be avoided. If a conductor wishes to employ a baton in performance, he should begin using it during the last chorus sessions.

When performing oratorio, be it in a concert hall or in church, questions of acoustics and seating arrangements must be part of advance planning to assure a satisfactory balance of vocal and instrumental sound. Equally important is the careful preparation of orchestra materials (see Chapter 35). It should be of interest to choral directors that Brahms, when leading performances of his *Ein deutsches Requiem*, made changes not included in printed scores, partly for expression, partly to improve balances (see p. 358; for a detailed report, see BACH, Volume VII, No. 4, published by the Riemenschneider Bach Institute, Berea, Ohio).

In view of the large number of eighteenth-century works in the standard oratorio repertory, the study of performance practices should be part of a choral director's training. For the performance of Bach's choral works, it should be kept in mind that they were intended to be sung by children and young adults to the accompaniment of small orchestras. Vocal opulence is therefore less important than simplicity of expression and a convincing delivery of the religious content of the text.

Finally, a word of advice to orchestral conductors without extensive choral experience. As in opera, the leader must identify with the singers at all times, not merely by giving cues, but by aiming for musical integration and clear projection of words. "Speaking with the chorus" helps the enunciation, while "breathing with the chorus" serves coordination. After the short breaks needed to take a breath, preparatory gestures secure unified attacks. Independence of the arms is essential to controlling the orchestra with the right hand, reserving left-hand motions to mold the phrasing of the vocal line.

Working with singers will be more successful when a conductor is familiar with the rudiments of vocal production, including pitch problems, projection of vowels, and enunciation of consonants. (For works performed in Latin, learn the meaning of the words and how they are pronounced!) Also, the conductor should arrange that, prior to the arrival of the orchestra at rehearsal, time is allowed for the chorus to warm up. This is done not only for vocal reasons but to refresh the feeling of ensemble. Rhythmically difficult passages will be sung with more precision if, during the warm-up period, the chorus is asked to speak the words in strict time.

Appendix A

DISCUSSION OF COMPLETE WORKS OR MOVEMENTS

THE FIRST THREE selections have been chosen to practice basic beating patterns, 3/4, 4/4, and 8/8, on music written for string orchestra. For comments on score study, see Chapter 31.

1.
George Frideric Handel
CONCERTO GROSSO IN G MINOR, OP. 6, NO. 6 — THIRD MOVEMENT (*MUSETTE*)

Use a score printed in *Urtext*. The piece employs two solo violins, one solo cello, and a small string group (*ripieno*). The figured bass is to be realized on a keyboard instrument, preferably a harpsichord. It is essential that the double basses always play the low E♭ instead of substituting the higher octave; if necessary, their fourth string must be retuned.

According to eighteenth-century authors, *Musette* was a dance of gentle nature, to be played at a fairly slow pace, smoothly and with a caressing expression. Characteristic for a *Musette* is a drone bass or an extended organ point. In this movement, an organ point of a few bars marks each beginning of the main theme.

In baroque music, Larghetto indicates a tempo within the Andante group. For a *Musette*, Quantz (see p. 362) suggested "one pulse for each beat." We assume a speed of ♩ = ca. 76.

According to the usage of the time, the absence of a sign for dynamics at the outset signified *forte* (translated into modern dynamics, *mf*). Use a decisive preparatory gesture to coordinate the low strings and the keyboard for a unified start, then apply a poco espressivo pattern that reflects the songlike nature of the music. *Two* in bars 3 and 4 is a neutral beat (non-espressivo), but *Three* prepares the next downbeat. In line with baroque practice, the 16th-notes can be slightly hurried although the beat remains steady. Similarly, 16th-notes such as in bar 5 can be short-

411

ened. In the 5th measure, the 1st violins may play on the G string. Note that in bar 14 the solo violins sustain their notes longer than the *ripieno* players. Do not "overconduct" the passages played by the three soloists alone. Prepare the tutti entrances on *Three* (bar 18, 22, and so forth). Bring out the celli in bar 30.

The first *piano* section begins in the 35th measure. This change in dynamics is to be reflected in your gesture. Whenever two eighth-notes are slurred, as in bar 35, they ought to be clearly phrased by a slight separation from the following notes. In all likelihood, the "inequality of notes" applies here. Direct the music with tender expression and do not increase the sonority prematurely. Begin bar 43 with a gentle downbeat, but before moving the baton to the right, prepare the *f* on *Two* (this works best by beating *One* diagonally to the left).

The phrasing for the sharply syncopated rhythm in bar 58 is obviously meant to continue throughout this passage; add slurs in bars where they are not notated. The soft chord in the 77th measure is to be played tenuto and, as the following three bars, with beauty of tone.

The cadence in bar 125 marks the end of a section. Baroque custom allows a slight ritard for the return to the main theme. Resume the original tempo in bar 126.

The *Urtext*, faithful to the source, does not add slurs in bars 134, 136, and so forth. It can be assumed that the composer expected the phrasing to continue (see bar 132). A comparison of bars 78 and 161 shows another discrepancy in phrasing—which seems to prove that *Urtext* editions do not always absolve conductors from making their own decisions.

For the concluding measure, beat only *One*. You may extend the length of the chord slightly before releasing it.

2.
Antonín Dvořák
SERENADE FOR STRINGS, OP. 22—FIRST MOVEMENT

Use the score of the Critical Edition (Prague, 1955).

You may pause for a moment, to prepare the quiet atmosphere. Then give the preliminary beat, $\quarternote$ = ca. 88, and direct the first 4 measures legato, poco espressivo. The celli are marked to play with more sonority than the 2nd violins. After bringing in the 1st violins and the bass pizzicato, increase the intensity of your gesture slightly for the crescendo. A left-hand motion may indicate espressivo for the melody. Adjust the beat to the diminuendo in bars 7 and 8 and to further changes in dynamics. For the detached notes beginning in bar 7 (1st violins), use gentle staccato beats. *Two* in bar 8 prepares the accent on *Three*.

Stay in tempo for the 2/4 measure. Use the left hand to assure very soft playing in the 13th bar, then from bar 16 on build a gradual but expressive crescendo. The *f* in the 20th measure is followed by a quick decrescendo: reduce the size of the beat markedly on *Three* and *Four*.

The two accented half-notes in the celli (bars 25-26) are prepared on *One*. Indicate the diminuendo that leads to *pp*, but do not reduce the speed in bars 28-30. Orchestra players tend to drag in soft passages of this kind unless directed with a steady beat.

Soft playing continues with the shift to major key, though with a change of articulation. Use light staccato. In bar 33, the $<$ $>$ requires a subtle adjustment of the gesture, but keep *Four* small. Bring in the bass pizzicato at the end of bar 35 and lead the two crescendos, beginning *p* again in bar 37. The beat is more forceful for the accents in bars 38 and 39 but must reflect the return to *pp*. *Espress.* for the celli (bar 43) calls for increased tone; address this section, still keeping the beat small to maintain the *pp* for the rest of the orchestra. Do not exaggerate crescendo or decrescendo.

For the fermata in bar 48, stop on *Three* and continue in tempo on *Four*. In the following measure, emphasize each of the four counts to bring out the phrasing. *Three* in the 50th measure requires a sudden switch to a fairly large gesture for the *cresc.* and to prepare the *fz* (*fp*) on *Four*. For the 16th-notes in the violins, the beat must remain absolutely steady. Beat light staccato, even when the articulation changes to legato (see p. 223).

Return to beating legato in bar 54. The orchestration is altered for the recapitulation, but the beating patterns are much the same as discussed for bars 1-24. The continuous use of 16th-notes in the 2nd violins (bars 54-59) makes a steady beat imperative. Also, the coordination of the leading voices, which drift from one section to another, demands clear leadership. For the *poco rit.* in bar 83, slow down the beat very gradually. In the final measure, stop on *Two*, sustain the chord, then cut.

3.
Johann Sebastian Bach
AIR FROM SUITE NO. 3 IN D MAJOR, BWV 1068

(For an authentic edition of Bach's Third Suite, consult volume VII/1 of the New Bach Edition [Bärenreiter].)

Subdivided 4-beat, ♪ = 69–74. The entire piece is done with a legato beat. The main function of the baton is to keep the rhythm moving steadily but unobtrusively and to bring out the various melodic impulses. The continuous flow of the melody must be maintained without undue emphasis of the 1st beat in each bar.

Use a gentle eighth-note preparation for the start and beat the 1st measure non-espressivo, though with clear definition to lead cellos and basses. The espressivo begins on the 2nd eighth in bar 2. Here you turn your eyes to the 1st violins, always beating in the center for all to see. Turn the palm of the left hand toward the 1st violins just before the 3rd bar, to insure a soft attack. At the same time, address the 2nd violins and lead their melody. Turn back to the 1st violins on the 5th eighth.

In a similar manner, bring out the various melodic ideas in the inner parts throughout the piece. To do this well, you must know the polyphonic structure and think with the four different parts as they move along. In places like the first half of bar 5 and the last half of bar 10, there is no melodic movement and consequently no espressivo is needed. When bar 6 is played the first time, lead the bass instruments in their 16th-note movement. For the second ending, use small non-espressivo beats while the orchestra is sustaining the half-note.

Most passages written in 16th-notes are given more importance than sustained notes as, for instance, at the end of the 14th bar. Here the violas begin a melodic line which, in the following measure, is taken up by 2nd and 1st violins. The fermata in the last bar applies only to the repeat; to conclude the piece stop on the 5th eighth-note and keep the baton up as long as you want to sustain the chord, then cut.

Since no dynamics are marked in the original score, each conductor must decide for himself how he wants to shade the music. In any event, the rise and fall of the melody requires changes in the size of the beat, depending on the individual interpretation. The subdivided beat, however, must be clear enough so that the players are never in doubt as to where you are.

Suggestions for embellishments:

The grace notes on *Two* in bar 2, and on *One* in bar 12, are played on the beat as 32nd-notes.

The appogiaturas on *Four* in bar 2, on *Three* in bar 8 (F♯), on *Three* in bar 10, on *Four* in bar 12, and on *Three* in bar 16, are played somewhat shorter than an eighth.

The three trills begin on the upper note, whereby the starting note can be tied to the preceding (identical) note. In bar 14, the trill has the length of an eighth and is followed by two 16th-notes (C♯ and B). The trills on the final measure are played as double trills (four 64th-notes).

4.
Ludwig van Beethoven
SYMPHONY NO. 7 IN A MAJOR, OP. 92 — THIRD MOVEMENT

SCHERZO. It is indispensable for conducting this music to know how the phrase groups are built. Thus, the 1st section up to the double bar is divided into phrases of 2, 4, 4, 6, 4, and 4 bars. The 2nd section starts with a 4-bar phrase in the strings followed by an 8-bar phrase in the flutes and clarinets, and a 4-bar phrase in the violins and violas. The next phrase ends with a sudden *ff*. The succeeding 16 bars are metrically similar. The following 5 bars (starting with the 61st measure) have the oboe and bassoon entrance 1 bar before the end of the 4-bar phrase in the strings; this overlapping entrance starts a 2-bar phrase all within bars 61-65. Now there are 4 phrases of 4 bars each, then 4 + 3, leading back to the repetition. Bars 89-98 are similar to the beginning but with different orchestration; the 8-bar inversion following this is new, as is the next 4-bar phrase divided between the strings and winds. After the 6-bar phrase (starting with the 111th measure) the section ends with 8 regular 4-bar phrases.

Familiarize yourself thoroughly with the orchestration, especially in connection with the phrase groups, and the dynamics.

Use 1-beat, staccato throughout. Start with an energetic full-staccato; the preliminary beat has upbeat character (see Ex.

153). Be sure that the sudden *p* in the 3rd bar is well expressed by the baton and left hand, which requires mental preparation on the part of the conductor. While the orchestra is playing the entire 2nd measure *f*, you must think of the *p* subito that is coming. In terms of gesture, this means that the right hand changes suddenly from a fairly large and vigorous beat to a small and light one. Increase the size for the crescendo and use sharper beats for *sf*.

Do not think it necessary to wave dramatically at each group of strings starting with bar 25. Beat straight ahead and look at the various groups, scarcely turning the head. Save the left hand for the *pp* in bar 33. For the sudden *ff*, avoid any emphasis on the downbeat in bar 43, but immediately snap the baton up to prepare the tutti chords. Return at once to the light *p* beat. Cue in the oboe and bassoon in the 63rd bar. To get an effective climax, lead in the string entrances just before the repetition.

In this fast 1-beat the *ff* must be expressed by the intensity of the beat, not the size; too large a beat would be awkward. Be careful of the sudden *p* in bars 99 and 117. The groups of wind chords starting in bar 118 must be light and delicate; how to direct this, using either hand, is up to the individual.

The rhythmic notation in bars 140ff. often remains unnoticed. Beethoven clearly distinguished between eighth-notes followed by eighth-rests, and quarter-notes.

The left hand sustains the *ff* of the last 4 bars (1st ending) before the double bar; the right hand beats *ff* only the 1st of these measures, then marks time with non-espressivo beats for 2 bars and uses the 4th for preparation. At the 2nd ending, use the left hand for the diminuendo. Some conductors make a ritardando in these 4 bars, or beat the last one in the tempo of the Trio to prepare the change to the slower tempo. This is not indicated by the composer, and the change of tempo can be executed just by starting off in the new tempo at "Assai meno presto"; the beat in the 2 first bars of the Trio must be very definite to establish the tempo.

TRIO. The first measure in the new tempo bears the number 149 (some editions have different bar numbering). Many conductors take the Trio at a considerably slower pace than that indicated by the composer (see p. 329). Stylistic reasons and the length of the movement (double repetition!) speak against dragging. The phrase groups in the Trio are quite regular and easy to analyze; the orchestration presents no particular problem.

Most of the Trio requires the legato beat. There should be some espressivo quality in it because of the $<\!\!>$, and to lead the melodic line, as in bar 154. This is more effective if you use neutral beats in bars 150 and 152, as well as in 155 and 156.

Starting with the 199th measure, there is an 8-bar syncopated passage with gradual crescendo. The beat must be very precise and may develop some staccato quality. As the beat becomes larger (crescendo) it approaches marcato. The downbeat in bar 205 should be especially emphasized to stimulate the entering instruments. It is more important here to watch the strings than the flutes and 1st horn. A very energetic marcato is used for the *ff*.

In the *ff* passage you may subdivide, beating *One-Three*, particularly in bars 213 and 214, to keep a firm hold on the rhythmic figure in the trumpets and tympani. For the *fp* in the horns, use a staccato beat changing immediately to non-espressivo. Subdivision in bar 235 leads the eighth-note in the low strings securely.

To change back to Presto, beat as if the passage were written:

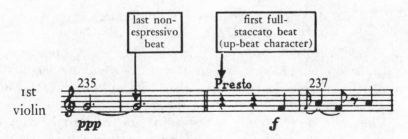

Starting with bar 260, the 1st section of the Scherzo is repeated, but *p*. The gestures are small and precise to insure a clear and delicate staccato from the orchestra. The left hand is especially needed in bar 285 where the 2nd section begins, also *p*. The tutti chords (bar 303) are now *pp*; the snappy preparation is extremely small.

CODA. While the change to "Assai meno presto" is done the same way as before, the attack of the last Presto requires a preparation strictly in tempo. For this, insert an extra (preliminary) presto beat, which also cuts off the strings, giving them a chance to lift the bow quickly for the *ff*. To direct the concluding 5 bars with downbeats would be rather pedantic. You may use a vigorous gesture similar to a 4-beat: One-Two-Three-Four-ONE!

In conducting this movement from memory, it is necessary to

have a clear picture of how the repetitions differ from one another:

SCHERZO. 1st section repeated
             2nd   "   "
TRIO.   1st   "   "   (repeat written out,
                                orchestration changed)
             2nd "   "
Transition
SCHERZO. 1st section repeated (repeat written out,
                                  dynamics changed)
             2nd   "   not repeated (dynamics changed)
TRIO   1st   "   same as 1st time
             2nd   "   repetition often omitted
Transition
SCHERZO. 1st   "   not repeated
             2nd "   "   "
CODA.

5.
Johannes Brahms
SYMPHONY NO. 4 IN E MINOR, OP. 98 — FIRST MOVEMENT

This *Allegro non troppo* requires flexible pacing, but tempo modifications should not exceed a span of about $\quad=66$-80. If handled skillfully and gradually, they will be hardly noticeable to the listener.

The tradition of a leisurely beginning goes back to the days of the composer. At one point, he intended to alter the start of the movement to prepare for an unhurried violin entrance. Later, however, he abandoned the idea. Here are the 4 bars that he crossed out in the autograph.

Ex. 514

Bar 1	For a well-coordinated and beautifully played beginning, the conductor needs the undivided attention of both violin sections. His gesture, 2-beat espressivo, must suggest a continual melodic line in which the half-notes are fully sustained.
Bar 4	The dynamic sign for the violins does not indicate diminuendo in the strict sense, but is a phrase accent (see pp. 354 and 359). Use a larger gesture on *Two* for preparation.
Bar 9	Emphasize *One for the*
Bar 12	After a minor crescendo, lead back to *p*.
Bar 17	Do not use large gestures for the *f*. The oboe solo will not be heard sufficiently if the other players overdo the *f*. If necessary, change their markings to *mf*.
Bar 19 ff.	Lead the violins; the winds accompany *leggiero* and need no encouragement.
Bar 26	*Two* is a staccato gesture.
Bar 27 ff.	Do not "work" for the crescendo too soon! The real crescendo is still to come in bar 33.
Bar 37 ff.	A staccato beat is needed for the syncopations. In bar 38, cue in the trumpets (their first entrance!).
Bar 45	Resume a legato beat. At this point the tempo has increased to about $\mathJ = 80$.
Bar 50	Bring out the second horn pair.
Bar 53 ff.	Beat staccato. Even when the celli, later the violins, play the melody, the gestures retain staccato quality to control the rhythm of the staccato accompaniment.
Bar 86	To make the crescendo more effective, mark the last quarter-note in the strings *mf*.
Bar 90	Change to legato beat. In bars 91 and 92, the violins divide the bow. The 2nd violins continue the same bowing in bar 93, but, for an effective diminuendo, the 1st violins should play bars 93 and 94 in one bow.

BAR 95	Espressivo beat.
BAR 97	The *pp* and the rhythm in the trumpets is controlled by a light-staccato beat.
BAR 110	For good ensemble, the strings must adjust to the articulation of the wind instruments.
BAR 117	Quick and intense crescendo.
BAR 119 FF.	Use incisive gestures (also for the off-beat accents.
BAR 123	If the trumpets sustain the D in *f*, they are likely to cover the woodwinds; their long note may have to be marked $>$ *mf*.
BAR 136	Wait on *One* for a moment before a gentle legato beat on *Two*.
BAR 139	If you have used very little forearm motion for the preceding measures, an increase in arm motion will lead the $<$ $>$ effectively.
BAR 153 FF.	Maintain the flow of this passage while controlling the delicate dynamics with gentle gestures.
BAR 168	Strong crescendo, especially in the winds. Change to marcato beat.
BAR 183	A slight ritard prepares the *ffp* and the gloomy passage that follows. Use a small but precise beat beginning with bar 184.
BAR 194	*Two* prepares the $<>$.
BAR 206	The energetic downbeat that prepares the *ff* attack is a sudden change from the preceding non-espressivo. Beat staccato until bar 218.
BAR 219	Use a legato beat from here on.
BAR 227 FF.	This passage is directed with subtle gestures that reflect the dynamics and, at the same time, secure continuity (no breaks between wind and string entrances!).
BAR 239	The left hand helps to indicate the sudden *pp*. Keep strict time with small gestures.
BAR 243	The double basses had a pause of no more than 15 measures; still, cue them in for a very soft pizzicato.

BAR 246	For the recapitulation, which begins here, the tempo will have slowed down to about ♩ = 72. Keep a steady pace for 12 measures.
BAR 258	Hold back slightly to lead the melody in the violins (*p* after the *pp*!) in the mood of the movement's beginning.
BARS 259–370	The comments on the performance of the exposition apply to the recapitulation.
BAR 371	The Coda starts here; the conducting patterns are much the same as those used for the preceding section.
BAR 377	Reduce the size and intensity of the beat for the sudden *f* after *ff*. In order to build the final climax the orchestra must "start afresh." Note that Brahms asks five times for more crescendo or for *più f*, even within a *ff*. These markings, which defy logic, must be understood as a composer's request for undiminished intensity.
BAR 388	According to the autograph the *f* in the timpani part is a misprint. Brahms clearly marked *ff* beginning with this measure. (Many conductors let the timpani make a crescendo of 2 bars, leading to the printed *ff*.)
BAR 392	From here the momentum increases more and more. The pace may be accelerated to about ♩ = 88.
BAR 422 FF.	Lead the accents with forceful gestures.
BAR 431	In this and the following measure bring out the first horn pair.
BARS 436–437	Strong gestures must lead these very short chords.
BAR 439	It has become a tradition to slow down the tempo for the 4 timpani notes. However, an exaggeration of this nuance would not be in line with the impetuous drive of the Coda.

6.
Ludwig van Beethoven
OVERTURE TO "EGMONT", Op. 84

In the introduction the 3/2-time is subdivided, and the tempo is generally taken ♩ = 72–76.

BAR 1	Use a quarter-note preparation (staccato). The opening fermata should be sustained for no fewer than 9 quarter-counts. The way in which you indicate the diminuendo depends on the orchestra's response. Use a quarter-beat for cut-off and preparation for bar 2.
BAR 2	Giving equal emphasis to each quarter-beat would result in the rhythmic figure ♩𝄽♩𝄽, but the notation leads us to assume that Beethoven wanted ♩.𝄾♩.𝄾. Therefore use the tenuto technique, with strong emphasis on the 1st and 3rd quarters; the 2nd quarter is used for a connecting gesture. The 4th is in the manner of a cut-off, and the 5th relatively weak. The 6th is a strong preliminary beat.
BAR 4	The 6th beat is done with a gentle staccato, now indicating *p*.
BAR 5	Beat non-espressivo with clear subdivision; elaborate gestures would be out of place here.
BAR 6	The 6th quarter may have a slight staccato quality to bring out the separation from the following note. Clear separations of this kind are typical of classic style and should always be carefully observed.
BAR 8	Indicate the expressive ◁▷ with the left hand; do not slow down the tempo, and use the accented upbeat on *Six*.
BAR 8	Indicate the crescendo with the left hand; do not slow down the tempo, and use the accented upbeat on *Six*.
BAR 9	Using *Six* for preparation would cut the players off and result in a quarter-rest. To

hold the *ff* unison as long as possible, you may use a shortened preparation for the next bar.

BAR 14 — Do not use too small a gesture for the *p* string entrance, since it is played with some vibrato. The *pp* gesture must be still smaller.

BAR 15 FF. — An unobtrusive staccato beat on *Six* secures the rhythmic emphasis for the motive in the cellos and basses.

BAR 22 — After the previous non-espressivo bars, a small espressivo gesture will be sufficient. The horn entrances should be controlled if necessary.

BAR 25 — The new tempo ($\downdownarrows$ = ca. 54) starts without time for preparation, and therefore this bar requires an unmistakably clear beat ($\downarrow$ = ca. 160). Indicate the crescendo by increasing the intensity, but not the size, of the beat. Throughout the Allegro, the beating pattern must remain flexible, from a straight 3-beat to a subdivided 1-beat or a regular 1-beat.

BAR 28 — The *sfp* is indicated by subdivision or by a sharp upbeat; legato beat follows.

BAR 42 — Change to staccato beat; no crescendo until marked in the score!

BAR 47 FF. — *Gradual* crescendo.

BAR 58, 62 — High rebound for strong preparation.

BAR 74 FF. — Beat marcato. By this time the tempo may have increased slightly, but the contrast to the second theme (bar 82) must not be too obvious.

BAR 82 — The tempo is slightly slower; the forceful chords on *One* and *Two* can be directed by using 3-beat, though not with the regular pattern, which would be too academic. Beat *Two* with a strong but quite small motion, carrying only slightly to the right. Also, *Three* should be comparatively small but incisive.

BAR 84 — 1-beat legato.

BAR 93 FF. — Indicate the crescendo by intensity of gesture,

	saving the first large motion for preparation of the *ff* in bar 99.
BAR 100 FF.	The *sf* may be indicated by a sharp upward motion on *Three*, or by the left hand.
BAR 116	Sudden change to legato gesture, leading into the lyric episode.
BAR 123	The *p* must not be disturbed by the way you lead the *f* chords. Use a sudden staccato gesture.
BAR 146 FF.	A legato gesture with clicking brings out both the melody in the low strings and the rhythmic motive in the violins.
BAR 153 FF.	The beat must remain very steady.
BAR 163 FF.	Because of the changed orchestration (winds) it may be necessary to add some staccato to the beat.
BAR 206	The wind chords are important for the modulation. A strong gesture should obtain the greatest possible volume from the winds.
BAR 215	A strong *One* must be addressed to the 1st violins.
BAR 259 FF.	Use a small but extremely intense gesture. Many conductors rearrange the notes of the horn quartet in bars 259–262 and 267–270 for a more balanced sound of the wind chords.
BAR 263 FF.	By contrast, the gesture must express the timid feeling of these 4 bars.
BAR 266	Subdivide *One-(two-) Three; Three* prepares the *ff*.
BAR 275	In this and the 2 following measures, the second horn pair can double the notes of the first and second horns (in Beethoven's time, the A was not available on horns in E♭). Note that clarinets and bassoons pause to allow the players to prepare for the *ppp*!
BAR 278	Beat *One-Three* (*Three* with a sideways motion) and stop abruptly.
BAR 279	After the pause use a whole-beat preparation

	or prepare with *Three*, in case you prefer to lead the wind passage with a small 3-beat.
BAR 281 FF.	Indicate the entrances very quietly.
BAR 286	The cut-off is usually the preliminary beat ($\mathbf{\jmath} = 168$) which must express the subdued excitement of the beginning of the Allegro con brio.
BAR 287 FF.	Do not make the crescendo too early.
BAR 294	Lead the trumpet ($p < ff$) and beat a subdivided 2-beat as transition to
BAR 295	Alla breve, but do not rush (not faster than $\mathbf{\jmath} = 92$).
BAR 313	At this point the gesture should not be too emphatic, to allow for the crescendo which follows.
BAR 317 FF.	Use marcato beats.
BAR 319	Bring out the trumpets.
BAR 329	The downbeat is also the preparation for the *sf* on *Two*.

7.
Johann Strauss
OVERTURE TO "DIE FLEDERMAUS"
("THE BAT")

The entrance cues will no longer be mentioned, since a thorough study of the score is presupposed and the techniques of cuing have been amply demonstrated.

Conductors differ widely in their interpretation of this work, there being no unanimity even among the Viennese. The following discussion is concerned mainly with baton technique.

The interpretation of this overture, whose entire thematic material is taken from the operetta, should reflect the relation between the music and the libretto to which it was written. Lack of familiarity with words and stage action must account for misjudgments in regard to tempi and expression. An authentic full score has been published; also, a facsimile of the overture's autograph is available.

BAR 1 FF.	$\flat$ = 132–138, full staccato. Only the preparatory beat is large, as is *Two* in bar 2. In this way, you direct the motive ♪♪♪♪ strongly and indicate the rhythm for the run with a minimum of gesture.
BAR 4	Here *Two* is not preparatory; the next preparation is on *One* in the next measure.
BAR 8	Use the left hand for the *p*.
BAR 12	The cut-off gesture should leave the baton at a medium height, to allow a convenient preparation for the next tempo.
BAR 13	$\flat$ = 84 (alla breve), non-espressivo.
BAR 15	The conductor may or may not lead the oboe solo; if he does, any exaggerated gestures should be avoided.
BAR 19	Address the 1st violins with an espressivo-legato beat.
BAR 21	*Two* is staccato to stimulate the piquant violin figure.
BAR 22	Address the 2nd violins; their staccato notes must be audible and played scherzando.
BAR 27	Sudden change to light staccato.
BAR 31 F.	Some conductors make a transition back to the original tempo by means of a stringendo, although this is not necessary. In any event, an intensive gesture is needed for the *p* $<$ *ff*.
BAR 37 F.	Syncopation beat.
BAR 41 FF.	$\flat$ = 58. Beat marcato on the *fp*, then use tenuto. The tenuto pattern, with its connecting gestures, produces a unified attack by flutes, oboe, and bell. They would not respond very well to a legato motion.
BAR 47	$\flat$ = 100. Light staccato. The first 2 beats in the Allegretto must be given so convincingly that the tempo is clear to the cellos and bassoon and that the violas have no doubt about their sixteenth-notes. It is possible to use the last eighth in the Lento to prepare the new

tempo; in this case, the eighth-beat must be lengthened so as to correspond to the following quarter-beat.

BAR 50	Change to poco espressivo.
BAR 55	Light-staccato.
BAR 58	Espressivo-legato, stringendo to about $\boldsymbol{\downarrow} = 112$.
BAR 69	Indicate a sharp *fz* (trumpets!) on *One* and do not fail to establish the slower tempo ($\boldsymbol{\downarrow} = 108$) decisively.
BAR 74 FF.	This passage is often taken slightly slower ($\boldsymbol{\downarrow} = 100$), although no tempo change is indicated by the composer (a *meno mosso* would require a minor ritard on *Two* in bar 73). Lead the music with freedom of gesture and bring out the alternation of staccato and legato.
BAR 82, 90	Many conductors hold back slightly on *Two*, but any exaggeration would be out of style.
BAR 97	Lead the cellos with an espressivo gesture.
BAR 99 FF.	The poco rit. is usually distributed over the next 5 bars and should not be overdone.
BAR 104	A tempo (or più mosso, about $\boldsymbol{\downarrow} = 116$) is traditional here. Beat light-staccato.
BAR 106	Prepare the pizzicato clearly.
BAR 107	Change to an espressivo gesture suggesting vibrato for the accompanying strings. These instruments have a tendency to drag at this point unless led convincingly.
BAR 108	According to the autograph, the poco rit. begins in this measure.
BAR 109	Give the flute and violins time for the eighth-note A.
BAR 110	$\boldsymbol{\downarrow} = 116$. Observe that the first $\boldsymbol{\flat}$ is still *p*, but beat it staccato.
BAR 114	Use small gestures for the *p*.
BAR 121	This bar can be held back slightly. The autograph leaves no doubt that the last note is D (some editions print C$\sharp$).

BAR 122	1-beat, about $\dotted{\quarter} = 69$ (*nicht zu schnell!*). In the autograph the *pp* is followed by a *crescendo molto* beginning in the next measure. Bars 122–125 have been subjected to various manipulations, none of which can claim authenticity. The frequently heard break before bar 126 is a mannerism.
BAR 126	Address the double basses strongly.
BAR 128	Beat a vigorous rebound for the accent on the 3rd quarter.
BAR 131	The ♪♩ ♩ ♩ requires a dynamic preparation. The same is true for the trombone attack in bar 141 ff.
BAR 165	The end of the musical thought is indicated by a strong marcato beat. Let a fraction of a second elapse before the next attack.
BAR 166	The composer did not indicate a ritard or a fermata on the D. Nevertheless, three different executions of this measure can be heard. They are explained here, though not recommended. (1) 3-beat with ritardando, (2) 3-beat with ⌢ on *One*, the 2 eighth-notes still played with ritardando, (3) 1-beat with ⌢ on the half-note and repeated beat without ritardando; the 2 eighth-notes are thus strictly in tempo.
BAR 181	A tempo relation is possible ($\dotted{\quarter} = \eighth$), which means $\quarter = 138$. Use small gestures.
BAR 200	Stop briefly on *One* to give the solo bassoon time to breathe. The fermata on *Two* is hardly needed.
BAR 201 FF.	$\quarter = 76$. Start beating non-espressivo and develop gradually to espressivo.
BAR 209	Change to staccato.
BAR 210	Resume the legato beat, emphasizing *One* for the off-beat accents.
BAR 215	A large gesture on *Three* brings the melody into sharper relief.

BAR 218	According to tradition, the oboe plays poco rubato. The conductor may lead the accompaniment unobtrusively or direct the melody, depending on his personality and that of the oboist.
BAR 224	An effect of comic exaggeration, intended by the composer, can be secured with an expressive tenuto beat on each count.
BAR 225	A tempo.
BAR 228	Usually a pause is made before the start of the new theme. For this, cut off the violins with the left hand so that the baton is spared for the preparatory *Two*. The last note is marked staccato at the corresponding place in the operetta (No. 4). Some conductors use a special gesture for this upbeat staccato and hesitate before attacking the next bar. The correct tempo marking is *Allegro moderato*. The accents in the melody always require an emphasized beat.
BAR 248 FF.	Use a light gesture to keep the playing from becoming too heavy. As a contrast, direct the motive ♪♪♪⁊ (bars 252 and 254) with a vigorous beat.
BAR 260	Indicate the *fp* and bring out the horn.
BAR 269	Precise upbeat so that the trumpet will not drag.
BAR 278 FF.	Except for the change in orchestration, this section is the same as when it occurred the first time (see bar 74).
BAR 315	A smooth transition can be made by beating *Two* so that ♩ = ♩. of the following waltz tempo.
BAR 351 FF.	If these bars are taken too rapidly, the double basses may produce disagreeable noises! The composer's mark is *Allegro moderato* (not faster than ♩ = 132).
BAR 371 FF.	Some conductors make a ritard, with the theme slightly held back and speeding up un-

til bar 380. However, it is at least as effective when played in tempo, accenting the octave jumps sharply and playing the theme with a sudden *p*.

BAR 388   ♩ = 160, with small gestures.

BAR 395   Beat *One* sharply in case the brass instruments tend to fall behind.

BAR 404   A definite indication is needed for this contrasting *p* subito.

BAR 412 FF.   Bring out the syncopated motive in the horns and trombones.

BAR 419   Lift the baton for a strong preparation to direct the concluding measure with one energetic stroke.

8.
Claude Debussy
"FÊTES" ("FESTIVALS")
(No. 2 from Nocturnes for Orchestra)

When Debussy revised the score of the *Nocturnes,* he not only corrected wrong notes but made radical changes in regard to orchestration, phrasing, and dynamics. This version bears the mark "Edition définitive réorchestrée par l'Auteur." Right at the beginning of *Fêtes,* the orchestration must include oboes, English horn, and clarinets; if it does not, the score is incorrect.

BAR 1   A speed of ♩ = 88 is in the best French tradition. Use a marcato gesture for the beginning with a straight, or subdivided, beat. Subdivision controls the rhythm more firmly, but it would stifle the flow of the music if applied continually.

BAR 3, 7   There is a marked difference in intensity of beat between *ff* and *f*, especially in the 3rd measure where three woodwinds must be heard against the entire violin section.

BAR 9   Light-staccato, wrist motion only!

BAR 10   Use a slightly larger beat for the crescendo, then immediately indicate the *pp* (bar 11) with the left hand.

Bar 13 f.	Indicate the accents.
Bar 23	The tempo is twice as slow. Beat this bar with a strong marcato, using a regular 4-beat. Include in *Three* the preparation for the timpani.
Bar 24	Sustain the *ff*.
Bar 25	Cut off the wind chord sharply and keep strictly in tempo during the *p* $>$ of the timpani. Subdivide *Four* and use the last eighth-beat to prepare the harp entrance.
Bar 26	4-beat in the tempo of the beginning ($\flat = \flat$).
Bar 27	The tempo is slightly faster ($\flat . = 184$). The pattern is 5-beat, grouped into $3+2$ by the composer. The *sfz* in strings and cymbal requires a sharp gesture on *One*, followed immediately by light staccato.
Bar 29	Same tempo in 3-beat. After the accented *One*, use small beats for a subdued accompaniment; the flutes and oboes play *f* on their own initiative.
Bar 39 ff.	Keep the tempo well in hand.
Bar 41	A slight $< >$ of this sort can be indicated effectively by adding a gentle motion of the forearm to the wrist movement.
Bar 44	Keep the beat small and precise. The difficult passages of the English horn and oboes will suffer if the tempo has been hurried previously.
Bar 46	Do not become so preoccupied with the main instruments that you forget the double bass entrance!
Bar 49	The larger gesture on *Three*, which prepares the next bar, will not disturb the flute passage.
Bar 52	Strong indication of the rapid diminuendo.
Bar 55	A slightly emphasized *Two* helps the oboe with the phrasing.
Bar 60	*Arco* for the basses is missing in the score.

BAR 63	A definite *One* brings the trumpets in precisely.
BAR 64	Weaken *Two* and *Three* so as not to conflict with the quadruplet.
BAR 70 FF.	Relax the pace slightly. Bring out the crescendo in the woodwinds by addressing only this group.
BAR 82	Indicate the *pp* subito in the 1st violins with a sudden left-hand gesture.
BAR 86 FF.	For this passage, the beat must be sufficiently flexible to express both legato and staccato. Stress *One* slightly, the pattern being the subdivided 1-beat rather than an actual 3-beat.
BAR 97	The left hand may be used for the *sfz* on *Three*.
BAR 102 FF.	The crescendo in the winds needs no indication; save your gesture until bar 106. Do not rush, let the strings sing!
BAR 116	$\quartnote = 88$ (twice as slow as the quarter-beat in the opening). Light-staccato.
BAR 124 FF.	The gesture must reflect the correct phrasing. All triplets are slurred! (This was confirmed by Debussy when asked by the conductor Pierre Monteux.)
BAR 138 FF.	Do not speed up the tempo.
BAR 149	Add $>$ to the horn parts, also in bar 151.
BAR 151 FF.	A well-balanced climax requires economy of gesture.
BAR 170 FF.	Use a heavy marcato gesture but without slowing down. (A steady tempo is necessary for the coming transition to I° Tempo.)
BAR 174	If the tempo has been maintained strictly, the last bar in 2/4 is exactly as long as 2 bars in the new 6/8 ($\eighthnote = \dottedquarternote = 176$).
BAR 190 FF.	The violins play 3 notes against 2 beats; therefore, weaken *Two*.
BAR 202	Here the faster tempo ($\dottedquarternote = 184$) is established.

BAR 209	Cue in the cymbal roll with the left hand.
BAR 221	Indicate the crescendo strongly.
BAR 233	Use a sharp wrist motion on *Three* for the pizzicato in the violas.
BAR 236 FF.	Small gestures with the utmost precision.
BAR 252	Slower tempo immediately. Since no preparation is possible, the 1st and 2nd beats must establish the new tempo very clearly.
BAR 260	A well-prepared *Three* leads the pizzicato and the *sf* in the horns, and brings in the English horn, clarinet, and 1st horn. Do this without slowing down.
BAR 264 F.	The 3rd beat must be flexible enough to allow the flutes and oboes time to play their triplet figure without rushing.
BAR 266	Sudden "a tempo."
BAR 269 FF.	Delicate handling of the baton and a clear mind are needed for directing the fleeting notes of the close.
BAR 278	You may wait slightly before the final downbeat.

9.
Béla Bartók
CONCERTO FOR ORCHESTRA — FIRST MOVEMENT

Bartók's sectional timings supplement his metronome indications as an additional guide for conductors. Right at the start, the first 34 measures (metronome $\quarternote = 73$–64) are calculated to last one minute and 38 seconds, including one acceleration and one ritard. The following section ($\quarternote = 64$) comprises 16 measures without any printed tempo modifications and is given a duration of one minute. This estimate implies some liberty in pacing, because when played at metronome speed these 16 measures last only 45 seconds.

Here again, metronome markings, though no more than an approximation to the music's inner pulse, fulfill an important function (see p. 328). Using the *Tranquillo* in bar 155 as an example, do not stick mechanically to the metronome's ticking

(. $= 70$), but rather, while remaining close to the indicated speed, sing to yourself the oboe and harp lines. Yet, you must sense the eighth-note units distinctly enough to apply them with certainty to the 4/8 measures that follow.

BAR 1 FF.	Use a poco espressivo beat.
BAR 6 FF.	The string tremolo must be played at the point of the bow. Note that only the violas, without mutes, play the tremolo near the bridge.
BAR 23 FF.	The tempo increases to about ♩ $= 84$, then slows down very gradually. *Three* in bar 29 prepares the flute entrance in the new tempo, ♩ $= 64$.
BAR 39 FF.	It can be assumed that the tempo modifications, implied in the composer's sectional timing, are related to the rendering of the trumpet passages; a hardly noticeable slowing down in the eighth-note motion of the strings may result.
BAR 51 FF.	Although the beat retains the legato pattern, it allows for gestures that reflect articulation and phrasing.
BAR 63 FF.	The phrase groups for the accelerando are $4 + 3 + 3 + 3$. Switch to 1-beat with the third phrase group. For a well-organized increase of tempo, "think" with the trumpets while speeding the quarter-beats. The 1-beat in bar 70 starts at ♩. $= 50\text{--}60$. Note that the composer marked the final measure ♩. $= 76$, no faster!
BAR 75	In this measure, use a quick and vigorous rebound for the short break. Having whipped up the baton, stop for a moment before bringing in the violins in the new tempo, ♩. $= 83$. This is a tempo change without a timed preparation (see p. 295).
BAR 76 FF.	Beat full-staccato. To direct the interspersed 2/8 bars with authority, the conductor's feeling for lopsided rhythms must be unshakable.
BAR 90	Incisive 3-beat. Cue in trombones and timpani.

Bar 95	Use legato gestures.
Bar 99 ff.	In case the winds are not heard clearly, the strings make a diminuendo and resume *f* in bar 102.
Bar 113	Address the 2nd violins with an espressivo gesture.
Bar 123 ff.	Clarinets and bassoons may have to double in order to stand out sufficiently; the string accompaniment must not be too heavy. Alternate between legato and staccato gestures in line with the orchestra's playing.
Bar 154 ff.	The transition to the new tempo, ♩. = 70, works best when the 4/8 bar is directed with a 2-beat, ♩ = 105. This brings in the oboe securely and helps to establish the eighth-note unit unmistakably. (Use a 2-beat also for the other 4/8 bars.) For this passage, apply a legato pattern that reflects the subtle nature of the music and still leaves no doubt about the rhythm. Note the temporary change of key in the clarinets.
Bar 192 ff.	A precise beat is needed to direct the strings (10 violins in all).
Bar 206	The rallentando of 2 measures is a very minor slowing down.
Bar 215 ff.	Trombones, English horn, and trumpet must be cued in. The composer's tempo instructions for this passage are not clear. The mark ♩. = 69 in bar 229 seems to be in contradiction to the "sempre più tranquillo," extended through 13 measures. Many conductors take the liberty of beginning a minor rallentando with the trumpet solo, then slow down more noticeably for the expressive low string passage. Bars 229 and 230 are played at ♩. = 60 (with or without subdivision).
Bar 231	Return to beating staccato and synchronize the *f* subito in the strings with the timpani cue.

BAR 239	This is the first piccolo cue (the 3rd flute had briefly participated in an earlier passage).
BAR 240	Control the diminuendo in the brass.
BAR 242	It is helpful to be aware of the phrase grouping: $6 + 6 + 4 + 3 + 4 + 4 + 3$.
BAR 248	Observe the simple f after the ff!
BAR 271	The "pochiss. allarg." together with the trombone and timpani cues on *Three* is best directed by means of a quick 3-beat ($\flat = 200$, wrist motion!).
BAR 272	After a brief stop, bring in the clarinet with a freely timed preparation. Use 1-beat, legato poco espressivo.
BAR 284	Indicate the pp, then slow down the beat slightly, without subdivision.
BAR 300 FF.	Cue in the wind players; English horn and piccolo should play very softly.
BAR 313	Before resuming the quicker tempo after the ritard, stop for a moment on the downbeat in bar 312, then use a regular preparatory beat to attack the Tempo I. For the passage that extends from here to bar 396, analyze the phrase groups in conjunction with the orchestration.
BAR 342 FF.	Study the brass setting thoroughly. The 3rd trombone has its first cue in bar 350!
BAR 380 FF.	Bring in the strings; the double basses enter f!
BAR 390	First percussion cue.
BAR 396	Subdivide skillfully to bring in the violins (p) after a brief pause. Resume the 1-beat in the next measure.
BAR 424	Direct the pizzicato together with the flute and oboe entrances.
BAR 425 FF.	Your gesture must remain clear to facilitate the coordination of the quadruplets in the harp and the quintuplets in the strings.
BAR 438	Do not "beat forte" for the harps!

BAR 456 FF.	Throughout this passage keep the legato beat smooth and steady. Cue in the trumpets.
BAR 468	Use a full-staccato gesture to prepare the robust *f* of the violas in the next bar, then immediately indicate *p* and resume beating legato while slowing the pace.
BAR 474	Subdivide for the flutes in this and the next measure ($\flat = 120$).
BAR 476	Having used the last eighth in bar 475 as a free preparation, return here to 1-beat at a speed of about $\downarrow. = 60$. Beat *f* staccato (disregarding the dynamics in the woodwinds as far as your beat is concerned) and increase the pace steadily so as to resume the Tempo I in bar 488.
BAR 494 FF.	Five phrase groups begin here, each of three measures, with changing rhythmic patterns. Note that the first two groups end with a lopsided beat. The sequence of bars in the next two groups, however, is short-long-short, while the last group shows the pattern short-long-long. For perfect coordination, the orchestra needs flawless direction by the conductor.
BAR 509	The dynamics are reduced to a simple *f* (*p* in the timpani) for a final intense crescendo.

10.
Felix Mendelssohn
VIOLIN CONCERTO IN E MINOR, OP. 64 — THIRD MOVEMENT

Start practicing at the Allegretto non troppo ($\downarrow = 100$). This short transition follows a fermata. Whether there is a pause, caused by applause or tuning, or whether the violinist proceeds directly, be ready for the solo entry. If you do not lift your arm until he starts playing, you will not arrive at the 1st beat in time. Keep the baton in the position of attention, and just as the violinist attacks the upbeat, make the preparatory gesture without hesitation. Follow the traditional rubato in bars 9 and 10, synchronizing *Three* in bar 10 exactly with the A. In the 13th measure the soloist is likely to slow down before the *pp*. Hence, delay the 3rd beat and follow delicately. In the next bar, watch the violin bow so as to end the fermata with the soloist.

Allegro molto vivace ($\flat$ = 88). Most of this movement is conducted with 2-beat, although in certain places a subdivided beat is used.

BAR 1	This is often done with 2-beat, using a half-note preparation. The rhythm may be more incisive with a subdivided beat, in which case the preliminary beat would be a quarter-note.
BAR 2	Most violinists like to hurry this figure, but the conductor keeps his tempo.
BAR 4	Use 2-beat from here.
BAR 9 FF.	Precision of gesture must be combined with lightness and elegance; too tense a beat would hamper the fluent movement.
BARS 18, 20 and 21	The entries after *One* must not be late; keep the beat moving to prevent any hesitation.
BAR 23	Neutral beats on the rest.
BAR 24	Be on the alert to catch the pizzicato exactly with the D$\sharp$ in the solo. The effectiveness of this depends on a skillful preparation on *One*.
BAR 25 F.	*Two* in this bar prepares the next attack and may be slightly hastened, using a gesture that is not too sharp but rather flexible. This may seem to contradict previous suggestions, but when such transparent passages occur in accompaniment, the conductor must rely to some extent upon his musicians having an attentive ear. An academic beat would not arouse the "chamber music" participation of the individual players which is essential here.
BAR 30	The best way to secure a perfect ensemble is to think with the solo violin. The clarinets will follow.
BAR 35	Use a slight syncopation beat without delaying.

Bar 41 ff.	The soloist's freedom of playing should not be restrained by the accompaniment; pick up the beat when necessary.
Bar 46	Address the 2nd violins.
Bar 55	For the handling of this passage, see Ex. 374. In case you must subdivide to prevent rushing, return to 2-beat for bars 57 and 58 so as not to lose the grazioso quality of the music.
Bar 63, 65	*fp* beat on *One*.
Bar 71 ff.	A lively gesture must maintain the swift pace of the movement and prevent the wind entrances from being late.
Bar 75 ff.	The beat must build the crescendo and prepare the bass entrance, leading to a strong *One* in bar 76. Change to legato in bar 77.
Bar 80	A slight ritardando is traditional; follow the soloist.
Bar 81 ff.	The violin resumes the fast tempo; concentrate upon the runs to be with the soloist all the time.
Bar 98 ff.	Watch the runs again and do not let the wind entrances drag. The violins also need some indication in bar 100 so as not to be late after the sustained note. The pizzicato in the low strings, together with the entrance of the flutes, needs a clear upbeat.
Bar 129	Slightly slower for the tranquillo. Beat *Two* exactly with the A in the violin to get the following pizzicato precisely in time.
Bar 184	Beat the rests, following the soloist strictly.
Bar 193	Follow the slight rubato which is customary and synchronize *Two* with the A, but catch up immediately in the next measure.
Bar 198	The soloist usually speeds up at this point; be sure to follow.
Bar 204 ff.	Subdue the accompaniment by using a small gesture (the crescendo in bar 206 applies only to the solo). The sforzati in the orchestra must

	not be too heavy and need not be reflected in your beat.
BAR 216	Address clarinets, bassoons, and double basses.
BAR 218	Follow the soloist closely, since he needs time to attack the high E.
BAR 222	Indicate *fp* strongly, then go along with the rapid movement of the solo instrument. The violinist will be grateful for not being hurried in bars 226–229. Trumpets and timpani should reduce the *ff* to *f*.

11.
Wolfgang Amadeus Mozart
RECITATIVE: "E SUSANNA NON VIEN"
From The Marriage of Figaro, Act III

The remarks made on page 135 are pertinent to this discussion. The words as well as the music of the vocal part should be studied so that the conductor knows on which counts the syllables fall.

No matter what liberties the singer takes with the rhythm, the conductor must always give a clear *One* in each bar. Whether or not to beat the other counts during sustained notes or rests depends upon the speed of the music. Beating on all counts is practicable in moderate tempo, using small and smooth gestures. In faster tempo or when the singer hurries, too many beats may become confusing, in which case it is advisable to skip all beats that are not necessary.

When the beat follows the singer's liberties, it is bound to become irregular and to affect the various preparatory beats. Therefore, since the conductor must be on time with the entrances, he might have to use free preparations.

For students who use a piano score: only the strings play in this recitative.

BAR 1	Synchronize *Three* with the singer. Beat in tempo ($\quarternote = 60$) on *Three-Four*, no matter how fast the first 2 quarters were. A gentle syncopation beat on *Three* brings in the orchestra.
BAR 2	Indicate the counts clearly with a slight

	gesture, unless the soprano rushes unduly so that you must hurry to the next downbeat.
BAR 3	Use a clear downbeat and cut off quietly on *Four*, preferably with the left hand.
BAR 4, 6	Procedure similar to bar 1. *Four* must be incisive to secure clear 32nd-notes.
BAR 7	If the singer hurries, it is better to skip *Three* and *Four* so as to be ready for the sharp downbeat in bar 8.
BAR 8	Do not beat *Three* before the singer reaches it. The tempo changes without preparation. Beat *Three* and *Four* clearly in the new tempo ($\jmath = 100$).
BAR 9	Wait on *Four*.
BAR 11	Downbeat only.
BAR 12	Use 4 beats, synchronizing *Three*.
BAR 14	If the singer's tempo is steady, the preparation for the *fp* is easy; but if she hesitates, you must wait on *Two* and then give a quick free preparation. Beat *Three* and *Four* in rapid succession, to be ready for the next downbeat.
BAR 15 F.	Here again, be sure not to fall behind the singer. The 2nd beat in bar 16 must coincide with the soprano's C♯ (the violas change to A!).
BAR 18	Beat the 1st and 4th counts only, following the vocal part.
BAR 19	If necessary, wait on *Two* and *Four*.
BAR 21 F.	The preparatory beats on *One* in each bar introduce contrasting accompaniment figures; the first is wistful, the second dramatic.
BAR 23	The conductor takes the lead in this bar, the tempo being identical with the previous Andante.
BAR 24 F.	Indicate *fp* strongly and follow the singer closely. A smooth and convincing gesture brings in the closing E-major chord, helped perhaps by the left hand.

12.
Ruggiero Leoncavallo
PROLOGUE TO "PAGLIACCI"

When the Prologue is performed on the concert stage, the orchestra begins 44 bars before the first vocal entry (No. 8 in the full score). The numbering of bars in this discussion starts at that point. The orchestration is listed for students who do not have access to the full score.

BAR 1	*Str. Cl. Bn. Hn. Trb. Timp.* 1-beat ($\downarrow$. = 88), marcato gesture.
BAR 3	*Fl. Ob. Cl.* Beat staccato.
BAR 9	*Tutti*
BAR 25	Beat this bar with a larger rebound so as to prepare the following "pesante" a trifle slower.
BARS 29–36	Gradual increase in tempo. Use a strong gesture for the secco effect in bar 36.
BAR 37	A tempo. Beat steadily in light staccato.
BAR 39	*Fl. Ob.*
BAR 43	*Cl.*
BAR 46	Synchronize a neutral downbeat with the vocal part.
BAR 47	*Str.* Give a clear staccato beat for the off-beat entrance.
BAR 50	*Pizzicato* After the fermata, wait for the upbeat until the singer, after a short pause, attacks the next phrase. In a case like this, the simplest thing to do is to watch the singer take his breath, thus timing your preparation so as to arrive together with him on *One* (bar 51).
BAR 51	*Str.* 4-beat, poco espressivo.
BAR 53	*Ob. Bn. enter after the 3rd count* Use a flexible gesture which allows for a possible rubato.

BAR 54	*Cl.Hn. added* A marcato 3rd beat straight toward the right brings out the second half of the measure emphatically.
BAR 55	There is no fermata in the full score. Follow the singer and stop on *Three*. Release the chord with the left hand, then beat *Four* to bring in the singer (together with the celli) after the count.
BAR 56	*Vc., melody with singer; Fl. Harp, upper staff; Vln.2 Vla. DB., lower staff* According to the vocal score, the beginning of the vocal line can be performed half-spoken. Actually, this is never done.
BAR 59	The vocal score does not conform to the orchestration: 2nd violins and violas sustain their chord throughout the 3rd count, which is treated as a fermata (*col canto*). The singer starts "in parte ei vuol" after flutes and harps have ended their passage. Beat *Three* with a short gesture to the left, wait, and repeat *Three* on the singer's F♯ to prepare the next bar.
BAR 60	*Vln.1, melody*
BAR 64	Tenuto is best for this type of chordal accompaniment; the quick connecting gestures enable you to follow the singer from one chord to the next.
BAR 65	Either separate cut-off and preparation or do both with the same gesture.
BAR 66	*Vc.Bn.*
BAR 67	Cue in the singer.
BAR 74	*Vln.1,2* "A tempo" here means maintain a steady tempo.
BAR 88	The sudden change to slower tempo is accomplished by retarding the rebound.
BAR 90	*Vc.D.B.*
BAR 91	*Vla. added (sf)*

There is a pause on the eighth-rest in the vocal part; beat tenuto, the upward motion leading into the next bar.

BAR 92
Cl. Bn. added
Follow the singer.

BAR 96 FF.
If the singer is very slow, the 1-beat may be subdivided or changed to 3-beat.

BAR 99
Cut the chord; for the execution of the pause see bar 50.

BAR 100
Str.
The tempo is faster (1-beat). Follow the singer with sharp and distinct beats until bar 105, then stop as though there were a over the rest, and wait. Watch the singer again.

BAR 111
Ob. Cl. Bn. added
Use subdivision, if needed, to follow the singer.

BAR 114
Fl. Hn. Harp enter on the 3rd eighth-note
3-beat; prepare the entrance on *Three* carefully.

BAR 117
Vc., melody; Vln. 1,2, accomp.
Use a calm, flexible espressivo 3-beat.

BAR 121
Ob. Bn. Vla. added

BAR 122
Change to a non-espressivo 2-beat.

BAR 124
Harp added

BAR 125
The vocal score is misleading: the first note (tied from the preceding bar) is an eighth-note.

BAR 126
Str. Harp

BAR 128
Bn. added
A tempo.

BAR 129 FF.
Vln. 1,2,Cl., melody; Vla. Vc. D.B. Bn. Hn., lower part
In these bars the tempo increases gradually as more instruments enter, and the espressivo is intensified.

BAR 139
Give the singer time for a good breath on the eighth-rest.

BAR 140	*Tutti* Use an energetic marcato gesture, but not so large that the orchestra will play too loudly and cover the voice.
BAR 142 FF.	Lead the heavy ritardando with clear beats, unperturbed by the syncopations! They can be controlled by decisive marcato gestures, without the need for subdivision, except perhaps at the end of the passage. Cut off the concluding A♭ with a sideways gesture, saving the upward motion for the following attack.
BAR 144	*Vln.1,2,Fl., melody; Vla.Vc. (joining the melody in bar 146),D.B.Cl.Bn.Hn.Hp., accompaniment* Here again the beat is very expressive, but should keep the orchestra subordinated to the singer.
BAR 148	*E.H. Hn., melody*
BAR 151	Hesitate slightly before *One* to give the singer a chance to breathe, and attack the beat with him.
BAR 152	The sudden *p* needs a definite indication.
BAR 156	Beat tenuto on *One* and subdivide the other counts. A fermata is customarily made on the first eighth-note of *Three* for a sustained "high note" (often changed to a A♭). Keep the baton perfectly still and (watching the singer!) use a swift connecting gesture leading to the next eighth-beat. These last 3 eighth-beats should not be too slow.
BAR 157	Only *Two* is subdivided; wait for the singer and use the subdivision to prepare *Three*, then proceed in tempo.
BAR 158	*Bn. enter on the 3rd count*
BAR 158	There is no fermata in the full score. Cut the chord and use *Two* to prepare the F♯-minor chord (three bassoons) on *Three*.
BAR 161	*Tutti* Energetic full-staccato; beat the rests with

small and relaxed gestures, except for the preparatory beats.

BAR 162   After the chord on *Three*, do not beat *Four* until the singer is about to slur down to his concluding note, then use *Four* to prepare I° Tempo (1-beat).

Appendix B

WAGNER'S INSTRUCTIONS REGARDING THE PERFORMANCE OF TWO OF HIS OVERTURES

1.
OVERTURE TO "TANNHÄUSER"

In August 1852 Wagner wrote an article *Über die Aufführung des Tannhäuser, Eine Mitteilung an die Dirigenten and Darsteller dieser Oper.* This "message to the conductors and singers of this opera" included performance instructions for the overture. Two months later Wagner announced in a music magazine that conductors intending to perform the work in concert should ask him for special information. His concern was caused by his dissatisfaction with performances of the overture.

Wagner's remarks are here presented in code form. The comments that appear in parentheses are based on notes made by Felix Mottl during Wagner's rehearsals for a *Tannhäuser* production in Vienna (1875). They are believed to be authentic. For the tempo of the introduction, see p. 357.

BAR 1	(Not dragging, in walking motion.)
BAR 2	The winds take a breath before the last quarter-note, also in bars 4, 6, etc.
BAR 4	Bassoons: change the dotted half-note to a half-note followed by a quarter-note.
BARS 38 FF.	Trombones and tuba: breathe whenever needed to sustain every note forcefully at full length.
BARS 38–53	All instruments, except trombones, tuba, and timpani, play *ff* $>$ in each measure.
BAR 81	(Allegro: begin very calmly, increase tempo only later.)
BAR 94	(Poco ritenuto.)
BAR 123	Increase tempo slightly.
BAR 124	Only slight ritenuto without any noticeable

change of tempo; sharply contrasting expression, languishing.

BAR 132   Change the *fp* to *p* in all instruments.

BAR 140   Do not speed up too much.

BAR 142   This theme, although to be played with passion, must not be conducted too fast. An all-too-quick tempo would give it the character of levity which must be strictly avoided. (Do not rush; broadly.)

BAR 195   For the 8-part divisi of the violins: the six lower lines of equal strength, the first line could be played as a solo, but the second line, beginning with bar 205, must be performed by the largest number of players.

BAR 196   (Calmer.)

BAR 202   Clarinet: separation between the long note and the triplet.

BAR 212–219   The clarinet has the most important part and must be heard distinctly; the first violins must not cover it.

BAR 219   (Molto ritenuto.)

BAR 220   (Begin calmly.)

BAR 228   Rather strong increase of tempo.

BAR 240   Hold back for the transition into the energetic tempo that is required here.

BAR 301–308   With full and steady force; any decrease in strength is to be avoided.

BAR 321   Violins from here on in utmost piano, like a whisper; the theme in the winds, though not played loudly, must catch the listener's attention immediately.

BAR 369   Increase the tempo gradually, but with striking effect, to prepare for the *ff* entrance in bar 379 where the tempo must be sufficiently fast for the rhythmically enlarged theme in the trombones. In order to make the melody understood, their notes must not appear to be played as single tones. Conductor and orchestra must make every effort to maintain the *ff* with the utmost energy and force to achieve the intended effect.

BAR 439   After the preceding renewed acceleration (bars 433–438) the last four bars must be slowed down for a broad and solemn tempo.

2.
PRELUDE TO "DIE MEISTERSINGER VON NÜRNBERG"

Wagner's comments are quoted, in free translation, from his essay *Über das Dirigieren*. They begin with a discussion of the prelude's basic tempo.

"The basic tempo *sehr mässig bewegt* would in older terminology equal an *Allegro maestoso*. No other tempo needs modification more than this one, especially when of long duration and marked by episodic treatment of the thematic content. It is a favored choice to combine a variety of motives because, within a regular 4/4-rhythm, its broad structure permits modifications with great ease. At moderate speed this rhythm is highly flexible. When conducted in forcefully 'moving' four beats it can express a real, lively Allegro (this is the intended basic tempo that appears most vividly in bars 89ff.), or else it can be applied to bars 122ff. with the character of a lively scherzando" (see Ex. 15). "It can even be understood as an alla breve conducted with two moderately slow beats per measure, in the sense of a real, deliberate *Tempo andante* of former times. This is to be applied to the passage beginning at bar 158."

The notes enclosed in brackets have been added by the author.

BAR 1   [*Sehr mässig bewegt* = *Allegro maestoso*, see p. 323; *sehr gehalten* does not refer to the tempo but indicates well-sustained notes in the winds.]

BAR 27   [Traditionally, the tempo is held back slightly. Although this is not mentioned by Wagner, the *ausdrucksvoll*, espressivo, justifies a minor modification.]

BAR 41   To be performed with vigorous, weighty quarter-beats.

BAR 58   Change to 2-beat in the sense of *Andante alla breve.*

BAR 59   A *cantabile* passage begins here with increasing intensity resulting from the natural feeling for the music and the modulating harmony.

BAR 85 (or 86?)   Return to 4-beat with the beginning of the new pattern, that is when the harmony changes on each quarter-note. [Wagner says that he marked this tempo change in the score; as the only marking is *ausdrucksvoll*, it is clear that the term indicates slowing down in this context.]

BAR 89   Basic tempo in its most lively form.

BAR 96   The *poco rallentando*, hardly noticeable, leads into the new tempo.

BAR 97   *Mässig im Hauptzeitmass* [moderately fast within the basic tempo]. To be played in straight 4/4 time. The tempo, together with an extremely tender expression, assumes a passionate, almost hasty, character, like a secretly whispered declaration of love. As passion and haste are clearly enough expressed by the lively figuration, the tempo must be held back somewhat, which means that the basic tempo is reduced here to its slowest *nuance* [italics added].

BAR 105   The theme assumes a more and more dominating restlessness, making it easy to lead the tempo eventually back to an Andante alla breve as previously explained. [Wagner's comments are by no means clear. Did he suggest a change to 2-beat at some point, or did he merely wish to indicate that the acceleration must lead to a lively Allegro in bar 118?]

BAR 122   A lively scherzando; each bar consists of two measures in 2/4.

BAR 158   Andante alla breve in two moderately slow beats.

BAR 188   With the return of the forceful, march-like fanfare, the broadening of the rhythm in 4/4 is in clear evidence.

BAR 196   The doubling in the figuration adds to the broadening of the tempo, so that it ends exactly the way it had begun. [If taken literally, this contradicts Wagner's initial remarks regarding the basic tempo. Traditionally, the tempo of the beginning is not resumed before bar 211, which is probably what the composer had in mind.]

Appendix C

THE FIRST VIOLIN PART OF MOZART'S SYMPHONY NO. 35 IN D MAJOR (K. 385) MARKED FOR PERFORMANCE

THE TEXT HAS BEEN corrected to conform to Mozart's autograph (published as facsimile). Bowings and some fingerings have been added. All other added markings, offered as suggestions, appear in brackets to set them apart from the original. When entered into orchestra parts for practical use, brackets would confuse the players and must be omitted.

First Movement

BAR 1
Most conductors use a 2-beat for the beginning. For this reason, the sign ¢ has been added to Mozart's C, but put in brackets. A speed of ♩ = 144–152 is recommended, also alternating 2-beat and 4-beat for certain passages (see p. 265, Ex. 415).

BAR 7
The added tenuto sign on C♯ prevents the players from "dropping" this note, a frequently heard habit in connection with appoggiaturas, which can lead to rendering such notes almost inaudible, especially in large halls.

BAR 10
The main theme consists of three motives: 5 bars (stately), 4 bars (songlike), and 4 bars (playful). The suggested bowing underlines the character of the third motive.

BAR 44
Mozart's phrasing is essential for an incisive syncopation. The musical context suggests that, in this case, *tr* stands for an inverted mordent (*Pralltriller*).

BAR 49
(*save*) warns the players to be economical with the bow during the sustained F♯.

452

Bar 62	Mozart wanted the *p* to commence on the 2nd quarter; for the added diminuendo, see p. 342.
Bar 74	(*ten.*) reminds the players to sustain the A to its full value. Technically, this requires very quick, almost abrupt, bow action.
Bar 77 ff.	The suggested bowing, though different from the original, is recommended in the interest of correctly sustained eighth-notes.
Bar 80	(*mf*) produces a better orchestral balance (see bars 110 and 186).
Bar 94	In general, whether or not to apply *divisi* to double and triple stops depends on intonation, articulation, and sound and is to be decided on the merits of each case. (Purists can rightly claim that in former times such chords used to be performed in unison.)

Second Movement

Bar 1	The authenticity of "Andante" is not proven.
Bar 2	The players must lift the bow before the triplet.
Bar 6	Dots have been added for phrasing.
Bar 9 ff.	Mozart's bowing secures a soft accompaniment (oboe and bassoon soli) and must not be changed. In bar 11 the violins should apply some vibrato.
Bar 15	In the autograph, the first B is followed by a dot, but B and D are clearly 32nd-notes, as they are in bar 13 where there is no dot. Thus, it can be assumed that Mozart intended even notes in both instances, in contrast to the dotted rhythm in the 14th measure.
Bar 23	A bow change on the second note would upset Mozart's logical phrasing. Besides, using the bow sparingly on the high C contributes to the beauty of the melodic line.
Bar 25	Mozart wished to tie the sustained D to the grace note (see also bar 74!) and to separate

the 32nd-note by marking it staccato. The short upbeat creates an element of surprise which would be destroyed by altering the original phrasing. (A different effect is intended in bar 74, another example of variety vs. analogy!)

BAR 33 F.   Here, and in bar 82 F., wedges indicate an accent (see Ex. 487).

BAR 43   Dots have been added (also in bar 45) to indicate the phrasing; a sustained legato would be contrary to the style.

Third Movement

BAR 3   Chords of this kind must not be routinely marked with successive down-bows!

BAR 25   This measure is to be played on the string.

BAR 26   Mozart marked the winds staccato; this probably also applies to the violins.

Fourth Movement

BAR 1   The autograph clearly shows ₵.

BAR 9   Here, successive down-bows assure "clipped" chords to let the eighth-notes in the low instruments stand out.

BAR 32   The change of phrasing is optional. Yet the suggested slurs are so "violinistic" that Mozart would probably have approved.

BAR 125   The violins must not play too heavily; a (repeated) p serves as warning.

BAR 126   The original phrasing would create a problem within a passage that is performed off-string.

BAR 137   Some editions print A as the last note for violas, cellos, and basses; the autograph has F♯ for all instruments.

BAR 223 FF.   This passage is distorted in printed parts by the omission of grace notes. Players unaccustomed to the original version may find them confusing, a problem that is easily remedied by some practice (slow!).

BAR 240   (*stay in the middle*) is a warning not to use too much bow, neither here nor in the following two measures. The entire passage, including bar 243, must be played softly and smoothly.

Wolfgang Amadeus Mozart
SYMPHONY NO. 35 IN D MAJOR (K. 385)

Violino I

Trills begin on the upper note, unless marked * (= inverted mordent).

460

LIST OF DIAGRAMS

INDEX OF MUSIC

(Page numbers in italics indicate musical illustrations;
numbers in roman indicate references in the text.)